Praise for *JavaScript Everywhere*

JavaScript Everywhere is an incredible book that will give you everything you need to build applications with JavaScript on any platform. The title is the truth: JavaScript is everywhere, and this book performs the unique feat of putting everything in context for developers at all levels. Read this book then write code and make technology decisions with confidence.

—*Eve Porcello, Software Developer and Instructor at Moon Highway*

JavaScript Everywhere is the perfect companion for navigating the ever-changing modern JavaScript ecosystem. Adam teaches React, React Native, and GraphQL in a clear, approachable way so you can build robust web, mobile, and desktop applications.

—*Peggy Rayzis, Engineering Manager at Apollo GraphQL*

JavaScript Everywhere

Building Cross-Platform Applications with
GraphQL, React, React Native, and Electron

Adam D. Scott

Beijing · Boston · Farnham · Sebastopol · Tokyo

JavaScript Everywhere

by Adam D. Scott

Published by O'Reilly Media, Inc., 1005 Gravenstein Highway North, Sebastopol, CA 95472.

O'Reilly books may be purchased for educational, business, or sales promotional use. Online editions are also available for most titles (*http://oreilly.com*). For more information, contact our corporate/institutional sales department: 800-998-9938 or *corporate@oreilly.com*.

Acquisitions Editor: Jennifer Pollock	**Indexer:** WordCo Indexing Services, Inc.
Development Editor: Angela Rufino	**Interior Designer:** David Futato
Production Editor: Christopher Faucher	**Cover Designer:** Karen Montgomery
Copyeditor: Rachel Monaghan	**Illustrator:** Rebecca Demarest
Proofreader: Christina Edwards	

February 2020:   First Edition

Revision History for the First Edition

2020-02-06:   First Release
2020-03-03:   Second Release

See *http://oreilly.com/catalog/errata.csp?isbn=9781492046981* for release details.

978-1-492-04698-1

[LSI]

For my dad, who both brought home my first hacked-together computer and proofread every paper that I wrote. I wouldn't be here without you. You are missed.

Table of Contents

Foreword

In 1997 I was a junior in high school. A friend and I were goofing around with the web-connected computer in our school library when he showed me that you could click View → Source to see the underlying code of a web page. A few days later, another friend showed me how to publish my own HTML. My mind was blown.

After that, I was hooked. I went around borrowing the bits of the websites I liked to construct my own Franken-site. I spent much of my free time at the pieced-together computer in my family's dining room tinkering away. I even "wrote" (OK, copied and pasted) my first JavaScript, to implement hover styles on links, which was not yet doable with simple CSS.

And in a turn of events that I've come to think of as a nerdy and wholesome version of the film *Almost Famous*, my homegrown music site gained reasonable popularity. Because of this, I received promotional CDs in the mail and was put on the guest list at concerts. More important to me, however, was that I was sharing my interests with other people around the world. I was a bored suburban teenager, in love with music, and was able to reach people I'd never meet. That was, and still is, such an empowering feeling.

Today, we can build powerful applications using only web technologies, but it can be daunting to get started. APIs are an invisible background that serves up data. View → Source shows concatenated and minified code. Authentication and security are mystifying. Putting all of these things together can be overwhelming. If we're able to look beyond these confusing details, we may notice that the same technologies I was fiddling with 20-some years ago can now be used to build powerful web applications, code native mobile applications, create powerful desktop applications, design 3D animations, and even program robots.

As an educator, I've found that many of us learn best by building new things, taking them apart, and adapting them for our own use cases. That is the goal of this book. If you know some HTML, CSS, and JavaScript but are unsure of how to take those components and build the robust applications that you've dreamed up, this book is for you. I'll guide you through building an API that can power the user interfaces of a web application, a native mobile application, and a desktop application. Most importantly, you'll gain an understanding of how all of these pieces fit together so that you can build and create wonderful things.

I can't wait to see what you make.

— Adam

Preface

The idea for this book came to me after writing my first Electron desktop application. Having made a career as a web developer, I was immediately smitten with the possibilities of using web technologies to build cross-platform applications. At the same time, React, React Native, and GraphQL were all taking off. I sought out resources to learn how all of these things fit together, but kept coming up short. This book represents the guide that I wished I had.

The ultimate goal of this book is to introduce the possibilities of using a single programming language, JavaScript, to build all sorts of applications.

Who This Book Is For

This book is for intermediate-level developers who have some experience with HTML, CSS, and JavaScript or ambitious beginners who are looking to learn the tools necessary to bootstrap a business or side project.

How This Book Is Organized

The book is designed to walk you through developing an example application for a variety of platforms. It can be broken down into the following sections:

- Chapter 1 guides you through setting up a JavaScript development environment.
- Chapters 2–10 cover building an API with Node, Express, MongoDB, and Apollo Server.
- Chapters 11–25 review the details of building cross-platform user interfaces using React, Apollo, and a variety of tools. Specifically:
  - Chapter 11 introduces user interface development and React.
  - Chapters 12–17 demonstrate how to build a web application with React, Apollo Client, and CSS-in-JS.

— Chapters 18–20 guide you through building simple Electron applications.

— Chapters 21–25 introduce using React Native and Expo to build mobile applications for iOS and Android.

Conventions Used in This Book

The following typographical conventions are used in this book:

Italic
> Indicates new terms, URLs, email addresses, filenames, and file extensions.

`Constant width`
> Used for program listings, as well as within paragraphs to refer to program elements such as variable or function names, databases, data types, environment variables, statements, and keywords.

`Constant width bold`
> Shows commands or other text that should be typed literally by the user.

`Constant width italic`
> Shows text that should be replaced with user-supplied values or by values determined by context.

 This element signifies a tip or suggestion.

 This element signifies a general note.

 This element indicates a warning or caution.

Using Code Examples

Supplemental material (code examples, exercises, etc.) is available for download at *https://github.com/javascripteverywhere*.

If you have a technical question or a problem using the code examples, please send email to *bookquestions@oreilly.com*.

This book is here to help you get your job done. In general, if example code is offered with this book, you may use it in your programs and documentation. You do not need to contact us for permission unless you're reproducing a significant portion of the code. For example, writing a program that uses several chunks of code from this book does not require permission. Selling or distributing examples from O'Reilly books does require permission. Answering a question by citing this book and quoting example code does not require permission. Incorporating a significant amount of example code from this book into your product's documentation does require permission.

We appreciate, but generally do not require, attribution. An attribution usually includes the title, author, publisher, and ISBN. For example: "*JavaScript Everywhere* by Adam D. Scott (O'Reilly). Copyright 2020 Adam D. Scott, 978-1-492-04698-1."

If you feel your use of code examples falls outside fair use or the permission given above, feel free to contact us at *permissions@oreilly.com*.

O'Reilly Online Learning

 For more than 40 years, *O'Reilly Media* has provided technology and business training, knowledge, and insight to help companies succeed.

Our unique network of experts and innovators share their knowledge and expertise through books, articles, conferences, and our online learning platform. O'Reilly's online learning platform gives you on-demand access to live training courses, in-depth learning paths, interactive coding environments, and a vast collection of text and video from O'Reilly and 200+ other publishers. For more information, please visit *http://oreilly.com*.

How to Contact Us

Please address comments and questions concerning this book to the publisher:

O'Reilly Media, Inc.
1005 Gravenstein Highway North
Sebastopol, CA 95472
800-998-9938 (in the United States or Canada)
707-829-0515 (international or local)
707-829-0104 (fax)

We have a web page for this book, where we list errata, examples, and any additional information. You can access this page at *https://oreil.ly/javascript-everywhere*.

Email *bookquestions@oreilly.com* to comment or ask technical questions about this book.

For more information about our books, courses, conferences, and news, see our website at *http://www.oreilly.com*.

Find us on Facebook: *http://facebook.com/oreilly*

Follow us on Twitter: *http://twitter.com/oreillymedia*

Watch us on YouTube: *http://www.youtube.com/oreillymedia*

Acknowledgments

Thanks to all of the wonderful people at O'Reilly, past and present, who have been universally welcoming and open to my ideas over the years. I want to particularly thank my editor, Angela Rufino, who has given me feedback, encouragement, and lots of helpful reminders. I want to also thank Mike Loukides, who has provided me with both caffeine and great conversation. Lastly, thanks to Jennifer Pollock, for her support and encouragement.

I am eternally grateful for the open source community, from which I have learned and benefited. Without the individuals and organizations who have created and maintained the many libraries I have written about, this book would not be possible.

Several technical reviewers helped make this book better, ensuring that things were accurate. Thank you, Andy Ngom, Brian Sletten, Maximiliano Firtman, and Zeeshan Chawdhary. It's a heck of a code review to undertake and I sincerely appreciate their efforts. Special thanks goes to my long-time colleague and friend, Jimmy Wilson, who I called in at the 11th hour to review and provide feedback. It was a lot to ask, but as with everything he does, he took it on with gusto. This book wouldn't be what it is without his help.

I've been incredibly lucky to surround myself with smart, passionate, supportive co-workers throughout my adult life. So many lessons big and small, both technical and nontechnical, have come through my time with them. The full list is too long for print, but I want to give a shout-out to Elizabeth Bond, John Paul Doguin, Marc Esher, Jenn Lassiter, and Jessica Schafer.

Music was my constant companion as I wrote, and this book may not exist without the wonderful sounds of Chuck Johnson, Mary Lattimore, Makaya McCraven, G.S. Schray, Sam Wilkes, Hiroshi Yoshimura, and many others.

Finally, I want to thank my wife, Abbey, and my children, Riley, Harrison, and Harlow, with whom I sacrificed a lot of time to write this book. Thank you for putting up with me while I was locked away in my office—or when I wasn't, but my mind still was. The four of you are the motivation for everything that I do.

## CHAPTER 1

Our Development Environment

John Wooden, the late coach of the UCLA men's basketball team, is one of the most successful coaches of all time, winning 10 national championships in a 12-year period. His teams consisted of top recruits, including hall-of-fame players such as Lew Alcindor (Kareem Abdul-Jabbar) and Bill Walton. On the first day of practice, Wooden would sit down each of his new recruits, players who had been the best in the United States in high school, and teach them to put on their socks properly. When asked about this, Wooden stated (*https://oreil.ly/lnZkf*) that "it's the little details that make the big things come about."

Chefs use the term *mise en place*, meaning "everything in its place," to describe the practice of preparing the tools and ingredients required for the menu prior to cooking. This preparation enables the kitchen's cooks to successfully prepare meals during busy rushes, as the small details have already been considered. Much like Coach Wooden's players and chefs preparing for a dinner rush, it is worth dedicating time to setting up our development environment.

A useful development environment does not require expensive software or top-of-the-line hardware. In fact, I'd encourage you to start simple, use open source software, and grow your tools with you. Though a runner prefers a specific brand of sneakers and a carpenter may always reach for her favorite hammer, it took time and experience to establish these preferences. Experiment with tools, observe others, and over time you will create the environment that works best for you.

In this chapter we'll install a text editor, Node.js, Git, MongoDB, and several helpful JavaScript packages as well as locate our terminal application. It's possible that you already have a development environment that works well for you; however, we will also be installing several required tools that will be used throughout the book. If you're like me and typically skip over the instruction manual, I'd still encourage you to read through this guide.

If you find yourself stuck at any point, please reach out to the JavaScript Everywhere community, via our Spectrum channel at *spectrum.chat/jseverywhere*.

Your Text Editor

Text editors are a lot like clothes. We all need them, but our preferences may vary wildly. Some like simple and well constructed. Some prefer the flashy paisley pattern. There's no wrong decision, and you should use whatever makes you most comfortable.

If you don't already have a favorite, I highly recommend Visual Studio Code (VSCode) (*https://code.visualstudio.com*). It's an open source editor that is available for Mac, Windows, and Linux. Additionally, it offers built-in features to simplify development and is easily modified with community extensions. It's even built using JavaScript!

The Terminal

If you're using VSCode, it comes with an integrated terminal. For most development tasks, this may be all you need. Personally, I find using a dedicated terminal client preferable as I find it easier to manage multiple tabs and use more dedicated window space on my machine. I'd suggest trying both and finding what works best for you.

Using a Dedicated Terminal Application

All operating systems come with a built-in terminal application and this is a great place to get started. On macOS it is called, fittingly enough, Terminal. On the Windows operating system, starting with Windows 7, the program is PowerShell. The name of the terminal for Linux distributions may vary, but often includes "Terminal."

Using VSCode

To access the terminal in VSCode, click Terminal → New Terminal. This will present you with a terminal window. The prompt will be present in the same directory as the current project.

Navigating the Filesystem

Once you've found your terminal, you'll need the critical ability to navigate the filesystem. You can do this using the cd command, which stands for "change directory."

Command-Line Prompts

Terminal instructions often include a $ or > at the start of the line. These are used to designate the prompt and should not be copied. In this book, I'll indicate the terminal prompt with a dollar sign ($). When entering instructions into your terminal application, do not type the $.

When you open your terminal application, you'll be presented with a cursor prompt, where you may enter commands. By default, you're in your computer's home directory. If you haven't already, I'd recommend making a *Projects* folder that is a subdirectory within your home directory. This folder can house all of your development projects. You create a *Projects* directory and navigate into that folder like so:

```
# first type cd, this will ensure you are in your root directory
$ cd
# next, if you don't already have a Projects directory, you can create one
# this will create Projects as a subfolder in your system's root directory
$ mkdir Projects
# finally you can cd into the Projects directory
$ cd Projects
```

In the future, you can navigate to your *Projects* directory as follows:

```
$ cd # ensure you are in the root directory
$ cd Projects
```

Now let's say you have a folder called *jseverywhere* in your *Projects* directory. You can type cd jseverywhere from the *Projects* directory to navigate into that folder. To navigate backward into a directory (in this case, to *Projects*), you would type cd .. (the cd command followed by two periods).

All together, this would look something like:

```
> $ cd # ensure you are in your root directory
> $ cd Projects # navigate from root dir to Projects dir
/Projects > $ cd jseverywhere # navigate from Projects dir to jsevewehre dir
/Projects/jseverwhere > $ cd .. # navigate back from jseverwhere to Projects
/Projects > $ # Prompt is currently in the Projects dir
```

If this is new to you, spend some time navigating through your files until you're comfortable. I've found that filesystem issues are a common tripping point for budding developers. Having a grasp of this will provide you with a solid foundation for establishing your workflows.

Command-Line Tools and Homebrew (Mac Only)

Certain command-line utilities are only available to macOS users once Xcode is installed. You can jump through this hoop, without installing Xcode, by installing xcode-select via your terminal. To do so, run the following command and click through the install prompts:

```
$ xcode-select --install
```

Homebrew is a package manager for macOS. It makes installing development dependencies, like programming languages and databases, as simple as running a command-line prompt. If you use a Mac, it will dramatically simplify your development environment. To install Homebrew, either head over to *brew.sh* to copy and paste the install command, or type the following in a single line:

```
$ /usr/bin/ruby -e "$(curl -fsSL
https://raw.githubusercontent.com/Homebrew/install/master/install)"
```

Node.js and NPM

Node.js (*https://nodejs.org*) is "a JavaScript runtime, built on Chrome's V8 JavaScript Engine." In practical terms this means that Node is a platform that allows developers to write JavaScript outside of a browser environment. Node.js comes with NPM, the default package manager. NPM enables you to install thousands of libraries and JavaScript tools within your projects.

Managing Node.js Versions

If you plan on managing a large number of Node projects, you may find that you also need to manage multiple versions of Node on your machine. If that's the case, I recommend using Node Version Manager (NVM) (*https://oreil.ly/fzBpO*) to install Node. NVM is a script that enables you to manage multiple active Node versions. For Windows users, I recommend nvm-windows (*https://oreil.ly/qJeej*). I won't be covering Node versioning, but it is a helpful tool. If this is your first time working with Node, I recommend proceeding with the following instructions for your system.

Installing Node.js and NPM for macOS

macOS users can install Node.js and NPM using Homebrew. To install Node.js, type the following command into your terminal:

```
$ brew update
$ brew install node
```

With Node installed, open your terminal application to verify it is working.

```
$ node --version
## Expected output v12.14.1, your version number may differ
$ npm --version
## Expected output 6.13.7, your version number may differ
```

If you see a version number after typing those commands, congratulations—you've successfully installed Node and NPM for macOS!

Installing Node.js and NPM for Windows

For Windows, the most straightforward way to install Node.js is to visit *nodejs.org* and download the installer for your operating system.

First, visit *nodejs.org* and install the LTS version (12.14.1 at the time of writing), following the installation steps for your operating system. With Node installed, open your terminal application to verify it is working.

```
$ node --version
## Expected output v12.14.1, your version number may differ
$ npm --version
## Expected output 6.13.7, your version number may differ
```

What is LTS?

LTS stands for "long-term support," meaning that the Node.js Foundation has committed to providing support and security updates for that major version number (in this case 12.x). The standard support window lasts for three years after the version's initial release. In Node.js, even-numbered releases are LTS versions. I recommend using an even-numbered release for application development.

If you see a version number after typing those commands, congratulations—you've successfully installed Node and NPM for Windows!

MongoDB

MongoDB is the database that we will be using while developing our API. Mongo is a popular choice for working with Node.js, because it treats our data as JSON (JavaScript Object Notation) documents. This means that it's comfortable for JavaScript developers to work with from the get-go.

Official MongoDB Installation Documentation

The MongoDB documentation offers a regularly updated guide for installing MongoDB Community Edition across operating systems. If you run into issues with the installation, I recommend consulting the documentation at *docs.mongodb.com/manual/administration/install-community*.

Installing and Running MongoDB for macOS

To install MongoDB for macOS, first install with Homebrew:

```
$ brew update
$ brew tap mongodb/brew
$ brew install mongodb-community@4.2
```

To start MongoDB, we can run it as a macOS service:

```
$ brew services start mongodb-community
```

This will start the MongoDB service and keep it running as a background process. Note that anytime you restart your machine and plan to develop with Mongo, you may need to run this command again to restart the MongoDB service. To verify that MongoDB has installed and is running, type **ps -ef | grep mongod** into your terminal. This will list the currently running Mongo processes.

Installing and Running MongoDB for Windows

To install MongoDB for Windows, first download the installer from the MongoDB Download Center (*https://oreil.ly/XNQj6*). Once the file has downloaded, run the installer following the installation wizard. I recommend choosing the Complete setup type, configuring it as a Service. All other values can remain as the defaults.

Once installation is complete, we may need to create the directory in which Mongo will write our data. Within your terminal, run the following commands:

```
$ cd C:\
$ md "\data\db"
```

To verify that MongoDB has installed and start the Mongo service:

1. Locate the Windows Services console.

2. Find the MongoDB service.

3. Right-click the MongoDB service.

4. Click Start.

Note that anytime you restart your machine and plan to develop with Mongo, you may need to restart the MongoDB service.

Git

Git is the most popular version control software, allowing you to do things like copy code repositories, merge code with others, and create branches of your own code that do not impact one another. Git will be helpful for "cloning" this book's sample code repositories, meaning it will allow you to directly copy a folder of sample code. Depending on your operating system, Git may already be installed. Type the following into your terminal window:

```
$ git --version
```

If a number is returned, congrats—you're all set! If not, visit *git-scm.com* to install Git, or use Homebrew for macOS. Once you've completed the installation steps, once again type **git --version** into your terminal to verify that it has worked.

Expo

Expo is a toolchain that simplifies the bootstrapping and development of iOS and Android projects with React Native. We will need to install the Expo command-line tool and, optionally (though recommended), the Expo app for iOS or Android. We'll cover this in more detail in the mobile application portion of the book, but if you're interested in getting a head start, visit *expo.io* to learn more. To install the command-line tools, type the following into your terminal:

```
npm install -g expo-cli
```

Using the -g global flag will make the expo-cli tool globally available to your machine's Node.js installation.

To install the Expo mobile application, visit the Apple App Store or Google Play Store on your device.

Prettier

Prettier is a code formatting tool with support for a number of languages, including JavaScript, HTML, CSS, GraphQL, and Markdown. It makes it easy to follow basic formatting rules, meaning that when you run the Prettier command, your code is automatically formatted to follow a standard set of best practices. Even better, you can configure your editor to do this automatically every time you save a file. This means that you'll never again have a project with issues like inconsistent spaces and mixed quotes.

I recommend installing Prettier globally on your machine and configuring a plug-in for your editor. To install Prettier globally, go to your command-line and type:

```
npm install -g prettier
```

Once you've installed Prettier, visit *Prettier.io* to find the plug-in for your text editor. With the editor plug-in installed, I recommend adding the following settings within your editor's settings file:

```
"editor.formatOnSave": true,
"prettier.requireConfig": true
```

These settings will automatically format files on save whenever a *.prettierrc* configuration file is within the project. The *.prettierrc* file specifies options for Prettier to follow. Now whenever that file is present, your editor will automatically reformat your code to meet the conventions of the project. Each project within this book will include a *.prettierrc* file.

ESLint

ESLint is a code linter for JavaScript. A linter differs from a formatter, such as Prettier, in that a linter also checks for code quality rules, such as unused variables, infinite loops, and unreachable code that falls after a return. As with Prettier, I recommend installing the ESLint plug-in for your favorite text editor. This will alert you to errors in real time as you write your code. You can find a list of editor plug-ins on the ESLint website (*https://oreil.ly/H3Zao*).

Similar to Prettier, projects can specify the ESLint rules they would like to follow within an *.eslintrc* file. This provides project maintainers with fine-grained control over their code preferences and a means to automatically enforce coding standards. Each of the projects within this book will include a helpful but permissive set of ESLint rules, aimed at helping you to avoid common pitfalls.

Making Things Look Nice

This is optional, but I've found that I enjoy programming just a bit more when I find my setup aesthetically pleasing. I can't help it; I have a degree in the arts. Take some time and test out different color themes and typefaces. Personally, I've grown to love the Dracula Theme (*https://draculatheme.com*), which is a color theme available for nearly every text editor and terminal, along with Adobe's Source Code Pro typeface (*https://oreil.ly/PktVn*).

Conclusion

In this chapter we've set up a working and flexible JavaScript development environment on our computer. One of the great joys of programming is personalizing your environment. I encourage you to experiment with the themes, colors, and tools that you use to make this environment your own. In the next section of the book, we will put this environment to work by developing our API application.

## CHAPTER 2

API Introduction

Picture yourself seated in a booth at a small, local restaurant where you've decided to order a sandwich. The server writes your order on a slip of paper and passes that paper to the cook. The cook reads the order, takes individual ingredients to build the sandwich, and passes the sandwich to the server. The server then brings the sandwich to you to eat. If you would then like some dessert, the process repeats.

An application programming interface (API) is a set of specifications that allows one computer program to interact with another. A web API works in much the same way as ordering a sandwich. A client requests some data, that data travels to a web server application over the HyperText Transfer Protocol (HTTP), the web server application takes the requests and processes the data, and the data is then sent to the client over HTTP.

In this chapter we'll explore the broad topic of web APIs and get started with our development by cloning the starter API project to our local machine. Before we do that, however, let's explore the requirements of the application that we'll be building.

What We're Building

Throughout the book we'll be building a social note application called Notedly. Users will be able to create an account, write notes in plain text or Markdown, edit their notes, view a feed of other users' notes, and "favorite" the notes of other users. In this portion of the book, we'll be developing the API to support this application.

In our API:

- Users will be able to create notes, as well as read, update, and delete the notes they've created.

- Users will be able to view a feed of notes created by other users, and read individual notes created by others, though they will not be able to update or delete them.
- Users will be able to create an account, log in, and log out.
- Users will be able to retrieve their profile information as well as the public profile information of other users.
- Users will be able to favorite the notes of other users as well as retrieve a list of their favorites.

Markdown

Markdown is a popular text markup language that is common in the programming community as well as in text applications such as iA Writer, Ulysses, Byword, and many more. To learn more about Markdown, take a look at the Markdown Guide website (*https://www.markdownguide.org*).

Though this sounds like a lot, I'll be breaking it down into small chunks throughout this portion of the book. Once you've learned to perform these types of interactions, you'll be able to apply them to building all sorts of APIs.

How We're Going to Build This

To build our API we'll be using the GraphQL API query language (*https://graphql.org*). GraphQL is an open source specification, first developed at Facebook in 2012. The advantage of GraphQL is that it allows the client to request precisely the data it needs, dramatically simplifying and limiting the number of requests. This also provides a distinct performance advantage when we're sending data to mobile clients, as we only need to send the data that the client needs. We'll be exploring how to write, develop, and consume GraphQL APIs throughout much of the book.

What about REST?

If you're familiar with Web API terminology, you've likely heard of REST (Representational State Transfer) APIs. The REST architecture has been (and continues to be) the dominant format for APIs. These APIs differ from GraphQL by relying upon the URL structure and query parameters to make requests to a server. While REST remains relevant, the simplicity of GraphQL, the robustness of tooling around GraphQL, and the potential performance gains of sending limited data over the wire make GraphQL my preference for modern platforms.

Getting Started

Before we can start development, we need to make a copy of the project starter files to our machine. The project's source code (*https://oreil.ly/mYKmE*) contains all of the scripts and references to third-party libraries that we will need to develop our application. To clone the code to your local machine, open the terminal, navigate to the directory where you keep your projects, **git clone** the project repository, and install the dependencies with **npm install**. It may also be helpful to create a *notedly* directory to keep all of the book's code organized:

```
$ cd Projects
$ mkdir notedly && cd notedly
$ git clone git@github.com:javascripteverywhere/api.git
$ cd api
$ npm install
```

> **Installing Third-Party Dependencies**
>
> By making a copy of the book's starter code and running npm install in the directory, you avoid having to run npm install again for any of the individual third-party dependencies.

The code is structured as follows:

/src

This is the directory where you should perform your development as you follow along with the book.

/solutions

This directory contains the solutions for each chapter. If you get stuck, these are available for you to consult.

/final

This directory contains the final working project.

Now that you have the code on your local machine, you'll need to make a copy of the project's *.env* file. This file is a place to keep environment-specific information or project secrets, such as the database URL, client IDs, and passwords. Because of this you never want to check it into source control. You'll need your own copy of the *.env* file. To do this, type the following into your terminal, from the *api* directory:

```
cp .env.example .env
```

You should now see an *.env* file in the directory. You don't yet need to do anything with this file, but we'll be adding information to it as we progress through the development of our API backend. The *.gitignore* file included with the project will ensure that you do not inadvertently commit your *.env* file.

Help, I Don't See the .env File!

By default, operating systems hide files that start with a period, as these are typically used by the system, not end users. If you don't see the *.env* file, try opening the directory in your text editor. The file should be visible in the file explorer of your editor. Alternately, typing `ls  -a` into your terminal window will list the files in the current working directory.

Conclusion

APIs provide an interface for data to flow from a database to applications. In doing so, they are the backbone of modern applications. By using GraphQL we can quickly develop modern, scalable API-based applications. In the next chapter we'll begin our API development by building a web server, using Node.js and Express.

## CHAPTER 3

A Web Application with Node and Express

Before implementing our API, we're going to build a basic server-side web application to serve as the basis for the backend of our API. We'll be using the Express.js framework (*https://expressjs.com*), a "minimalist web framework for Node.js," meaning that it does not ship with a lot of features, but is highly configurable. We'll be using Express.js as the foundation of our API server, but Express can also be used to build fully featured server-side web applications.

User interfaces, such as websites and mobile applications, communicate with web servers when they need to access data. This data could be anything from the HTML required to render a page in a web browser to the results of a user's search. The client interface communicates with the server using HTTP. The data request is sent from the client via HTTP to the web application that is running on the server. The web application then processes the request and returns the data to the client, again over HTTP.

In this chapter we'll build a small server-side web application, which will be the basis for our API. To do this, we'll use the Express.js framework to build a simple web application that sends a basic request.

Hello World

Now that you understand the basics of server-side web applications, let's jump in. Within the *src* directory of our API project, create a file named *index.js* and add the following:

```
const express = require('express');
const app = express();

app.get('/', (req, res) => res.send('Hello World'));
```

```
app.listen(4000, () => console.log('Listening on port 4000!'));
```

In this example, first we require the express dependency and create the app object, using the imported Express.js module. We then use the app object's get method to instruct our application to send a response of "Hello World" when a user accesses the root URL (/). Lastly, we instruct our application to run on port 4000. This will allow us to view the application locally at the URL *http://localhost:4000*.

Now to run the application, type **node src/index.js** in your terminal. After doing so, you should see a log in your terminal that reads Listening on port 4000!. If that's the case, you should be able to open a browser window to *http://localhost:4000* and see the result in Figure 3-1.

Figure 3-1. The results of our Hello World server code in the browser

Nodemon

Now, let's say that the output of this example doesn't properly express our excitement. We want to change our code so that it adds an exclamation mark to our response. Go ahead and do that, changing the res.send value to read Hello World!!!. The full line should now be:

```
app.get('/', (req, res) => res.send('Hello World!!!'));
```

If you go to your web browser and refresh the page, you'll notice that the output hasn't changed. This is because any changes we make to our web server require us to restart it. To do so, switch back to your terminal and press Ctrl + C to stop the server.

Now restart it by again typing **node index.js**. Now, when you navigate back to your browser and refresh the page, you should see the updated response.

As you can imagine, stopping and restarting our server for every change can quickly become tedious. Thankfully, we can use the Node package nodemon to automatically restart the server on changes. If you take a look at the project's *package.json* file, you'll see a dev command within the scripts object, which instructs nodemon to watch our *index.js* file:

```
"scripts": {
  ...
  "dev": "nodemon src/index.js"
  ...
}
```

package.json Scripts

There are a handful of other helper commands within the scripts object. We will explore those in future chapters.

Now, to start the application from the terminal, type:

```
npm run dev
```

Navigating to your browser and refreshing the page, you'll see that things are working as before. To confirm that nodemon automatically restarts the server, let's once again update our res.send value so that it reads:

```
res.send('Hello Web Server!!!')
```

Now, you should be able to refresh the page in your browser and see the update without manually restarting the server.

Extending Port Options

Currently our application is served on port 4000. This works great for local development, but we will need the flexibility to set this to a different port number when deploying the application. Let's take the steps to update this now. We'll start by adding a port variable:

```
const port = process.env.PORT || 4000;
```

This change will allow us to dynamically set the port in the Node environment, but fall back to port 4000 when no port is specified. Now let's adjust our app.listen code to work with this change and use a template literal to log the correct port:

```
app.listen(port, () =>
  console.log(`Server running at http://localhost:${port}`)
);
```

Our final code should now read:

```
const express = require('express');

const app = express();
const port = process.env.PORT || 4000;

app.get('/', (req, res) => res.send('Hello World!!!'));

app.listen(port, () =>
  console.log(`Server running at http://localhost:${port}`)
);
```

With this, we now have the basics of our web server code up and running. To test that everything is working, verify that no errors are present in your console and reload your web browser at *http://localhost:4000*.

Conclusion

Server-side web applications are the foundation of API development. In this chapter, we built a basic web application using the Express.js framework. When developing Node-based web applications, you have a wide array of frameworks and tools to choose from. Express.js is a great choice due to its flexibility, community support, and maturity as a project. In the next chapter, we'll turn our web application into an API.

## CHAPTER 4

Our First GraphQL API

Presumably, if you are reading this, you are a human being. As a human you have a number of interests and passions. You also have family members, friends, acquaintances, classmates, and colleagues. Those people also have their own social relationships, interests, and passions. Some of these relationships and interests overlap, while others do not. All together, we each have a connected graph of the people in our lives.

These types of interconnected data are exactly the challenge that GraphQL initially set out to solve in API development. By writing a GraphQL API we are able to efficiently connect data, which reduces the complexity and number of requests while allowing us to serve a client precisely the data they need.

Does that all sound like a bit of overkill for a notes application? Perhaps it does, but as you'll see, the tools and techniques provided by the GraphQL JavaScript ecosystem both enable and simplify all types of API development.

In this chapter we'll build a GraphQL API, using the `apollo-server-express` package. To do so, we'll explore fundamental GraphQL topics, write a GraphQL schema, develop code to resolve our schema functions, and access our API using the GraphQL Playground user interface.

Turning Our Server into an API (Sort Of)

Let's begin our API development by turning our Express server into a GraphQL server using the `apollo-server-express` package. Apollo Server (*https://oreil.ly/ 1fNt3*) is an open source GraphQL server library that works with a large number of Node.js server frameworks, including Express, Connect, Hapi, and Koa. It enables us to serve data as a GraphQL API from a Node.js application and also provides helpful tooling such as the GraphQL Playground, a visual helper for working with our API in development.

To write our API we'll be modifying the web application code we wrote in the previous chapter. Let's start by including the `apollo-server-express` package. Add the following to the top of your *src/index.js* file:

```
const { ApolloServer, gql } = require('apollo-server-express');
```

Now that we've imported `apollo-server`, we'll set up a basic GraphQL application. GraphQL applications consist of two primary components: a schema of type definitions and resolvers, which resolve the queries and mutations performed against the data. If that all sounds like nonsense, that's OK. We'll implement a "Hello World" API response and will further explore these GraphQL topics throughout the development of our API.

To begin, let's construct a basic schema, which we will store in a variable called `type Defs`. This schema will describe a single `Query` named `hello` that will return a string:

```
// Construct a schema, using GraphQL schema language
const typeDefs = gql`
  type Query {
    hello: String
  }
`;
```

Now that we've set up our schema, we can add a resolver that will return a value to the user. This will be a simple function that returns the string "Hello world!":

```
// Provide resolver functions for our schema fields
const resolvers = {
  Query: {
    hello: () => 'Hello world!'
  }
};
```

Lastly, we'll integrate Apollo Server to serve our GraphQL API. To do so, we'll add some Apollo Server–specific settings and middleware and update our `app.listen` code:

```
// Apollo Server setup
const server = new ApolloServer({ typeDefs, resolvers });

// Apply the Apollo GraphQL middleware and set the path to /api
server.applyMiddleware({ app, path: '/api' });

app.listen({ port }, () =>
  console.log(
    `GraphQL Server running at http://localhost:${port}${server.graphqlPath}`
  )
);
```

Putting it all together, our *src/index.js* file should now look like this:

```javascript
const express = require('express');
const { ApolloServer, gql } = require('apollo-server-express');

// Run the server on a port specified in our .env file or port 4000
const port = process.env.PORT || 4000;

// Construct a schema, using GraphQL's schema language
const typeDefs = gql`
  type Query {
    hello: String
  }
`;

// Provide resolver functions for our schema fields
const resolvers = {
  Query: {
    hello: () => 'Hello world!'
  }
};

const app = express();

// Apollo Server setup
const server = new ApolloServer({ typeDefs, resolvers });

// Apply the Apollo GraphQL middleware and set the path to /api
server.applyMiddleware({ app, path: '/api' });

app.listen({ port }, () =>
  console.log(
    `GraphQL Server running at http://localhost:${port}${server.graphqlPath}`
  )
);
```

If you've left the nodemon process running, you can head straight to your browser; otherwise, you must type npm run dev within the terminal application to start the server. Then visit *http://localhost:4000/api*, where you'll be greeted with the GraphQL Playground (Figure 4-1). This web app, which comes bundled with Apollo Server, is one of the great benefits of working with GraphQL. From here, you can run GraphQL queries and mutations and see the results. You can also click the Schema tab to access automatically created documentation for the API.

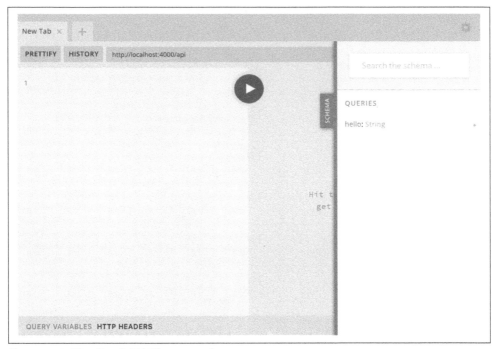

Figure 4-1. The GraphQL Playground

 GraphQL Playground has a dark colored default syntax theme. Throughout the book, I'll be using the "light" theme for its higher contrast. This is configurable in GraphQL Playground's settings, which can be accessed by clicking the gear icon.

We can now write our query against our GraphQL API. To do so, type the following into the GraphQL Playground:

```
query {
  hello
}
```

When you click the Play button, the query should return the following (Figure 4-2):

```
{
  "data": {
    "hello": "Hello world!"
  }
}
```

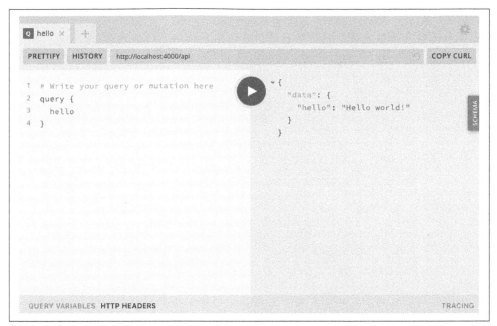

Figure 4-2. The hello query

And that's it! We now have a working GraphQL API that we've accessed via the GraphQL Playground. Our API takes a query of `hello` and returns the string `Hello world!`. More importantly, we now have the structure in place to build a fully featured API.

GraphQL Basics

In the previous section we dove right in and developed our first API, but let's take a few moments to step back and look at the different pieces of a GraphQL API. The two primary building blocks of a GraphQL API are *schemas* and *resolvers*. By understanding these two components, you can apply them more effectively to your API design and development.

Schemas

A schema is a written representation of our data and interactions. By requiring a schema, GraphQL enforces a strict plan for our API. This is because your API can only return data and perform interactions that are defined within the schema.

The fundamental component of GraphQL schemas are object types. In the previous example we created a GraphQL object type of `Query` with a field of `hello`, which returned a scalar type of `String`. GraphQL contains five built-in scalar types:

String
    A string with UTF-8 character encoding

Boolean
    A true or false value

Int
    A 32-bit integer

Float
    A floating-point value

ID
    A unique identifier

With these basic components we can construct a schema for an API. We do so by first defining the type. Let's imagine that we're creating an API for a pizza menu. In doing so, we might define a GraphQL schema type of `Pizza` like so:

```
type Pizza {
}
```

Now, each pizza has a unique ID, a size (such as small, medium, or large), a number of slices, and optional toppings. The `Pizza` schema might look something like this:

```
type Pizza {
  id: ID
  size: String
  slices: Int
  toppings: [String]
}
```

In this schema, some field values are required (such as ID, size, and slices), while others may be optional (such as toppings). We can express that a field must contain a value by using an exclamation mark. Let's update our schema to represent the required values:

```
type Pizza {
  id: ID!
  size: String!
  slices: Int!
  toppings: [String]
}
```

In this book, we'll be writing a basic schema, which will enable us to perform the vast majority of operations found in a common API. If you'd like to explore all of the GraphQL schema options, I'd encourage you to read the GraphQL schema documentation (*https://oreil.ly/DPT8C*).

Resolvers

The second piece of our GraphQL API will be resolvers. Resolvers perform exactly the action their name implies; they *resolve* the data that the API user has requested. We will write these resolvers by first defining them in our schema and then implementing the logic within our JavaScript code. Our API will contain two types of resolvers: queries and mutations.

Queries

A query requests specific data from an API, in its desired format. In our hypothetical pizza API we may write a query that will return a full list of pizzas on the menu and another that will return detailed information about a single pizza. The query will then return an object, containing the data that the API user has requested. A query never modifies the data, only accesses it.

Mutations

We use a mutation when we want to modify the data in our API. In our pizza example, we may write a mutation that changes the toppings for a given pizza and another that allows us to adjust the number of slices. Similar to a query, a mutation is also expected to return a result in the form of an object, typically the end result of the performed action.

Adapting Our API

Now that you have a good understanding of the components of GraphQL, let's adapt our initial API code for our notes application. To begin, we'll write some code to read and create notes.

The first thing we'll need is a little bit of data for our API to work with. Let's create an array of "note" objects, which we'll use as the basic data served by our API. As our project evolves, we'll replace this in-memory data representation with a database. For now, we will store our data in a variable named notes. Each note in the array will be an object with three properties, id, content, and author:

```
let notes = [
  { id: '1', content: 'This is a note', author: 'Adam Scott' },
  { id: '2', content: 'This is another note', author: 'Harlow Everly' },
  { id: '3', content: 'Oh hey look, another note!', author: 'Riley Harrison' }
];
```

Now that we have some data, we'll adapt our GraphQL API to work with it. Let's begin by focusing on our schema. Our schema is GraphQL's representation of our data and how it will be interacted with. We know that we will have notes, which will be queried and mutated. These notes will, for now, contain an ID, content, and an author field. Let's create a corresponding note type within our `typeDefs` GraphQL schema. This will represent the properties of a note within our API:

```
type Note {
  id: ID!
  content: String!
  author: String!
}
```

Now, let's add a query that will allow us to retrieve the list of all notes. Let's update the Query type to include a `notes` query, which will return the array of note objects:

```
type Query {
  hello: String!
  notes: [Note!]!
}
```

Now, we can update our resolver code to perform the work of returning the array of data. Let's update our Query code to include the following `notes` resolver, which returns the raw data object:

```
Query: {
    hello: () => 'Hello world!',
    notes: () => notes
  },
```

If we now go to the GraphQL playground, running at *http://localhost:4000/api*, we can test the `notes` query. To do so, type the following query:

```
query {
  notes {
    id
    content
    author
  }
}
```

Then, when you click the Play button, you should see a data object returned, which contains the data array (Figure 4-3).

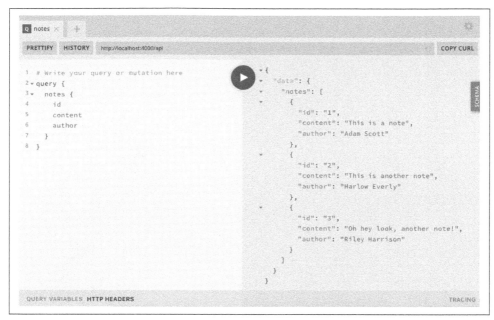

Figure 4-3. The notes query

To try out one of the coolest aspects of GraphQL, we can remove any of our requested fields, such as id or author. When we do so, the API returns precisely the data that we've requested. This allows the client that consumes the data to control the amount of data sent within each request and limit that data to exactly what is required (Figure 4-4).

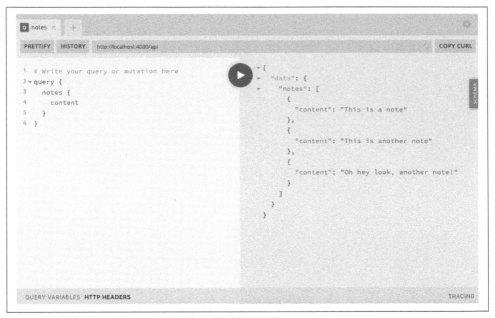

Figure 4-4. A notes query with only content data requested

Now that we can query our full list of notes, let's write some code that will allow us to query for a single note. You can imagine the usefulness of this from a user interface perspective, for displaying a view that contains a single, specific note. To do so, we'll want to request a note with a specific `id` value. This will require us to use an *argument* in our GraphQL schema. An argument allows the API consumer to pass specific values to the resolver function, providing the necessary information for it to resolve. Let's add a `note` query, which will take an argument of `id`, with the type `ID`. We'll update our `Query` object within our `typeDefs` to the following, which includes the new `note` query:

```
type Query {
  hello: String
  notes: [Note!]!
  note(id: ID!): Note!
}
```

With our schema updated, we can write a query resolver to return the requested note. To do this, we'll need to be able to read the API user's argument values. Helpfully, Apollo Server passes the following useful parameters to our resolver functions:

parent
    The result of the parent query, which is useful when nesting queries.

args
    These are the arguments passed by the user in the query.

context

Information passed along from the server application to the resolver functions. This could include things such as the current user or database information.

info

Information about the query itself.

We'll be exploring these further as needed within our code. If you're curious, you can learn more about these parameters in Apollo Server's documentation (*https://oreil.ly/ l6mL4*). For now, we'll need only the information contained within the second parameter, args.

The note query will take the note id as an argument and find it within our array of note objects. Add the following to the query resolver code:

```
note: (parent, args) => {
  return notes.find(note => note.id === args.id);
}
```

The resolver code should now look as follows:

```
const resolvers = {
  Query: {
    hello: () => 'Hello world!',
    notes: () => notes,
    note: (parent, args) => {
      return notes.find(note => note.id === args.id);
    }
  }
};
```

To run our query, let's go back to our web browser and visit the GraphQL Playground at *http://localhost:4000/api*. We can now query a note with a specific id as follows:

```
query {
  note(id: "1") {
    id
    content
    author
  }
}
```

When you run this query, you should receive the results of a note with the requested id value. If you attempt to query for a note that doesn't exist, you should receive a result with a value of null. To test this, try changing the id value to return different results.

Let's wrap up our initial API code by introducing the ability to create a new note, using a GraphQL mutation. In that mutation, the user will pass in the note's content. For now, we'll hardcode the author of the note. Let's begin by updating our `typeDefs` schema with a `Mutation` type, which we will call `newNote`:

```
type Mutation {
  newNote(content: String!): Note!
}
```

We'll now write a mutation resolver, which will take in the note content as an argument, store the note as an object, and add it in memory to our `notes` array. To do this, we'll add a `Mutation` object to our resolvers. Within the `Mutation` object, we'll add a function called `newNote`, with `parent` and `args` parameters. Within this function, we'll take the argument `content` and create an object with `id`, `content`, and `author` keys. As you may have noticed, this matches the current schema of a note. We will then push this object to our `notes` array and return the object. Returning the object allows the GraphQL mutation to receive a response in the intended format. Go ahead and write this code as follows:

```
Mutation: {
  newNote: (parent, args) => {
    let noteValue = {
      id: String(notes.length + 1),
      content: args.content,
      author: 'Adam Scott'
    };
    notes.push(noteValue);
    return noteValue;
  }
}
```

Our *src/index.js* file will now read like so:

```
const express = require('express');
const { ApolloServer, gql } = require('apollo-server-express');

// Run our server on a port specified in our .env file or port 4000
const port = process.env.PORT || 4000;

let notes = [
  { id: '1', content: 'This is a note', author: 'Adam Scott' },
  { id: '2', content: 'This is another note', author: 'Harlow Everly' },
  { id: '3', content: 'Oh hey look, another note!', author: 'Riley Harrison' }
];

// Construct a schema, using GraphQL's schema language
const typeDefs = gql`
  type Note {
    id: ID!
    content: String!
    author: String!
```

```
    }

    type Query {
      hello: String
      notes: [Note!]!
      note(id: ID!): Note!
    }

    type Mutation {
      newNote(content: String!): Note!
    }
  `;

// Provide resolver functions for our schema fields
const resolvers = {
  Query: {
    hello: () => 'Hello world!',
    notes: () => notes,
    note: (parent, args) => {
      return notes.find(note => note.id === args.id);
    }
  },
  Mutation: {
    newNote: (parent, args) => {
      let noteValue = {
        id: String(notes.length + 1),
        content: args.content,
        author: 'Adam Scott'
      };
      notes.push(noteValue);
      return noteValue;
    }
  }
};

const app = express();

// Apollo Server setup
const server = new ApolloServer({ typeDefs, resolvers });

// Apply the Apollo GraphQL middleware and set the path to /api
server.applyMiddleware({ app, path: '/api' });

app.listen({ port }, () =>
  console.log(
    `GraphQL Server running at http://localhost:${port}${server.graphqlPath}`
  )
);
```

With the schema and resolver updated to accept a mutation, let's try it out in GraphQL Playground at *http://localhost:4000/api*. In the playground, click the + sign to create a new tab and write the mutation as follows:

```
mutation {
  newNote (content: "This is a mutant note!") {
   content
   id
   author
   }
}
```

When you click the Play button, you should receive a response containing the content, ID, and author of our new note. You can also see that the mutation worked by rerunning the `notes` query. To do so, either switch back to the GraphQL Playground tab containing that query, or type the following:

```
query {
  notes {
    content
    id
    author
   }
}
```

When this query runs, you should now see four notes, including the recently added one.

Data Storage

We are currently storing our data in memory. This means that anytime we restart our server, we will lose that data. We'll be persisting our data using a database in the next chapter.

We've now successfully implemented our query and mutation resolvers and tested them within the GraphQL Playground user interface.

Conclusion

In this chapter we've successfully built a GraphQL API, using the `apollo-server-express` module. We can now run queries and mutations against an in-memory data object. This setup provides us a solid foundation on which to build any API. In the next chapter we'll explore the ability to persist data by using a database.

## CHAPTER 5

Database

When I was a kid, I obsessively collected sports cards of all types. A big part of collecting the cards was organizing them. I kept the star players in one box, basketball superstar Michael Jordan had an entire box dedicated to his cards, and the rest of my cards were kept organized by sport, and suborganized by team. This organization method enabled me to store the cards safely and easily find the card that I was looking for at any given time. Little did I know, but a storage system like this is the tangible equivalent to a database. At its core, a database allows us to store information and retrieve it later.

When I first started out with web development, I found databases intimidating. I would see instructions for running a database and entering obscure SQL commands, and it felt like an additional level of abstraction that I couldn't wrap my head around. Thankfully, I was eventually able to scale the wall and am no longer intimidated by a SQL table join, so if you are where I was, I want you to know that it is possible to navigate the world of databases.

In this book we'll be using MongoDB (*https://www.mongodb.com*) as our database of choice. I've chosen Mongo because it is a popular choice in the Node.js ecosystem and is a great database to get started with for anyone who is new to the topic. Mongo stores our data in "documents" that work like JavaScript objects. This means that we will be able to write and retrieve information in a format that is familiar to any JavaScript developer. However, if you have a database that you strongly prefer, such as PostgreSQL, the topics covered in this book are transferable to any type of system with a little work.

Before we can work with Mongo, we will need to ensure that the MongoDB server is running locally. This is something that is required throughout development. To do so, follow the instructions for your system in Chapter 1.

Getting Started with MongoDB

With Mongo running, let's explore how we can interact with Mongo directly from our terminal, using the Mongo shell. Begin by opening the MongoDB shell by typing the `mongo` command:

```
$ mongo
```

After running this command, you should see information about your MongoDB shell, the local server connection, and some additional information printed to the terminal. We can now interact directly with MongoDB from within the terminal application. We can create a database as well as switch to a new database with the `use` command. Let's create a database called `learning`:

```
$ use learning
```

In my card collection, described at the beginning of the chapter, I kept my cards organized in separate boxes. MongoDB brings with it the same concept, called *collections*. A collection is how we group similar documents together. For example, a blog application may have a collection for posts, another for users, and a third for comments. If we were to compare a collection to a JavaScript object, it would be the top-level object, while documents are the individual objects within. We can visualize it like so:

```
collection: {
  document: {},
  document: {},
  document: {}.
  ...
}
```

With this information in hand, let's create a document within a collection in our `learning` database. We'll create a `pizza` collection where we will store documents with a pizza type. Enter the following into the MongoDB shell:

```
$ db.pizza.save({ type: "Cheese" })
```

If this is successful, we should see a returned result that reads:

```
WriteResult({ "nInserted" : 1 })
```

We can also write multiple entries into the database at once:

```
$ db.pizza.save([{type: "Veggie"}, {type: "Olive"}])
```

Now that we've written some documents to our database, let's retrieve them. To do so, we'll use MongoDB's `find` method. To see all of the documents in the collection, run a `find` command with empty parameters:

```
$ db.pizza.find()
```

We should now see all three entries in the database. In addition to storing the data, MongoDB automatically assigns a unique ID to each entry. The results should look something like this:

```
{ "_id" : ObjectId("5c7528b223ab40938c7dc536"), "type" : "Cheese" }
{ "_id" : ObjectId("5c7529fa23ab40938c7dc53e"), "type" : "Veggie" }
{ "_id" : ObjectId("5c7529fa23ab40938c7dc53f"), "type" : "Olive" }
```

We can also find individual documents, both by property values as well as with Mongo's assigned ID:

```
$ db.pizza.find({ type: "Cheese" })
$ db.pizza.find({ _id: ObjectId("A DOCUMENT ID HERE") })
```

Not only do we want to be able to find documents, but it's also useful to be able to update them. We can do so by using Mongo's `update` method, which accepts a first parameter of a document to change and a second parameter of the change to the document. Let's update our `Veggie` pizza to be a `Mushroom` pizza:

```
$ db.pizza.update({ type: "Veggie" }, { type: "Mushroom" })
```

Now, if we run `db.pizza.find()`, we should see that your document has been updated:

```
{ "_id" : ObjectId("5c7528b223ab40938c7dc536"), "type" : "Cheese" }
{ "_id" : ObjectId("5c7529fa23ab40938c7dc53e"), "type" : "Mushroom" }
{ "_id" : ObjectId("5c7529fa23ab40938c7dc53f"), "type" : "Olive" }
```

As with updating a document, we can also remove one using Mongo's `remove` method. Let's remove the mushroom pizza from our database:

```
$ db.pizza.remove({ type: "Mushroom" })
```

Now if we perform a `db.pizza.find()` query, we will see only two entries within our collection. If we decided that we no longer wanted to include any of the data, we could run the `remove` method without an empty object parameter, which will wipe out our entire collection:

```
$ db.pizza.remove({})
```

We've now successfully used the MongoDB shell to create a database, add documents to a collection, update those documents, and remove them. These fundamental database operations will provide a solid footing as we integrate a database into our project. In development, we can also access our database using the MongoDB shell. This can prove helpful for tasks such as debugging and manually removing or updating entries.

Connecting MongoDB to Our Application

Now that you've learned a bit about using MongoDB from the shell, let's connect it to our API application. To do this, we'll be using the Mongoose Object Document Mapper (ODM) (*https://mongoosejs.com*). Mongoose is a library that simplifies working with MongoDB in Node.js applications by reducing and streamlining boilerplate code, through the use of its schema-based modeling solution. Yes, you read that right —another schema! As you'll see, once we've defined our database schema, working with MongoDB via Mongoose is similar to the types of commands we wrote within the Mongo shell.

We will first need to update our *.env* file with the URL of our local database. This will allow us to set the database URL in whatever environment we are working (such as local development and production). The default URL of a local MongoDB server is *mongodb://localhost:27017*, to which we'll add the name of our database. So, within our *.env* file, we will set a DB_HOST variable with the URL of our Mongo database instance as follows:

```
DB_HOST=mongodb://localhost:27017/notedly
```

The next step in working with a database in our application is to connect to it. Let's write some code that will connect our application to our database at startup. To do this, we'll first create a new file within the *src* directory, named *db.js*. Within *db.js* we'll write our database connection code. We'll also include a function to close our database connection, which will prove useful for testing the application.

In *src/db.js*, enter the following:

```
// Require the mongoose library
const mongoose = require('mongoose');

module.exports = {
  connect: DB_HOST => {
    // Use the Mongo driver's updated URL string parser
    mongoose.set('useNewUrlParser', true);
    // Use findOneAndUpdate() in place of findAndModify()
    mongoose.set('useFindAndModify', false);
    // Use createIndex() in place of ensureIndex()
    mongoose.set('useCreateIndex', true);
    // Use the new server discovery and monitoring engine
    mongoose.set('useUnifiedTopology', true);
    // Connect to the DB
    mongoose.connect(DB_HOST);
    // Log an error if we fail to connect
    mongoose.connection.on('error', err => {
      console.error(err);
      console.log(
        'MongoDB connection error. Please make sure MongoDB is running.'
      );
```

```
      process.exit();
    });
  },

  close: () => {
    mongoose.connection.close();
  }
};
```

Now we'll update our *src/index.js* to call this connection. To do so, we will first import our *.env* configuration as well as the *db.js* file. Within the imports, at the top of the file, add these imports:

```
require('dotenv').config();
const db = require('./db');
```

I like to store the DB_HOST value that is defined in the *.env* file as a variable. Add this variable directly below the port variable definition:

```
const DB_HOST = process.env.DB_HOST;
```

We can then call our connection, by adding the following to the *src/index.js* file:

```
db.connect(DB_HOST);
```

The *src/index.js* file will now read as follows:

```
const express = require('express');
const { ApolloServer, gql } = require('apollo-server-express');
require('dotenv').config();

const db = require('./db');

// Run the server on a port specified in our .env file or port 4000
const port = process.env.PORT || 4000;
// Store the DB_HOST value as a variable
const DB_HOST = process.env.DB_HOST;

let notes = [
  {
    id: '1',
    content: 'This is a note',
    author: 'Adam Scott'
  },
  {
    id: '2',
    content: 'This is another note',
    author: 'Harlow Everly'
  },
  {
    id: '3',
    content: 'Oh hey look, another note!',
    author: 'Riley Harrison'
  }
```

```
];

// Construct a schema, using GraphQL's schema language
const typeDefs = gql`
  type Note {
    id: ID
    content: String
    author: String
  }

  type Query {
    hello: String
    notes: [Note]
    note(id: ID): Note
  }

  type Mutation {
    newNote(content: String!): Note
  }
`;

// Provide resolver functions for our schema fields
const resolvers = {
  Query: {
    hello: () => 'Hello world!',
    notes: () => notes,
    note: (parent, args) => {
      return notes.find(note => note.id === args.id);
    }
  },
  Mutation: {
    newNote: (parent, args) => {
      let noteValue = {
        id: notes.length + 1,
        content: args.content,
        author: 'Adam Scott'
      };
      notes.push(noteValue);
      return noteValue;
    }
  }
};

const app = express();

// Connect to the database
db.connect(DB_HOST);

// Apollo Server setup
const server = new ApolloServer({ typeDefs, resolvers });

// Apply the Apollo GraphQL middleware and set the path to /api
```

```
server.applyMiddleware({ app, path: '/api' });

app.listen({ port }, () =>
  console.log(
    `GraphQL Server running at http://localhost:${port}${server.graphqlPath}`
  )
);
```

Though the actual functionality has not changed, if you run npm run dev, the application should successfully connect to the database and run without errors.

Reading and Writing Data from Our Application

Now that we can connect to our database, let's write the code needed to read and write data to it from within the application. Mongoose allows us to define how the data will be stored in our database as a JavaScript object, and we can then store and act upon data that fits that model structure. With this in mind, let's create our object, referred to as a Mongoose schema.

First, create a folder within our *src* directory called *models* to house this schema file. In this folder, create a file named *note.js*. Within *src/models/note.js*, we'll start by defining the basic setup of the file:

```
// Require the mongoose library
const mongoose = require('mongoose');

// Define the note's database schema
const noteSchema = new mongoose.Schema();

// Define the 'Note' model with the schema
const Note = mongoose.model('Note', noteSchema);
// Export the module
module.exports = Note;
```

Next, we will define our schema, within the noteSchema variable. Similar to the in-memory data example, our current schema will, for now, include the content of the note as well as a hardcoded string representing the author. We'll also include the option to include timestamps for our notes, which will be automatically stored when a note is created or edited. We'll be adding functionality to our note schema as we go.

Our Mongoose schema will be structured as follows:

```
// Define the note's database schema
const noteSchema = new mongoose.Schema(
  {
    content: {
      type: String,
      required: true
    },
    author: {
```

```
      type: String,
      required: true
    }
  },
  {
    // Assigns createdAt and updatedAt fields with a Date type
    timestamps: true
  }
);
```

Data Permanence

We'll be updating and changing our data model throughout development, at times removing all of the data from our database. As a result, I wouldn't recommend using this API to store important things like class notes, a list of your friends' birthdays, or the directions to your favorite pizza place.

Our overall *src/models/note.js* file should now read as follows:

```
// Require the mongoose library
const mongoose = require('mongoose');

// Define the note's database schema
const noteSchema = new mongoose.Schema(
  {
    content: {
      type: String,
      required: true
    },
    author: {
      type: String,
      required: true
    }
  },
  {
    // Assigns createdAt and updatedAt fields with a Date type
    timestamps: true
  }
);

// Define the 'Note' model with the schema
const Note = mongoose.model('Note', noteSchema);
// Export the module
module.exports = Note;
```

To simplify importing our models into our Apollo Server Express application, we'll add an *index.js* file to the *src/models* directory. This will combine our models into a single JavaScript module. While this isn't strictly necessary, I find it to be a good pattern to follow as applications and database models grow. In *src/models/index.js* we'll import our note model and add it to a `models` object to be exported:

```
const Note = require('./note');

const models = {
  Note
};

module.exports = models;
```

We can now incorporate our database models into our Apollo Server Express application code by importing our models into the *src/index.js* file:

```
const models = require('./models');
```

With our database model code imported, we can adapt our resolvers to save and read from the database, rather than an in-memory variable. To do this, we'll rewrite the `notes` query to pull the notes from the database by using the MongoDB `find` method:

```
notes: async () => {
  return await models.Note.find();
},
```

With our server running, we can visit the GraphQL Playground in our browser and run our `notes` query:

```
query {
  notes {
    content
    id
    author
  }
}
```

The expected result will be an empty array, since we have yet to add any data to our database (Figure 5-1):

```
{
  "data": {
    "notes": []
  }
}
```

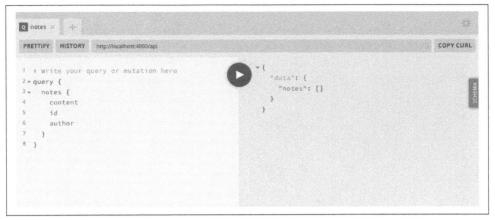

Figure 5-1. A notes query

To update our `newNote` mutation to add a note to our database, we'll use our Mon-goDB model's `create` method, which we'll accept an object. For now, we will continue to hardcode the author's name:

```
newNote: async (parent, args) => {
  return await models.Note.create({
    content: args.content,
    author: 'Adam Scott'
  });
}
```

We can now visit the GraphQL Playground and write a mutation that will add a note to our database:

```
mutation {
  newNote (content: "This is a note in our database!") {
    content
    author
    id
  }
}
```

Our mutation will return a new note, which contains the content we placed in our argument, the author's name, as well as a MongoDB-generated ID (Figure 5-2).

Figure 5-2. A mutation creates a new note in the database

If we now rerun our `notes` query, we should see our note retrieved from the database! (See Figure 5-3.)

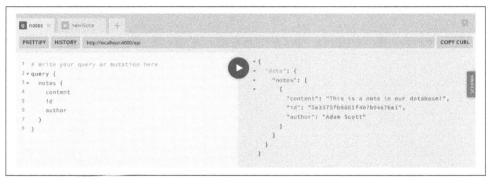

Figure 5-3. Our notes query returns the data from the database

The last step is to rewrite our notes query to pull a specific note from our database, using the unique ID that MongoDB assigns to each entry. To do so, we'll use Mongoose's findById method:

```
note: async (parent, args) => {
  return await models.Note.findById(args.id);
}
```

We can now write a query, using the unique ID we see in our notes query or newNote mutation, to retrieve an individual note from our database. To do so, we'll write a note query with an id argument (Figure 5-4):

```
query {
  note(id: "5c7bff794d66461e1e970ed3") {
    id
    content
    author
  }
}
```

Your Note ID

The ID used in the previous example is unique to my local database. Be sure to copy an ID from your own query or mutation results.

Figure 5-4. A query for an individual note

Our final *src/index.js* file will look as follows:

```
const express = require('express');
const { ApolloServer, gql } = require('apollo-server-express');
require('dotenv').config();

const db = require('./db');
const models = require('./models');
```

```javascript
// Run our server on a port specified in our .env file or port 4000
const port = process.env.PORT || 4000;
const DB_HOST = process.env.DB_HOST;

// Construct a schema, using GraphQL's schema language
const typeDefs = gql`
  type Note {
    id: ID
    content: String
    author: String
  }

  type Query {
    hello: String
    notes: [Note]
    note(id: ID): Note
  }

  type Mutation {
    newNote(content: String!): Note
  }
`;

// Provide resolver functions for our schema fields
const resolvers = {
  Query: {
    hello: () => 'Hello world!',
    notes: async () => {
      return await models.Note.find();
    },
    note: async (parent, args) => {
      return await models.Note.findById(args.id);
    }
  },
  Mutation: {
    newNote: async (parent, args) => {
      return await models.Note.create({
        content: args.content,
        author: 'Adam Scott'
      });
    }
  }
};

const app = express();

db.connect(DB_HOST);

// Apollo Server setup
const server = new ApolloServer({ typeDefs, resolvers });

// Apply the Apollo GraphQL middleware and set the path to /api
```

```
server.applyMiddleware({ app, path: '/api' });

app.listen({ port }, () =>
  console.log(
    `GraphQL Server running at http://localhost:${port}${server.graphqlPath}`
  )
);
```

We can now read and write data from our database with our GraphQL API! Try adding more notes, viewing the full list of notes using the notes query, and viewing the content of individual notes by utilizing the note query.

Conclusion

In this chapter you learned to use MongoDB and the Mongoose library with our API. A database, such as MongoDB, allows us to securely store and retrieve our application's data. An object modeling library, such as Mongoose, simplifies working with a database by providing tools for database queries and data validation. In the next chapter, we'll update our API to have full CRUD (create, read, update, and delete) functionality with our database content.

## CHAPTER 6

CRUD Operations

The first time I heard the term "CRUD application," I wrongfully assumed that it referred to an application that did something dirty or tricky. Admittedly, "CRUD" sounds as if it refers to something that would be scraped off the bottom of a shoe. In fact, the acronym was first popularized in the early 1980s by British technology author James Martin in reference to applications that create, read, update, and delete data. Though the term has been around for well over a quarter of a century, it still applies to many applications developed today. Consider the applications that you interact with daily—to-do lists, spreadsheets, content management systems, text editors, social media websites, and several others—and chances are that many of them fall into the CRUD application format. A user creates some data, accesses or reads data, and may update or delete that data.

Our Notedly application will follow the CRUD pattern. Users will be able to create, read, update, and delete their own notes. In this chapter, we'll implement the essential CRUD functionality of our API by connecting our resolvers and database.

Separating Our GraphQL Schema and Resolvers

Currently our *src/index.js* file is home to our Express/Apollo server code as well as our API's schema and resolvers. As you can imagine, this could get a bit unwieldy as our codebase grows. Before this happens, let's take some time to do a minor refactor that separates our schema, resolvers, and server code.

To begin, let's move our GraphQL schema to its own file. First, we'll make a new file called *src/schema.js* in the *src* folder and then move our schema content, found in our typeDefs variable, to that file. To do so, we'll also need to import the gql schema language that comes with the apollo-server-express package and export our schema as a module, using Node's `module.exports` method. While we're at it, we can also remove the `hello` query, which we won't need in our final application:

```
const { gql } = require('apollo-server-express');

module.exports = gql`
  type Note {
    id: ID!
    content: String!
    author: String!
  }

  type Query {
    notes: [Note!]!
    note(id: ID!): Note!
  }

  type Mutation {
    newNote(content: String!): Note!
  }
`;
```

We can now update our *src/index.js* file to use this external schema file by importing it and removing the `gql` import from `apollo-server-express` like so:

```
const { ApolloServer } = require('apollo-server-express');

const typeDefs = require('./schema');
```

Now that we have isolated our GraphQL schema to its own file, let's do something similar for our GraphQL resolver code. Our resolver code will encompass the vast majority of our API's logic, so first we'll create a folder to house this code, called *resolvers*. Within the *src/resolvers* directory we'll begin with three files: *src/resolvers/index.js*, *src/resolvers/query.js*, and *src/resolvers/mutation.js*. Similar to the pattern we followed in our database models, the *src/resolvers/index.js* file will be used to import our resolver code into a single exported module. Go ahead and set up this file like so:

```
const Query = require('./query');
const Mutation = require('./mutation');

module.exports = {
  Query,
  Mutation
};
```

Now you can set up the *src/resolvers/query.js* for the API query code:

```
module.exports = {
  notes: async () => {
    return await models.Note.find()
  },
  note: async (parent, args) => {
```

```
    return await models.Note.findById(args.id);
  }
 }
```

Then move the mutation code to the *src/resolvers/mutation.js* file:

```
module.exports = {
  newNote: async (parent, args) => {
    return await models.Note.create({
      content: args.content,
      author: 'Adam Scott'
    });
  }
}
```

Next, the server to import the resolver code by adding the following line to the *src/ index.js* file:

```
const resolvers = require('./resolvers');
```

The final step in refactoring our resolvers is to connect them to our database models. As you may have noticed, our resolver modules reference these models, but have no way of accessing them. To fix this problem, we'll use a concept that Apollo Server calls *context*, which allows us to pass specific information along from our server code to an individual resolver with each request. For now, this may feel excessive, but it will be useful for incorporating user authentication into our application. To do this, we'll update our Apollo Server setup code in *src/index.js* with a `context` function that will return our database models:

```
// Apollo Server setup
const server = new ApolloServer({
  typeDefs,
  resolvers,
  context: () => {
    // Add the db models to the context
    return { models };
  }
});
```

Now we'll update each of our resolvers to make use of this context by adding { `models` } as the third parameter in each function.

Do the following in *src/resolvers/query.js*:

```
module.exports = {
  notes: async (parent, args, { models }) => {
    return await models.Note.find()
  },
  note: async (parent, args, { models }) => {
    return await models.Note.findById(args.id);
  }
}
```

Move the mutation code to the *src/resolvers/mutation.js* file:

```
module.exports = {
  newNote: async (parent, args, { models }) => {
    return await models.Note.create({
      content: args.content,
      author: 'Adam Scott'
    });
  }
}
```

Our *src/index.js* file will now be simplified as follows:

```
const express = require('express');
const { ApolloServer } = require('apollo-server-express');
require('dotenv').config();

// Local module imports
const db = require('./db');
const models = require('./models');
const typeDefs = require('./schema');
const resolvers = require('./resolvers');

// Run our server on a port specified in our .env file or port 4000
const port = process.env.PORT || 4000;
const DB_HOST = process.env.DB_HOST;

const app = express();

db.connect(DB_HOST);

// Apollo Server setup
const server = new ApolloServer({
  typeDefs,
  resolvers,
  context: () => {
    // Add the db models to the context
    return { models };
  }
});

// Apply the Apollo GraphQL middleware and set the path to /api
server.applyMiddleware({ app, path: '/api' });

app.listen({ port }, () =>
  console.log(
    `GraphQL Server running at http://localhost:${port}${server.graphqlPath}`
  )
);
```

Writing Our GraphQL CRUD Schema

Now that we've refactored our code for flexibility, let's begin implementing our CRUD operations. We are already able to Create and Read notes, which leaves us with implementing our Update and Delete functionality. First, we'll want to update our schema.

Since update and delete operations will make changes to our data, they will be mutations. Our update note will require an ID argument to locate the note as well as the new note content. The update query will then return the newly updated note. For our delete operation, our API will return a Boolean value of `true` to inform us that the note deletion was successful.

Update the `Mutation` schema in *src/schema.js* as follows:

```
type Mutation {
  newNote(content: String!): Note!
  updateNote(id: ID!, content: String!): Note!
  deleteNote(id: ID!): Boolean!
}
```

With these additions, our schema is now ready to perform CRUD operations.

CRUD Resolvers

With our schema in place, we can now update our resolvers to either remove or update a note. Let's begin with our `deleteNote` mutation. To delete a note, we will use Mongoose's `findOneAndRemove` method and pass it the `id` of the item that we want to delete. If our item is found and deleted, we'll return `true` to the client, but if our item fails to delete, we'll return `false`.

In *src/resolvers/mutation.js*, add the following, within the `module.exports` object:

```
deleteNote: async (parent, { id }, { models }) => {
  try {
    await models.Note.findOneAndRemove({ _id: id});
    return true;
  } catch (err) {
    return false;
  }
},
```

Now we can run our mutation in the GraphQL Playground. In a new tab in the Playground, write the following mutation, being sure to use an ID from one of the notes in your database:

```
mutation {
  deleteNote(id: "5c7d1aacd960e03928804308")
}
```

If the note was successfully deleted, you should receive a response of `true`:

```
{
  "data": {
    "deleteNote": true
  }
}
```

If you pass a nonexistent ID, you'll receive a response of `"deleteNote": false`.

With our delete functionality in place, let's write our `updateNote` mutation. To do this, we will use Mongoose's `findOneAndUpdate` method. This method will take an initial parameter of a query to find the correct note in the database, followed by a second parameter where we'll `$set` new note content. Lastly, we'll pass a third parameter of `new: true`, which instructs the database to return the updated note content to us.

In *src/resolvers/mutation.js*, add the following within the `module.exports` object:

```
updateNote: async (parent, { content, id }, { models }) => {
  return await models.Note.findOneAndUpdate(
    {
      _id: id,
    },
    {
      $set: {
        content
      }
    },
    {
      new: true
    }
  );
},
```

We can now visit the GraphQL Playground in our browser to try out our `updateNote` mutation. In a new tab in the playground, write a mutation with the parameters of an `id` and `content`:

```
mutation {
  updateNote(
    id: "5c7d1f0a31191c4413edba9d",
    content: "This is an updated note!"
  ){
    id
    content
  }
}
```

If our mutation worked as intended, the GraphQL response should read as follows:

```
{
  "data": {
    "updateNote": {
```

```
      "id": "5c7d1f0a31191c4413edba9d",
      "content": "This is an updated note!"
    }
  }
}
```

If we pass an incorrect ID, the response fails and we will receive an internal server error with an `Error updating note` message.

We are now able to create, read, update, and delete notes. With this we have full CRUD functionality in our API.

Date and Time

When we created our database schema, we requested that Mongoose automatically store timestamps to record when entries are created and updated in the database. This information will be useful in our application, as it will allow us to show the user when a note was created or last edited within our user interface. Let's add `createdAt` and `updatedAt` fields to our schema so we can return these values.

You may recall that GraphQL allows for the default types of `String`, `Boolean`, `Int`, `Float`, and `ID`. Unfortunately GraphQL does not come with a built-in date scalar type. We *could* use the `String` type, but this would mean that we wouldn't be taking advantage of the type validation that GraphQL offers, ensuring that our dates and times are actually dates and times. Instead, we'll create a custom scalar type. A custom type allows us to define a new type and validate it against every query and mutation that requests data of that type.

Let's update our GraphQL schema in *src/schema.js* by adding a custom scalar at the top of our `GQL` string literal:

```
module.exports = gql`
  scalar DateTime
  ...
`;
```

Now, within the `Note` type, add the `createdAt` and `updatedAt` fields:

```
type Note {
  id: ID!
  content: String!
  author: String!
  createdAt: DateTime!
  updatedAt: DateTime!
}
```

The last step is to validate this new type. While we can write our own validation, for our use case we'll use the `graphql-iso-date` package (*https://oreil.ly/CtmP6*). To do so we'll add validation to any resolver function that requests a value with a type of `DateTime`.

In the *src/resolvers/index.js* file, import the package and add a `DateTime` value to the exported resolvers like so:

```
const Query = require('./query');
const Mutation = require('./mutation');
const { GraphQLDateTime } = require('graphql-iso-date');

module.exports = {
  Query,
  Mutation,
  DateTime: GraphQLDateTime
};
```

Now if we visit the GraphQL Playground in our browser and refresh the page, we can validate that our custom types work as intended. If we consult our schema, we can see that the `createdAt` and `updatedAt` fields have a type of `DateTime`. As Figure 6-1 shows, the documentation of this type states that it is a "date-time string at UTC."

Figure 6-1. Our schema now features DateTime types

To test this, let's write a `newNote` mutation in the GraphQL Playground that includes our date fields:

```
mutation {
  newNote (content: "This is a note with a custom type!") {
    content
    author
    id
    createdAt
    updatedAt
  }
}
```

This will return `createdAt` and `updatedAt` values as an ISO-formatted date. If we then run an `updateNote` mutation against the same note, we'll see an `updatedAt` value that differs from the `createdAt` date.

For more information on defining and validating custom scalar types, I recommend Apollo Server's "Custom scalars and enums" documentation (*https://oreil.ly/0rWAC*).

Conclusion

In this chapter we added create, read, update, and delete (CRUD) functionality to our API. CRUD applications are an incredibly common pattern used by many applications. I encourage you to look at the applications that you interact with daily and think about how their data may fit into this pattern. In the next chapter, we will add functionality to our API to create and authenticate user accounts.

## CHAPTER 7

User Accounts and Authentication

Picture yourself walking down a dark alley. You are on your way to join the "Secret Club for Super Cool People" (if you're reading this, you are a well-deserving member). As you enter the hidden door to the club, you are greeted by a receptionist who hands you a form to complete. On the form, you must enter your name and a password, which will be known only by you and the receptionist.

Once you have completed the form, you hand it back to the receptionist, who goes to the back room of the club. In the back room, the receptionist uses a secret key to encrypt your password and then stores the encrypted password in a locked file vault. The receptionist then stamps a coin, on which is pressed your unique membership ID. Upon returning to the front room, the receptionist hands you the coin, which you tuck away in your pocket. Now each time you return to the club, you need only show your coin to gain entrance.

This interaction may sound like something out of a low-budget spy movie, but it's nearly identical to the process that is followed each time we sign up for a web application. In this chapter, we'll learn how to build GraphQL mutations that will allow a user to create an account and sign in to our application. We'll also learn how to encrypt the user's password and return a token to the user, which they can use to verify their identity when they interact with our application.

Application Authentication Flow

Before we get started, let's step back and map out the flow users will follow when they sign up for an account and log in to an existing account. If you don't yet understand all of the concepts covered here, don't worry: we will approach them bit by bit. First, let's review the account creation flow:

1. A user enters their intended email, username, and password into a field in a user interface (UI), such as the GraphQL Playground, a web application, or a mobile application.

2. The UI sends a GraphQL mutation to our server with the user's information.

3. The server encrypts the password and stores the user's information in the database.

4. The server returns a token to the UI, which contains the user's ID.

5. The UI stores this token, for a specified period of time, and sends it with every request to the server to verify the user.

Now let's look at the user sign-in flow:

1. A user enters their email or username and password into a field in a UI.

2. The UI sends a GraphQL mutation to our server with this information.

3. The server decrypts the password stored in the database and compares it with the one the user entered.

4. If the passwords match, the server returns a token to the UI, which contains the user's ID.

5. The UI stores this token, for a specified period of time, and sends it with every request to the server.

As you can see, these flows are very similar to our "secret club" flow. In this chapter we'll focus on implementing the API portions of these interactions.

Password Reset Flow

You'll notice that our application does not allow users to change their password. We could allow users to reset their password with a single mutation resolver, but it is much more secure to verify the reset request via email first. For brevity's sake we won't be implementing password reset functionality in this book, but if you are interested in examples and resources for creating a password reset flow, please visit the JavaScript Everywhere Spectrum community (*https://spectrum.chat/jseverywhere*).

Encryption and Tokens

In our exploration of the user authentication flow, I mentioned encryption and tokens. These sound like mythological dark arts, so let's take a moment to look at each of these in more detail.

Encrypting Passwords

To effectively encrypt user passwords, we should use a combination of hashing and salting. *Hashing* is the act of obscuring a string of text by turning it into a seemingly random string. Hashing functions are "one way," meaning that once the text is hashed it cannot be reverted to the original string. When a password is hashed, the plain text of the password is never stored in our database. *Salting* is the act of generating a random string of data that will be used in addition to the hashed password. This ensures that even if two user passwords are the same, the hashed and salted versions will be unique.

bcrypt is a popular hashing function based on the blowfish cipher (*https://oreil.ly/4VjII*) and commonly used within a range of web frameworks. In Node.js development we can use the bcrypt module (*https://oreil.ly/t2Ppc*) to both salt and hash our passwords.

In our application code we would require the bcrypt module and write a function to handle the salting and hashing.

Salting and Hashing Examples

The following example is for illustrative purposes. We will integrate password salting and hashing with bcrypt later in the chapter.

```
// require the module
const bcrypt = require('bcrypt');

// the cost of processing the salting data, 10 is the default
const saltRounds = 10;

// function for hashing and salting
const passwordEncrypt = async password => {
  return await bcrypt.hash(password, saltRounds)
};
```

In this example, I could pass a password of PizzaP@rty99, which generates a salt of $2a$10$HF2rs.iYSvX1l5FPrX6970 and the hashed and salted password of $2a$10$HF2rs.iYSvX1l5FPrX69709dYF/O2kwHuKdQTdy.7oaMwVga54bWG (which is the salt plus an encrypted password string).

Now when checking a user's password against the hashed and salted password, we will use the bcrypt's compare method:

```
// password is a value provided by the user
// hash is retrieved from our DB
const checkPassword = async (plainTextPassword, hashedPassword) => {
  // res is either true or false
```

```
      return await bcrypt.compare(hashedPassword, plainTextPassword)
    };
```

With the user passwords encrypted, we are able to safely store them in a database.

JSON Web Tokens

As a user it would be extremely frustrating if we needed to enter our username and password each time we wanted to access a single protected page of a site or application. Instead, we can securely store a user's ID on their device within a JSON Web Token (*https://jwt.io*). With each request the user makes from the client, they can send that token, which the server will use to identify the user.

A JSON Web Token (JWT) consists of three parts:

Header
General information about the token and type of signing algorithm that is being used

Payload
The information that we've intentionally stored within the token (such as the username or ID)

Signature
A means to verify the token

If we were to look at the token, it would appear to be made up of random characters with each part separated by a period: xx-header-xx.yy-payload-yy.zz-signature-zz.

In our application code we can use the jsonwebtoken module (*https://oreil.ly/IYxkH*) to generate and validate our tokens. To do this we pass in the information we wish to store, along with a secret password, which would typically be stored within our *.env* file.

```
const jwt = require('jsonwebtoken');

// generate a JWT that stores a user id
const generateJWT = await user => {
  return await jwt.sign({ id: user._id }, process.env.JWT_SECRET);
}

// validate the JWT
const validateJWT = await token => {
  return await jwt.verify(token, process.env.JWT_SECRET);
}
```

By using JWTs, we can securely return and store a user's ID with the client application.

Integrating Authentication into Our API

Now that you have a solid understanding of the components of user authentication, we'll implement the ability for users to sign up and sign in to our application. To do this we'll be updating both our GraphQL and Mongoose schemas, writing `signUp` and `signIn` mutation resolvers that generate a user token, and validating the token on each request to the server.

User Schemas

To begin we will update our GraphQL schema by adding a `User` type and updating the `Note` type's `author` field to reference the `User`. To do so, update the *src/schema.js* file as follows:

```
type Note {
 id: ID!
 content: String!
 author: User!
 createdAt: DateTime!
 updatedAt: DateTime!
}

type User {
 id: ID!
 username: String!
 email: String!
 avatar: String
 notes: [Note!]!
}
```

When a user signs up for our application, they will submit a username, email address, and password. When a user signs in to our application, they will send a mutation containing their username or email address along with a password. If a sign-up or sign-in mutation is successful, the API will return a token as a string. To accomplish this in our schema, we will need to add two new mutations to our *src/schema.js* file, each of which will return a String, which will be our JWT:

```
type Mutation {
  ...
  signUp(username: String!, email: String!, password: String!): String!
  signIn(username: String, email: String, password: String!): String!
}
```

Now that our GraphQL schema has been updated, we also need to update our database models. To do this we'll create a Mongoose schema file in *src/models/user.js*. This file will be set up similarly to our note model file, with fields for username, email, password, and avatar. We will also require the username and email fields to be unique in our database by setting index: { unique: true }.

To create the user database model, enter the following in your *src/models/user.js* file:

```
const mongoose = require('mongoose');

const UserSchema = new mongoose.Schema(
  {
    username: {
      type: String,
      required: true,
      index: { unique: true }
    },
    email: {
      type: String,
      required: true,
      index: { unique: true }
    },
    password: {
      type: String,
      required: true
    },
    avatar: {
      type: String
    }
  },
  {
    // Assigns createdAt and updatedAt fields with a Date type
    timestamps: true
  }
);

const User = mongoose.model('User', UserSchema);
module.exports = User;
```

With our user model file in place, we now must update the *src/models/index.js* to export the model:

```
const Note = require('./note');
const User = require('./user');

const models = {
  Note,
  User
};

module.exports = models;
```

Authentication Resolvers

With our GraphQL and Mongoose schemas written, we can implement the resolvers that will allow a user to sign up and sign in to our application.

First, we need to add a value to the JWT_SECRET variable in our *.env* file. This value should be a string without spaces. It will be used to sign our JWT, which allows us to verify them when they are decoded.

```
JWT_SECRET=YourPassphrase
```

Once we have created this variable, we can import the required packages within our *mutation.js* file. We will utilize the third-party bcrypt, jsonwebtoken, mongoose, and dotenv packages as well as importing Apollo Server's AuthenticationError and For biddenError utilities. Additionally, we'll import the gravatar utility function, which I've included with the project. This will generate a Gravatar image URL (*https://en.gravatar.com*) from a user's email address.

In *src/resolvers/mutation.js*, enter the following:

```
const bcrypt = require('bcrypt');
const jwt = require('jsonwebtoken');
const {
  AuthenticationError,
  ForbiddenError
} = require('apollo-server-express');
require('dotenv').config();

const gravatar = require('../util/gravatar');
```

Now we can write our signUp mutation. This mutation will accept a username, email address, and password as parameters. We will normalize the email address and username by trimming any whitespace and converting it to all lowercase. Next, we will encrypt the user's password using the bcrypt module. We will also generate a Gravatar image URL for user avatars by using our helper library. Once we have performed these actions, we will store the user in the database and return a token to the user. We can set this all up within a try/catch block, so that our resolver returns an intention-ally vague error to the client if there are any issues with the sign-up process.

To accomplish all of this, write the signUp mutation as follows within the *src/resolvers/mutation.js* file:

```
signUp: async (parent, { username, email, password }, { models }) => {
  // normalize email address
  email = email.trim().toLowerCase();
  // hash the password
  const hashed = await bcrypt.hash(password, 10);
  // create the gravatar url
  const avatar = gravatar(email);
  try {
    const user = await models.User.create({
      username,
      email,
      avatar,
      password: hashed
    });

    // create and return the json web token
    return jwt.sign({ id: user._id }, process.env.JWT_SECRET);
  } catch (err) {
    console.log(err);
    // if there's a problem creating the account, throw an error
    throw new Error('Error creating account');
  }
},
```

Now, if we switch over to the GraphQL Playground in our browser, we can try out our signUp mutation. To do so we'll write a GraphQL mutation with username, email, and password values:

```
mutation {
  signUp(
    username: "BeeBoop",
    email: "robot@example.com",
    password: "NotARobot10010!"
  )
}
```

When we run the mutation, our server will return a token like this (Figure 7-1):

```
"data": {
  "signUp": "eyJhbGciOiJIUzI1NiIsInR5cCI6..."
}
}
```

Figure 7-1. The signUp mutation in the GraphQL Playground

The next step will be to write our signIn mutation. This mutation will accept the user's username, email, and password. It will then find the user in the database, based on the username or email address. Once the user is located, it will decrypt the password stored in the database and compare it with the one the user has entered. If the user and password match, our application will return a token to the user. If they don't match, we'll want to throw an error.

Write this mutation as follows in the *src/resolvers/mutation.js* file:

```
signIn: async (parent, { username, email, password }, { models }) => {
  if (email) {
    // normalize email address
    email = email.trim().toLowerCase();
  }

  const user = await models.User.findOne({
    $or: [{ email }, { username }]
  });

  // if no user is found, throw an authentication error
  if (!user) {
    throw new AuthenticationError('Error signing in');
  }

  // if the passwords don't match, throw an authentication error
  const valid = await bcrypt.compare(password, user.password);
  if (!valid) {
    throw new AuthenticationError('Error signing in');
  }

  // create and return the json web token
  return jwt.sign({ id: user._id }, process.env.JWT_SECRET);
}
```

We can now visit the GraphQL Playground in our browser and try out the `signIn` mutation, using the account we created with our `signUp` mutation:

```
mutation {
  signIn(
    username: "BeeBoop",
    email: "robot@example.com",
    password: "NotARobot10010!"
  )
}
```

Again, if successful, our mutation should resolve with a JWT (Figure 7-2):

```
{
  "data": {
    "signIn": "<TOKEN VALUE>"
  }
}
```

Figure 7-2. The signIn mutation in the GraphQL Playground

With these two resolvers in place, users will be able to both sign up for and sign in to our application using JWTs. To experiment with this, try adding more accounts and even intentionally entering incorrect information, such as passwords that do not match, to see what the GraphQL API returns.

Adding the User to the Resolver Context

Now that a user can use a GraphQL mutation to receive a unique token, we'll need to verify that token on each request. Our expectation will be that our client, whether it be web, mobile, or desktop, will send the token with the request in an HTTP header named `Authorization`. We can then read the token from the HTTP header, decode it using our `JWT_SECRET` variable, and pass along the user's information with the context to each GraphQL resolver. By doing this, we can determine if a signed-in user is making a request, and if so, which user it is.

First, import the `jsonwebtoken` module into the *src/index.js* file:

```
const jwt = require('jsonwebtoken');
```

With the module imported, we can add a function that will verify the validity of the token:

```
// get the user info from a JWT
const getUser = token => {
  if (token) {
    try {
      // return the user information from the token
      return jwt.verify(token, process.env.JWT_SECRET);
    } catch (err) {
      // if there's a problem with the token, throw an error
      throw new Error('Session invalid');
    }
  }
};
```

Now, within each GraphQL request we will grab the token from the header of the request, attempt to verify the validity of the token, and add the user's information to the context. Once this is done, each GraphQL resolver will have access to the user ID we stored in the token.

```
// Apollo Server setup
const server = new ApolloServer({
  typeDefs,
  resolvers,
  context: ({ req }) => {
    // get the user token from the headers
    const token = req.headers.authorization;
    // try to retrieve a user with the token
    const user = getUser(token);
    // for now, let's log the user to the console:
    console.log(user);
    // add the db models and the user to the context
    return { models, user };
  }
});
```

Though we're not yet performing user interactions, we can test our user context within the GraphQL Playground. In the lower-left corner of the GraphQL Playground UI, there is a space labeled HTTP Headers. In that portion of the UI, we can add a header that contains a JWT that was returned in either our `signUp` or `signIn` mutation as follows (Figure 7-3):

```
{
  "Authorization": "<YOUR_JWT>"
}
```

QUERY VARIABLES **HTTP HEADERS (1)**

```
1  {
2    "Authorization": "eyJhbGciOiJIUzI1NiIsInR5cCI6IkpXVCJ9.eyJpZCI6IjV
3  }
```

Figure 7-3. The authorization header in the GraphQL Playground

We can test this authorization header by passing it along with any query or mutation in the GraphQL Playground. To do this, we'll write a simple `notes` query and include the `Authorization` header (Figure 7-4).

```
query {
  notes {
    id
  }
}
```

Figure 7-4. The authorization header and query in the GraphQL Playground

If our authentication is successful, we should see an object containing the user's ID logged to our terminal application's output, as shown in Figure 7-5.

```
→ nodemon solutions/05-Authentication/index.js
[nodemon] 1.18.7
[nodemon] to restart at any time, enter `rs`
[nodemon] watching: *.*
[nodemon] starting `node solutions/05-Authentication/index.js`
GraphQL Server running at http://localhost:4000/api
{ id: '5caa03539ce19b9970872fb4', iat: 1554647357 }
```

Figure 7-5. The user object in our terminal's console.log output

With all of these pieces in place, we are now able to authenticate users in our API.

Conclusion

User account creation and sign-in flows can feel mysterious and overwhelming, but by taking it piece by piece, we can implement a stable and secure authentication flow in our API. In this chapter, we created both sign-up and sign-in user flows. These are a small fragment of the account management ecosystem, but will provide us with a stable foundation on which to build. In the next chapter we'll implement user-specific interactions in our API, which will assign ownership to notes and activities within the application.

## CHAPTER 8

User Actions

Imagine you had just joined a club (remember the "Secret Club for Super Cool People"?), but when you showed up for the first time there was nothing to do. The club was a big, empty room with people wandering in and out with no way of interacting with the club or one another. I'm a bit of an introvert, so this doesn't sound *that* bad, but I wouldn't be willing to pay a membership fee for it.

Right now our API is essentially a big, useless club. We have a way to create data and a way for users to sign in, but nothing allows a user to own that data. In this chapter, we'll be addressing this by adding user interactions. We'll write the code that will enable a user to own the notes they create, limit who can delete or modify a note, and enable users to "favorite" a note that they like. Additionally, we'll enable API users to make nested queries, allowing our UIs to write simple queries that relate users to notes.

Before We Get Started

In this chapter, we'll be making some pretty significant changes to our notes files. Since we have a small amount of data in our database, you may find it easier to remove the existing notes from your local database. This isn't necessary, but can reduce confusion as you work through this chapter.

To do this, we'll go into the MongoDB shell, ensure that we're referencing the `notedly` database (the name of the database in our *.env* file), and use MongoDB's `.remove()` method. From your terminal, type the following:

```
$ mongo
$ use notedly
$ db.notes.remove({})
```

Attach a User to New Notes

In the previous chapter we updated our *src/index.js* file so that when a user makes a request, we check for a JWT. If the token exists, we decode it and add the current user to our GraphQL context. This allows us to send the user's information to each resolver function that we call. We'll update our existing GraphQL mutations to verify the user's information. To do this we'll utilize Apollo Server's `AuthenticationError` and `ForbiddenError` methods, which will allow us to throw appropriate errors. These will help us both debug in development as well as send appropriate responses to the client.

Before we get started, we'll need to import the `mongoose` package into our *mutations.js* resolver file. This will allow us to appropriately assign cross-referencing MongoDB object IDs to our fields. Update the module imports at the top of *src/resolvers/mutation.js* as follows:

```
const mongoose = require('mongoose');
```

Now, in our `newNote` mutation, we'll add `user` as a function parameter, then check to see if a user is passed into the function. If a user ID is not found, we'll throw an `AuthenticationError`, as a person must be signed in to our service to create a new note. Once we have verified that the request has been made by an authenticated user, we can create the note in the database. In doing so, we will now assign the author the user ID that is passed to the resolver. This will allow us to reference the creating user from the note itself.

In *src/resolvers/mutation.js*, add the following:

```
// add the users context
newNote: async (parent, args, { models, user }) => {
  // if there is no user on the context, throw an authentication error
  if (!user) {
    throw new AuthenticationError('You must be signed in to create a note');
  }

  return await models.Note.create({
    content: args.content,
    // reference the author's mongo id
    author: mongoose.Types.ObjectId(user.id)
  });
},
```

The last step is to apply the cross-referencing to the data in our database. To do this, we will need to update the `author` field of our MongoDB notes schema. In */src/models/note.js*, update the `author` field as follows:

```
author: {
  type: mongoose.Schema.Types.ObjectId,
  ref: 'User',
```

```
    required: true
}
```

With this reference in place, all new notes will accurately record and cross-reference the author from the context of the request. Let's try this out by writing a `newNote` mutation in the GraphQL Playground:

```
mutation {
  newNote(content: "Hello! This is a user-created note") {
    id
    content
  }
}
```

When writing the mutation, we also must be sure to pass a JWT in the `Authorization` header (see Figure 8-1):

```
{
  "Authorization": "<YOUR_JWT>"
}
```

How to Retrieve a JWT

If you don't have the JWT handy, you can perform a `signIn` mutation to retrieve one.

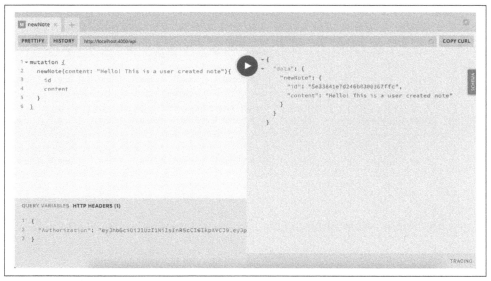

Figure 8-1. A newNote mutation in the GraphQL Playground

For now, our API doesn't return the author information, but we can verify that the author was added correctly by looking up the note in the MongoDB shell. In a terminal window, type the following:

```
mongo
db.notes.find({_id: ObjectId("A DOCUMENT ID HERE")})
```

The returned value should include an author key, with a value of an object ID.

User Permissions for Updates and Deletes

Now we can add user checks to our deleteNote and updateNote mutations as well. These will require that we check both that a user is passed to the context and whether that user is the owner of the note. To accomplish this, we'll check if the user ID stored in the author field of our database matches the user ID that is passed into the resolver context.

In *src/resolvers/mutation.js*, update the deleteNote mutation as follows:

```
deleteNote: async (parent, { id }, { models, user }) => {
  // if not a user, throw an Authentication Error
  if (!user) {
    throw new AuthenticationError('You must be signed in to delete a note');
  }

  // find the note
  const note = await models.Note.findById(id);
  // if the note owner and current user don't match, throw a forbidden error
  if (note && String(note.author) !== user.id) {
    throw new ForbiddenError("You don't have permissions to delete the note");
  }

  try {
    // if everything checks out, remove the note
    await note.remove();
    return true;
  } catch (err) {
    // if there's an error along the way, return false
    return false;
  }
},
```

Now, also in *src/resolvers/mutation.js*, update the updateNote mutation as follows:

```
updateNote: async (parent, { content, id }, { models, user }) => {
  // if not a user, throw an Authentication Error
  if (!user) {
    throw new AuthenticationError('You must be signed in to update a note');
  }

  // find the note
```

```
      const note = await models.Note.findById(id);
      // if the note owner and current user don't match, throw a forbidden error
      if (note && String(note.author) !== user.id) {
        throw new ForbiddenError("You don't have permissions to update the note");
      }

      // Update the note in the db and return the updated note
      return await models.Note.findOneAndUpdate(
        {
          _id: id
        },
        {
          $set: {
            content
          }
        },
        {
          new: true
        }
      );
    },
```

User Queries

With our existing mutations updated to include user checks, let's also add some user-specific queries. To do this, we'll add three new queries:

user
> Given a specific username, returns the user's information

users
> Returns a list of all users

me
> Returns the user information for the current user

Before we write the query resolver code, add these queries to the GraphQL *src/ schema.js* file like so:

```
type Query {
  ...
  user(username: String!): User
  users: [User!]!
  me: User!
}
```

Now in the *src/resolvers/query.js* file, write the following resolver query code:

```
module.exports = {
  // ...
  // add the following to the existing module.exports object:
```

```
user: async (parent, { username }, { models }) => {
  // find a user given their username
  return await models.User.findOne({ username });
},
users: async (parent, args, { models }) => {
  // find all users
  return await models.User.find({});
},
me: async (parent, args, { models, user }) => {
  // find a user given the current user context
  return await models.User.findById(user.id);
}
}
```

Let's see how these look in our GraphQL Playground. First, we can write a user query to look up the information of a specific user. Be sure to use a username that you've already created:

```
query {
  user(username:"adam") {
    username
    email
    id
  }
}
```

This will return a data object, containing the username, email, and ID values for the specified user (Figure 8-2).

Figure 8-2. The user query in the GraphQL Playground

Now to look up all of the users in our database, we can use the `users` query, which will return a data object containing the information of all users (Figure 8-3):

```
query {
  users {
    username
    email
    id
  }
}
```

Figure 8-3. The users query in GraphQL Playground

Now we can use a JWT, passed in the HTTP header, to look up information about the signed-in user, using the `me` query.

First, be sure to include the token in the HTTP header portion of the GraphQL Playground:

```
{
  "Authorization": "<YOUR_JWT>"
}
```

Now, perform the `me` query like so (Figure 8-4):

```
query {
  me {
    username
    email
    id
```

```
    }
}
```

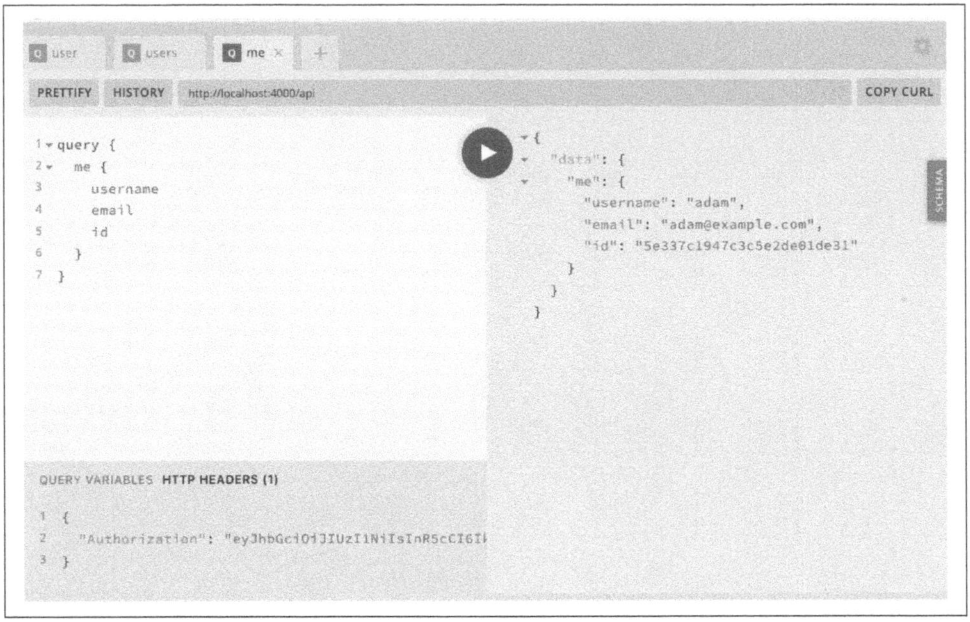

Figure 8-4. The me query in GraphQL Playground

With these resolvers in place, we can now query our API for user information.

Toggling Note Favorites

We have one last piece of functionality to add to our user interactions. You may recall that our application specifications stated that "users will be able to favorite the notes of other users as well as retrieve a list of their favorites." Similar to Twitter "hearts" and Facebook "likes," we'd like our users to be able to mark (and unmark) a note as a favorite. To implement this behavior, we'll follow our standard pattern of updating the GraphQL schema, then the database model, and lastly the resolver function.

First, we will update our GraphQL schema in *./src/schema.js* by adding two new properties to our Note type. favoriteCount will track the total number of "favorites" that a note has received. favoritedBy will contain an array of users who have favorited a note.

```
type Note {
  // add the following properties to the Note type
  favoriteCount: Int!
  favoritedBy: [User!]
}
```

We'll also add the list of favorites to our User type:

```
type User {
  // add the favorites property to the User type
  favorites: [Note!]!
}
```

Next, we will add a mutation in *./src/schema.js* called `toggleFavorite`, which will resolve by either adding or removing a favorite for the specified note. This mutation will take a note ID as a parameter and return the specified note.

```
type Mutation {
  // add toggleFavorite to the Mutation type
  toggleFavorite(id: ID!): Note!
}
```

Next, we need to update our note model to include the `favoriteCount` and `favoritedBy` properties in our database. `favoriteCount` will be a `Number` type with a default value of `0`. `favoritedBy` will be an array of objects, containing references to user object IDs in our database. Our full *./src/models/note.js* file will look as follows:

```
const noteSchema = new mongoose.Schema(
  {
    content: {
      type: String,
      required: true
    },
    author: {
      type: String,
      required: true
    },
    // add the favoriteCount property
    favoriteCount: {
      type: Number,
      default: 0
    },
    // add the favoritedBy property
    favoritedBy: [
      {
        type: mongoose.Schema.Types.ObjectId,
        ref: 'User'
      }
    ]
  },
  {
    // Assigns createdAt and updatedAt fields with a Date type
    timestamps: true
  }
);
```

With our GraphQL schema and database models updated, we can write the `toggleFavorite` mutation. This mutation will receive a note ID as a parameter and check to see if the user is already listed in the favoritedBy array. If the user is listed, we will remove the favorite by decreasing the favoriteCount and removing the user from the list. If the user has not yet favorited the note, we will increment the favoriteCount by 1 and add the current user to the favoritedBy array. To do all of this, add the following code to the *src/resolvers/mutation.js* file:

```
toggleFavorite: async (parent, { id }, { models, user }) => {
  // if no user context is passed, throw auth error
  if (!user) {
    throw new AuthenticationError();
  }

  // check to see if the user has already favorited the note
  let noteCheck = await models.Note.findById(id);
  const hasUser = noteCheck.favoritedBy.indexOf(user.id);

  // if the user exists in the list
  // pull them from the list and reduce the favoriteCount by 1
  if (hasUser >= 0) {
    return await models.Note.findByIdAndUpdate(
      id,
      {
        $pull: {
          favoritedBy: mongoose.Types.ObjectId(user.id)
        },
        $inc: {
          favoriteCount: -1
        }
      },
      {
        // Set new to true to return the updated doc
        new: true
      }
    );
  } else {
    // if the user doesn't exist in the list
    // add them to the list and increment the favoriteCount by 1
    return await models.Note.findByIdAndUpdate(
      id,
      {
        $push: {
          favoritedBy: mongoose.Types.ObjectId(user.id)
        },
        $inc: {
          favoriteCount: 1
        }
      },
      {
        new: true
      }
    );
```

```
    }
  },
```

With this code in place, let's test our ability to toggle a note favorite in the GraphQL Playground. Let's do this with a freshly created note. We'll begin by writing a newNote mutation, being sure to include an Authorization header with a valid JWT (Figure 8-5):

```
mutation {
  newNote(content: "Check check it out!") {
    content
    favoriteCount
    id
  }
}
```

Figure 8-5. A newNote mutation

You'll notice that the favoriteCount of this new note is automatically set to 0, because that's the default value we set in our data model. Now, let's write a toggleFavorite mutation to mark it as a favorite, passing the ID of the note as a parameter. Again, be sure to include the Authorization HTTP header, with a valid JWT.

```
mutation {
  toggleFavorite(id: "<YOUR_NOTE_ID_HERE>") {
    favoriteCount
```

```
    }
  }
```

After you run this mutation, the value of the note's `favoriteCount` should be 1. If you rerun the mutation, the `favoriteCount` will reduce to 0 (Figure 8-6).

Figure 8-6. The toggleFavorite mutation

Users can now mark and unmark notes as favorites. More importantly, I hope that this functionality demonstrates how you can add new features to a GraphQL application's API.

Nested Queries

One of the great things about GraphQL is that we can *nest* queries, allowing us to write a single query that returns precisely the data we need, rather than multiple queries. Our GraphQL schema's `User` type includes a list of notes by the author in an array format, while our `Notes` type includes a reference to its author. As a result, we can pull a list of notes from a user query or get the author information from a note query.

This means that we can write a query that looks like this:

```
query {
  note(id: "5c99fb88ed0ca93a517b1d8e") {
    id
```

```
      content
      # the information about the author note
      author {
        username
        id
      }
    }
  }
}
```

If we currently try to run a nested query like the preceding one, we'll receive an error. This is because we haven't yet written the resolver code that performs the database lookup for this information.

To enable this functionality, we'll add two new files in our *src/resolvers* directory.

In *src/resolvers/note.js*, add the following:

```
module.exports = {
  // Resolve the author info for a note when requested
  author: async (note, args, { models }) => {
    return await models.User.findById(note.author);
  },
  // Resolved the favoritedBy info for a note when requested
  favoritedBy: async (note, args, { models }) => {
    return await models.User.find({ _id: { $in: note.favoritedBy } });
  }
};
```

In *src/resolvers/user.js*, add this:

```
module.exports = {
  // Resolve the list of notes for a user when requested
  notes: async (user, args, { models }) => {
    return await models.Note.find({ author: user._id }).sort({ _id: -1 });
  },
  // Resolve the list of favorites for a user when requested
  favorites: async (user, args, { models }) => {
    return await models.Note.find({ favoritedBy: user._id }).sort({ _id: -1 });
  }
};
```

Now we need to update our *src/resolvers/index.js* to import and export these new resolver modules. Overall the *src/resolvers/index.js* file should now look as follows:

```
const Query = require('./query');
const Mutation = require('./mutation');
const Note = require('./note');
const User = require('./user');
const { GraphQLDateTime } = require('graphql-iso-date');

module.exports = {
  Query,
  Mutation,
  Note,
```

```
  User,
  DateTime: GraphQLDateTime
};
```

Now if we write a nested GraphQL query or mutation, we will receive the information that we expect. You can try this out by writing the following note query:

```
query {
  note(id: "<YOUR_NOTE_ID_HERE>") {
    id
    content
    # the information about the author note
    author {
      username
      id
    }
  }
}
```

This query should correctly resolve with the author's username and ID. Another practical example would be to return information about users who have "favorited" a note:

```
mutation {
  toggleFavorite(id: "<YOUR NOTE ID>") {
    favoriteCount
    favoritedBy {
      username
    }
  }
}
```

With nested resolvers in place, we can write precise queries and mutations that return exactly the data that we need.

Conclusion

Congratulations! In this chapter our API graduated to being something that users can truly interact with. This API demonstrates the true power of GraphQL by integrating user actions, adding new features, and nesting resolvers. We've also followed a tried-and-true pattern for adding new code to our projects: first write the GraphQL schema, then write the database model, and finally write the resolver code to query or update the data. By breaking down the process into these three steps, we can add all sorts of features to our applications. In the next chapter we'll look at the final steps needed to make our API production ready, including pagination and security.

## CHAPTER 9

Details

When the now-near-ubiquitous air freshener Febreze was first released, it was a dud. The original ads showed people using the product to remove specific bad smells, such as cigarette smoke, resulting in poor sales. Faced with this disappointing outcome, the marketing team shifted focus to using Febreze as a finishing detail. Now, the ads depicted someone cleaning a room, fluffing the pillows, and completing the tasks of refreshing a room with a spritz of Febreze. This reframing of the product caused sales to skyrocket.

This is a great example of the fact that *details matter*. Right now we have a working API, but it's lacking the finishing touches that will allow us to put it into production. In this chapter we'll implement some web and GraphQL application security and user experience best practices. These details, far exceeding a spritz of air freshener, will be critical to the safety, security, and usability of our application.

Web Application and Express.js Best Practices

Express.js is the underlying web application framework that powers our API. We can make a few small tweaks to our Express.js code to provide a solid basis for our application.

Express Helmet

The Express Helmet middleware (*https://oreil.ly/NGae1*) is a collection of small security-minded middleware functions. These will adjust our application's HTTP headers to be more secure. While many of these are specific to browser-based applications, enabling Helmet is a simple step to protect our application from common web vulnerabilities.

To enable Helmet, we'll require the middleware in our application and instruct Express to use it early in our middleware stack. In the *./src/index.js* file, add the following:

```
// first require the package at the top of the file
const helmet = require('helmet')

// add the middleware at the top of the stack, after const app = express()
app.use(helmet());
```

By adding the Helmet middleware, we're quickly enabling common web security best practices for our application.

Cross-Origin Resource Sharing

Cross-Origin Resource Sharing (CORS) is the means by which we allow resources to be requested from another domain. Because our API and UI code will live separately, we'll want to enable credentials from other origins. If you're interested in learning the ins and outs of CORS, I highly recommend the Mozilla CORS Guide (*https://oreil.ly/ E1lXZ*).

To enable CORS, we'll use the Express.js CORS middleware (*https://oreil.ly/lYr7g*) package in our *.src/index.js* file:

```
// first require the package at the top of the file
const cors = require('cors');

// add the middleware after app.use(helmet());
app.use(cors());
```

By adding the middleware in this way, we are enabling cross-origin requests from *all* domains. This works well for us for now, as we're in development mode and will likely be using domains generated by our hosting providers, but by using the middleware, we could also limit the requests to those of specific origins.

Pagination

Currently our `notes` and `users` queries return the full list of notes and users in the database. This works fine for local development, but as our application grows it will become unsustainable, as a query that returns potentially hundreds (or thousands) of notes is expensive and will slow down our database, server, and network. Instead, we can paginate those queries, returning only a set number of results.

There are two common types of pagination that we could implement. The first type, *offset pagination*, works by the client passing an offset number and returning a limited amount of data. For example, if each page of data were limited to 10 records, and we wanted to request the third page of data, we could pass an offset of 20. While this is the most straightforward approach conceptually, it can run into scaling and performance issues.

The second type of pagination is *cursor-based pagination*, in which a time-based cursor or unique identifier is passed as a starting point. We then request a specific amount of data that follows this record. This approach gives us the greatest control over our pagination. Additionally, because Mongo's object IDs are ordered (they begin with a 4-byte time value), we can easily utilize them as our cursor. To learn more about Mongo's object ID, I recommend reading the corresponding MongoDB documentation (*https://oreil.ly/GPE1c*).

If this sounds overly conceptual to you, that's OK. Let's walk through implementing a paginated feed of notes as a GraphQL query. First, let's define what we'll be creating, followed by our schema updates, and lastly our resolver code. For our feed we'll want to query our API while optionally passing a cursor as a parameter. The API should then return a limited amount of data, a cursor point representing the last item in the data set, and a Boolean value if there is an additional page of data to query.

With this description, we can update our *src/schema.js* file to define this new query. First, we'll need to add a `NoteFeed` type to our file:

```
type NoteFeed {
  notes: [Note]!
  cursor: String!
  hasNextPage: Boolean!
}
```

Next, we'll add our `noteFeed` query:

```
type Query {
  # add noteFeed to our existing queries
  noteFeed(cursor: String): NoteFeed
}
```

With our schema updated, we can write the resolver code for our query. In *./src/resolvers/query.js*, add the following to the exported object:

```
noteFeed: async (parent, { cursor }, { models }) => {
  // hardcode the limit to 10 items
  const limit = 10;
  // set the default hasNextPage value to false
  let hasNextPage = false;
  // if no cursor is passed the default query will be empty
  // this will pull the newest notes from the db
  let cursorQuery = {};

  // if there is a cursor
  // our query will look for notes with an ObjectId less than that of the cursor
  if (cursor) {
    cursorQuery = { _id: { $lt: cursor } };
  }
```

```
// find the limit + 1 of notes in our db, sorted newest to oldest
let notes = await models.Note.find(cursorQuery)
  .sort({ _id: -1 })
  .limit(limit + 1);

// if the number of notes we find exceeds our limit
// set hasNextPage to true and trim the notes to the limit
if (notes.length > limit) {
  hasNextPage = true;
  notes = notes.slice(0, -1);
}

// the new cursor will be the Mongo object ID of the last item in the feed array
const newCursor = notes[notes.length - 1]._id;

return {
  notes,
  cursor: newCursor,
  hasNextPage
};
}
```

With this resolver in place, we can query our `noteFeed`, which will return a maximum of 10 results. In the GraphQL Playground, we can write a query as follows to receive a list of notes, their object IDs, their "created at" timestamp, the cursor, and the next page boolean:

```
query {
  noteFeed {
    notes {
      id
      createdAt
    }
    cursor
    hasNextPage
  }
}
```

Since we have more than 10 notes in our database, this returns a cursor as well as a `hasNextPage` value of `true`. With that cursor, we can query the second page of the feed:

```
query {
  noteFeed(cursor: "<YOUR OBJECT ID>") {
    notes {
      id
      createdAt
    }
    cursor
    hasNextPage
```

```
    }
  }
```

We can continue to do this for each cursor where the `hasNextPage` value is `true`. With this implementation in place, we've created a paginated feed of notes. This will both allow our UI to request a specific feed of data as well as reduce the burden on our server and database.

Data Limitations

In addition to establishing pagination, we'll want to limit the amount of data that can be requested through our API. This prevent queries that could overload our server or database.

A simple first step in this process is to limit the amount of data that a query can return. Two of our queries, `users` and `notes`, return all of the matching data from the database. We could address this by setting a `limit()` method on our database queries. For example, in our *.src/resolvers/query.js* file, we can update our `notes` query as follows:

```
notes: async (parent, args, { models }) => {
  return await models.Note.find().limit(100);
}
```

While limiting data is a solid start, currently our queries can be written with an unlimited depth. This means that a single query could be written to retrieve a list of notes, the author information for each of those notes, the list of favorites of each author, the author information for each of those favorites, and so on. That's a lot of data in one query, and we could keep going! To prevent these types of overnested queries, we can *limit the depth* of queries against our API.

Additionally, we might have complex queries that are not overly nested, but still require heavy computation to return the data. We can protect against these types of requests by *limiting query complexity*.

We can implement these limits by using the `graphql-depth-limit` and `graphql-validation-complexity` packages in our *./src/index.js* file:

```
// import the modules at the top of the file
const depthLimit = require('graphql-depth-limit');
const { createComplexityLimitRule } = require('graphql-validation-complexity');

// update our ApolloServer code to include validationRules
const server = new ApolloServer({
  typeDefs,
  resolvers,
  validationRules: [depthLimit(5), createComplexityLimitRule(1000)],
  context: async ({ req }) => {
    // get the user token from the headers
```

```
        const token = req.headers.authorization;
        // try to retrieve a user with the token
        const user = await getUser(token);
        // add the db models and the user to the context
        return { models, user };
    }
});
```

With these package additions, we've added extra query protection to our API. For more information on securing a GraphQL API from malicious queries, check out the fantastic article (*https://oreil.ly/_r5tl*) from Max Stoiber, CTO of Spectrum.

Other Considerations

After building our API, you should have a solid understanding of the fundamentals of GraphQL development. If you're eager to dig in more on the topics, some excellent places to go next would be testing, GraphQL subscriptions, and Apollo Engine.

Testing

OK, I'll admit it: I feel guilty for not writing about tests in this book. Testing our code is important because it allows us to comfortably make changes and improves our collaboration with other developers. One of the great things about our GraphQL setup is that resolvers are simply functions, taking some parameters and returning data. This makes our GraphQL logic straightforward to test.

Subscriptions

Subscriptions are an incredibly powerful feature of GraphQL, which offers a straightforward way to integrate the publish-subscribe pattern in our application. This means that a UI can subscribe to be notified or updated when data is published on the server. This makes GraphQL servers an ideal solution for applications that work with real-time data. For more information about GraphQL subscriptions, take a look at the Apollo Server documentation (*https://oreil.ly/YwI5_*).

Apollo GraphQL Platform

Throughout the development of our API, we've been using the Apollo GraphQL library. In future chapters we'll also be using the Apollo client libraries to interface with our API. I've chosen these libraries because they are industry standards and offer a great developer experience for working with GraphQL. If you take your application to production, Apollo, the company who maintains these libraries, also offers a platform that provides monitoring and tooling for GraphQL APIs. You can learn more at Apollo's website (*https://www.apollographql.com*).

Conclusion

In this chapter we added some finishing touches to our application. Though there are many other options we could implement, at this point we have developed a solid MVP (minimum viable product). In this state, we are ready to launch our API! In the next chapter, we'll deploy our API to a public web server.

## CHAPTER 10

Deploying Our API

Imagine if each time a user wanted to access our API to create, read, update, or delete a note we had to go meet them, laptop in tow. Currently, this is how our API works, as it is running only on our individual computer. We can resolve this by *deploying* our application to a web server.

In this chapter we'll take two steps:

1. First, we'll set up a remote database that our API can access.

2. Second, we'll deploy our API code to a server and connect it to the database.

Once we've followed these steps, we can access our API from any web-connected computer, including the web, desktop, and mobile interfaces that we will develop.

Hosting Our Database

For the first step we'll use a hosted database solution. For our Mongo database, we'll be using MongoDB Atlas. This is a fully managed cloud offering backed by the organization behind Mongo itself. Additionally, they offer a free tier that will work well for our initial deployment. Let's walk through the steps of deploying to MongoDB Atlas.

First, visit *mongodb.com/cloud/atlas* and create an account. Once you've created an account, you'll be prompted to create a database. From this screen you can manage the settings of your sandbox database, but I recommend sticking with the defaults for now. These are:

- Amazon's AWS as the database host, though Google's Cloud Platform and Microsoft's Azure are also offered as options

- The closest region with a "free tier" option
- Cluster Tier with a default value of "M0 Sandbox (Shared RAM, 512MB Storage)"
- Additional Settings, which we can leave as the defaults
- Cluster Name, which we can leave as the default

From here, click Create Cluster, at which point it will take a few minutes for Mongo to set up the database (Figure 10-1).

Figure 10-1. The MongoDB Atlas database creation screen

Next, you'll see the Clusters page, where you can manage your individual database cluster (Figure 10-2).

Figure 10-2. MongoDB Atlas Cluster

From the Clusters screen, click Connect, where you'll be prompted to set up your connection security. The first step will be to whitelist your IP address. Because our application will have a dynamic IP address, you'll need to open this to any IP address by using `0.0.0.0/0`. With all IP addresses whitelisted, you'll then need to set up a secure username and password for accessing the data (Figure 10-3).

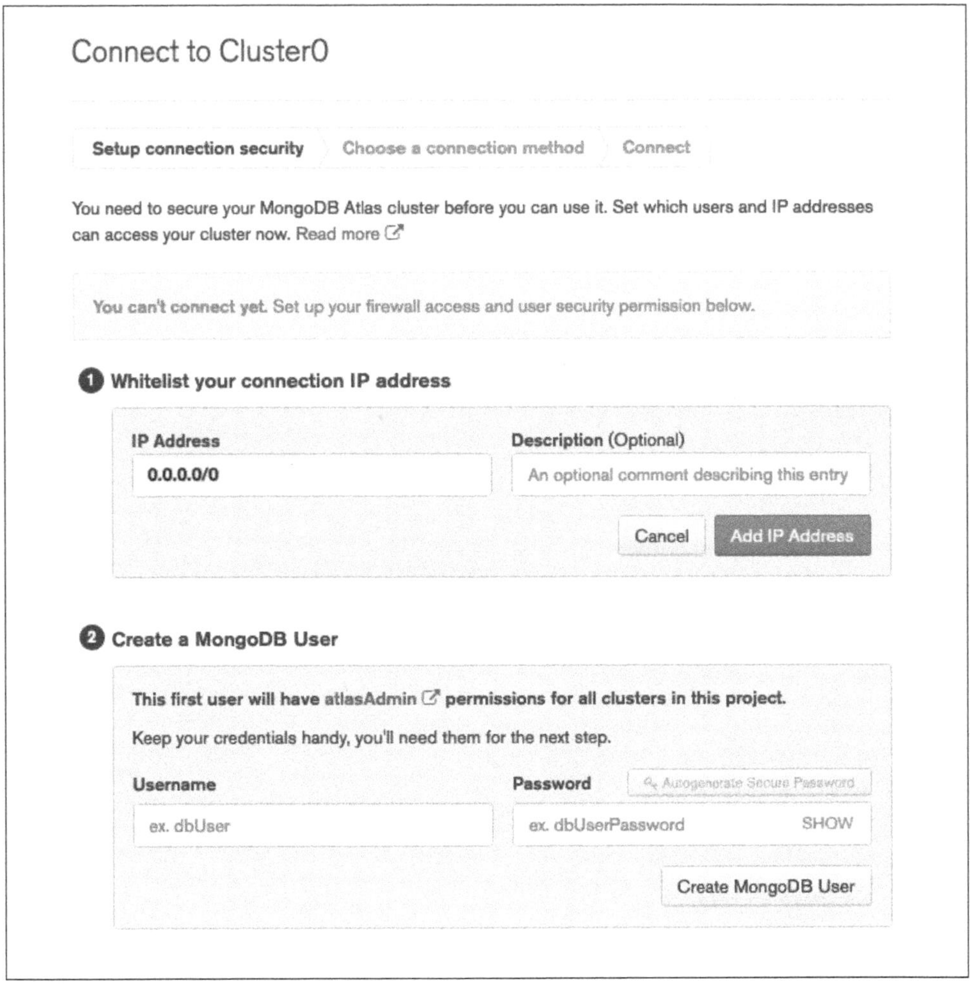

Figure 10-3. MongoDB Atlas IP whitelist and user account management

Once your IP has been whitelisted and your user account has been created, you'll choose the connection method for the database. In this case, it will be an "Application" connection (Figure 10-4).

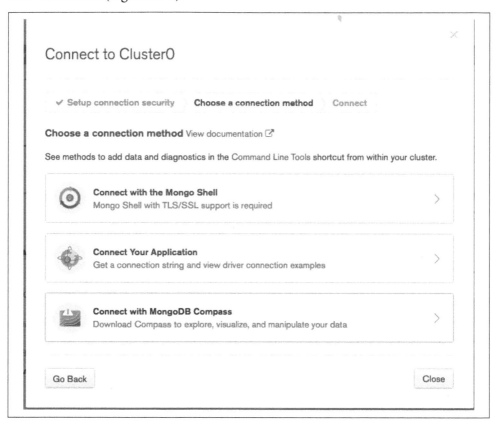

Figure 10-4. Selecting a connection type in MongoDB Atlas

From here, you can copy the connection string, which we'll be using in our production *.env* file (Figure 10-5).

Figure 10-5. MongoDB Atlas's database connection string

Mongo Passwords

MongoDB Atlas *hex-encodes* special characters within passwords. This means that if you use (and you should!) any nonalpha or numeric value, you will need to use the hex value for that code when adding your password to the connection string. The site *ascii.cl* offers the corresponding hex codes for all special characters. For example, if your password was Pizz@2! you would need to encode the @ and ! characters. You do this with a % followed by the hex value. The resulting password would be Pizz%402%21.

With our MongoDB Atlas managed database up and running, we now have a hosted data store for our application. In the next step we'll host our application code and connect it to our database.

Deploying Our Application

The next step in our deployment setup is to deploy our application code. For the purpose of this book we will use the cloud application platform Heroku. I've chosen Heroku due to its excellent user experience and generous free tier, but other cloud platforms such as Amazon Web Services, Google Cloud Platform, Digital Ocean, or Microsoft Azure all provide alternative hosting environments for Node.js applications.

Before we begin, you will need to visit Heroku's website (*https://heroku.com/apps*) and create an account. Once your account has been created, you'll need to install the Heroku command-line tools (*https://oreil.ly/Vf2Q_*) for your operating system.

For macOS you can install the Heroku command-line tools using Homebrew as follows:

```
$ brew tap heroku/brew && brew install heroku
```

For Windows users, visit the Heroku command-line tools guide and download the appropriate installer.

Project Setup

With the Heroku command-line tools installed, we can set up our project within the Heroku website. Create a new Heroku project by clicking New → Create New App (Figure 10-6).

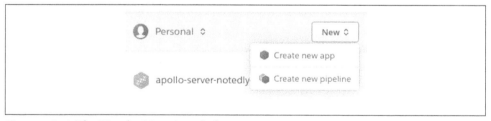

Figure 10-6. The Heroku New App dialog

From here you'll be prompted to give the application a unique name, after which you can click the Create App button (Figure 10-7). Going forward, use this name anywhere you see YOUR_APP_NAME.

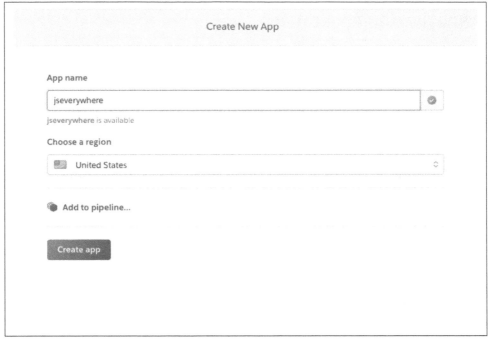

Figure 10-7. Provide a unique application name

Now we can add environment variables. Similar to how we used our *.env* file locally, we can manage our production environment variables within the Heroku website interface. To do so, click Settings followed by the Reveal Config Vars button. From this screen, add the following configuration variables (Figure 10-8):

```
NODE_ENV production
JWT_SECRET A_UNIQUE_PASSPHRASE
DB_HOST YOUR_MONGO_ATLAS_URL
```

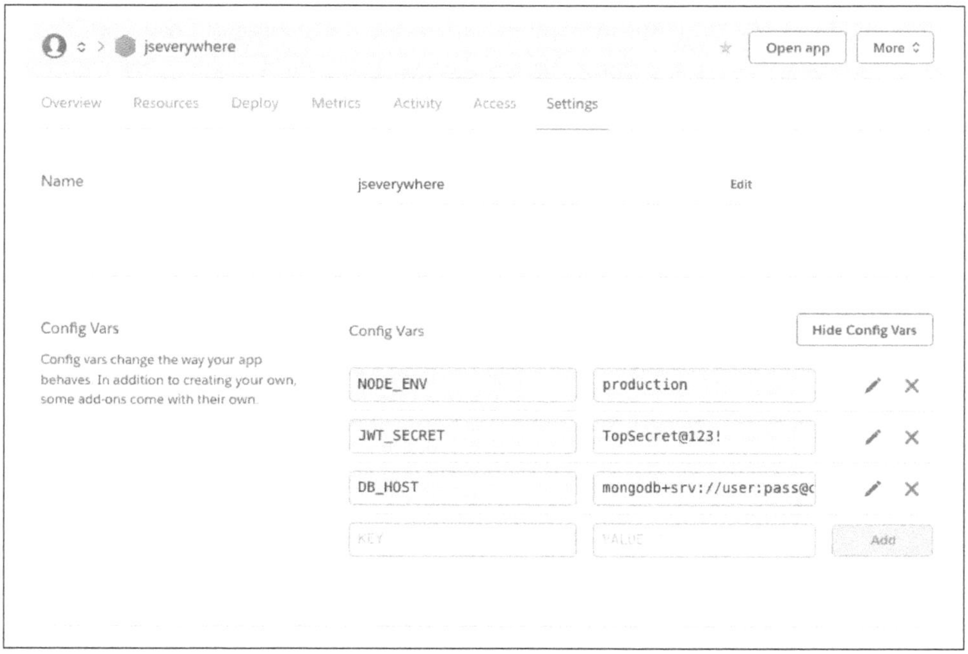

Figure 10-8. Heroku's environment variable configuration

With our application configured, we're ready to deploy our code.

Deployment

Now we're ready to deploy our code to Heroku's servers. To do this, we can use straightforward Git commands from our terminal application. We'll set Heroku as a remote endpoint, then add and commit our changes, and finally push our code to Heroku. To do this, run the following commands within your terminal application:

```
$ heroku git:remote -a <YOUR_APP_NAME>
$ git add .
$ git commit -am "application ready for production"
$ git push heroku master
```

You should see output in your terminal while Heroku builds and deploys the files. Once complete, Heroku will use the run script within our *package.json* file to run our application on their servers.

Testing

Once our application has been successfully deployed, we will be able to make GraphQL API requests to our remote server. By default, the GraphQL Playground UI is disabled in production, but we can test our application using curl from our terminal application. To run a curl request, enter the following in your terminal application:

```
$ curl \
  -X POST \
  -H "Content-Type: application/json" \
  --data '{ "query": "{ notes { id } }" }' \
  https://YOUR_APP_NAME.herokuapp.com/api
```

If the test is successful, we should receive a response containing an empty notes array, since our production database does not yet contain any data:

```
{"data":{"notes":[]}}
```

With this, we have deployed our application!

Conclusion

In this chapter we used cloud services to deploy a database and our application code. Services such as MongoDB Atlas and Heroku enable developers to launch small applications and scale them anywhere from hobby projects to heavily trafficked business. With our API deployed, we have successfully developed the backend services of our applications' stack. In the following chapters, we will focus on the UIs of our app.

## CHAPTER 11

User Interfaces and React

In 1979 Steve Jobs famously visited Xerox Parc, where he saw a demo of the Xerox Alto personal computer. While other computers at the time were controlled by typed commands, the Alto utilized a mouse and featured a graphic interface of windows, which could be opened and closed. Jobs went on to borrow these ideas in the creation of the original Apple Macintosh. The popularity of the original Mac led to the proliferation of computer UIs. Today, in a typical day we may interact with dozens of graphic user interfaces, which may include personal computers as well as smartphones, tablets, ATMs, game consoles, payment kiosks, and many more. UIs now surround us, working across all sorts of devices, content types, screen sizes, and interaction formats.

As an example, I recently traveled to a different city for a meeting. That morning, I woke up and checked my flight status on my phone. I drove to the airport in my car, where a screen showed a map and allowed me to choose the music that I was listening to. On the way, I stopped at an ATM to retrieve some cash, punching in my PIN and tapping out instructions on a touchscreen. When I arrived at the airport, I checked in to my flight at a flight kiosk. As I waited at the gate, I responded to a few emails on my tablet. On the flight, I read a book on an e-ink display device. Once I landed, I summoned a ride through an application on my phone and stopped for lunch, tapping out my custom order on a display screen. In the meeting, a slide deck was projected onto the screen, while many of us took notes on our laptops. Back at my hotel, later that evening, I browsed the television and movie offerings found through the hotel's television on-screen guide. My day was full of many UIs and screen sizes used to complete tasks related to core elements of life such as transportation, finance, and entertainment.

In this chapter we'll take a brief look at the history of JavaScript user interface development. With that background knowledge, we'll then explore the basics of React, the JavaScript library that we'll be using throughout the remainder of the book.

JavaScript and UIs

Originally designed in the mid-1990s (infamously, in 10 days (*https://oreil.ly/BNhvL*)) to enhance web interfaces, JavaScript provided an embedded scripting language in the web browser. This allowed web designers and developers to add small interactions to a web page that weren't possible with HTML alone. Unfortunately, browser vendors each had varying implementations of JavaScript, making it difficult to rely on. This is one of the factors that led to the proliferation of applications designed to work in a single browser.

In the mid-2000s jQuery (as well as similar libraries, such as MooTools) took off in popularity. jQuery allowed developers to write JavaScript with a simple API that worked well across browsers. Soon we were all removing, adding, replacing, and animating things on our web pages. Around the same time, Ajax (short for "asynchronous JavaScript and XML") allowed us to fetch data from a server and inject it into the page. The combination of these two technologies provided an ecosystem to create powerful interactive web applications.

As the complexity of these applications grew, the need for organization and boilerplate code grew in parallel. By the early 2010s frameworks such as Backbone, Angular, and Ember came to dominate the JavaScript application landscape. These frameworks worked by imposing structure and implementing common application patterns into the framework code. These frameworks were often modeled after the Model, View, Controller (MVC) pattern of software design. Each framework was prescriptive about all of the layers of the web application, providing a structured way to handle templating, data, and user interactions. While this had many benefits, it also meant that the effort of integrating new or nonstandard technologies could be quite high.

Meanwhile, desktop applications continued to be written in system-specific programming languages. This meant that developers and teams were often forced to make either/or style choices (either a Mac app or a Windows app, either a web app or a desktop app, etc.). Mobile applications were in a similar position. The rise of responsive web design meant that designers and developers could create truly incredible sites and applications for the mobile web browser, but choosing to build a web-only application locked them out of the mobile platform app stores. Apple's iOS applications were written in Objective C (and more recently Swift), while Android relied upon the Java programming language (not to be confused with our friend JavaScript). This meant that the web, consisting of HTML, CSS, and JavaScript, was the only truly cross-platform user interface platform.

Declarative Interfaces with JavaScript

In the early 2010s developers at Facebook began to face challenges in the organization and management of their JavaScript code. In response, the software engineer Jordan Walke wrote React, inspired by Facebook's PHP library, XHP. React differed from other popular JavaScript frameworks in that it focused solely on the rendering of the UI. To do this, React took a "declarative" programming approach, meaning that it provides an abstraction that allows developers to focus on describing what the state of the UI should be.

With the rise of React, and similar libraries such as Vue.js, we have seen a shift in the way that developers are writing UIs. These frameworks provide a means to manage the state of a UI at the component level. This allows applications to feel smooth and seamless to users, while providing an excellent development experience. With tooling such as Electron for building desktop apps and React Native for cross-platform native mobile applications, developers and teams are now able to leverage these paradigms in all of their applications.

Just Enough React

Throughout the remaining chapters, we'll be relying on the React library to build our UIs. You do not need to have any prior experience with React to follow along, but it may help to get a sense of the syntax before jumping in. To do this, we'll use `create-react-app` (*https://oreil.ly/dMQyk*) to scaffold out a new project. `create-react-app` is a tool developed by the React team that allows us to quickly set up a new React project and helpfully abstracts away the underlying build tooling, such as Webpack and Babel.

In your terminal application `cd` into your projects directory and run the following commands, which will create a new React application in a folder named *just-enough-react*:

```
$ npx create-react-app just-enough-react
$ cd just-enough-react
```

Running these commands will output a directory in *just-enough-react*, which contains all of the project structure, code dependencies, and development scripts to build a full-featured application. Start the application by running:

```
$ npm start
```

Our React application will now be visible in our browser at *http://localhost:3000* (Figure 11-1).

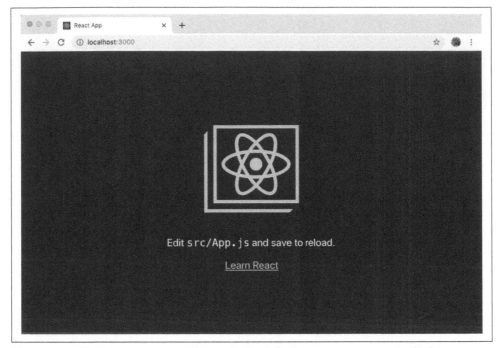

Figure 11-1. Typing npm start will launch the default create-react-app in the browser

We can now begin to edit our application by making changes to the *src/App.js* file. This file contains our primary React component. After requiring some dependencies, it consists of a function that returns some HTML-like markup:

```
function App() {
  return (
    // markup is here
  )
}
```

The markup used within the component is something called *JSX*. JSX is an XML-based syntax, similar to HTML, which allows us to precisely describe our UI and couple it with user actions within our JavaScript files. If you know HTML, picking up JSX is a matter of learning a few minor differences. The big difference in this example is that HTML's `class` property is replaced by `className` to avoid collisions with JavaScript's native class syntax.

JSX? Yuck!

If, like me, you come from a background of web standards and a strict decoupling of concerns, this may feel very icky to you. I admit that the first time that I encountered JSX, I immediately took a strong disliking to it. However, the coupling of UI logic with the rendering output presents many compelling advantages that may grow on you over time.

Let's begin to customize our app by removing most of the boilerplate code and reducing it to a simple "Hello World!":

```
import React from 'react';
import './App.css';

function App() {
  return (
    <div className="App">
      <p>Hello world!</p>
    </div>
  );
}

export default App;
```

You may notice the enclosing `<div>` tag that wraps all of our JSX content. Each React UI component must be contained within a parent HTML element or use a React fragment, which represents a non-HTML element container, such as:

```
function App() {
  return (
    <React.Fragment>
      <p>Hello world!</p>
    </React.Fragment>
  );
}
```

One of the most powerful things about React is that we can use JavaScript directly within our JSX by enclosing it within curly brackets, {}. Let's update our `App` function to make use of some variables:

```
function App() {
  const name = 'Adam'
  const now = String(new Date())
  return (
    <div className="App">
      <p>Hello {name}!</p>
      <p>The current time is {now}</p>
      <p>Two plus two is {2+2}</p>
    </div>
```

```
  );
}
```

In the preceding example, you can see that we're making use of JavaScript directly in our interface. How cool is that?

Another useful feature of React is the ability to turn each UI feature into its own component. A good rule of thumb is if an aspect of the UI behaves in an independent manner, it should be separated out into its own component. Let's create a new component. To begin, create a new file at *src/Sparkle.js* and declare a new function:

```
import React from 'react';

function Sparkle() {
  return (
    <div>

    </div>
  );
}

export default Sparkle;
```

Now let's add some functionality. Whenever a user clicks a button it will add a sparkle emoji to our page (critical functionality for any application). In order to do this, we'll import React's useState component and define some initial state for our component, which will be an empty string (in other words, no sparkle).

```
import React, { useState } from 'react';

function Sparkle() {
  // declare our initial component state
  // this a variable of 'sparkle' which is an empty string
  // we've also defined an 'addSparkle' function, which
  // we'll call in our click handler
  const [sparkle, addSparkle] = useState('');

  return (
    <div>
      <p>{sparkle}</p>
    </div>
  );
}

export default Sparkle;
```

What Is State?

We'll cover state in more detail in Chapter 15, but for now it may be helpful to know that the *state* of a component represents the current status of any information that may change within the component. For example, if a UI component has a checkbox, it has a state of `true` when checked and `false` when it is not checked.

Now we can complete our component by adding a button with `onClick` functionality. Note the camel casing, which is required within JSX:

```
import React, { useState } from 'react';

function Sparkle() {
  // declare our initial component state
  // this a variable of 'sparkle' which is an empty string
  // we've also defined an 'addSparkle' function, which
  // we'll call in our click handler
  const [sparkle, addSparkle] = useState('');

  return (
    <div>
      <button onClick={() => addSparkle(sparkle + '\u2728')}>
        Add some sparkle
      </button>
      <p>{sparkle}</p>
    </div>
  );
}

export default Sparkle;
```

To use our component we can import it into our *src/App.js* file and declare it as a JSX element as follows:

```
import React from 'react';
import './App.css';

// import our Sparkle component
import Sparkle from './Sparkle'

function App() {
  const name = 'Adam';
  let now = String(new Date());
  return (
    <div className="App">
      <p>Hello {name}!</p>
      <p>The current time is {now}</p>
      <p>Two plus two is {2+2}</p>
      <Sparkle />
    </div>
  );
```

```
}

export default App;
```

Now if you visit our application in the browser, you should see our button and be able to click it to add sparkle emojis to the page! This represents one of the true superpowers of React. We're able to re-render individual components, or elements of components, in isolation from the rest of our application (Figure 11-2).

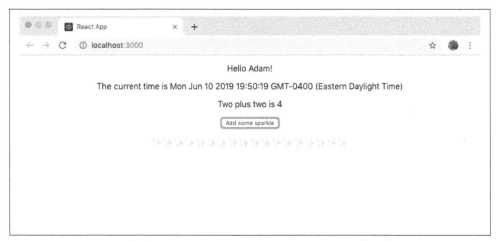

Figure 11-2. Clicking the button updates the component state and adds content to our page

We have now created a new application using `create-react-app`, updated our `Appli cation` component's JSX, created a new component, declared a component state, and dynamically updated a component. With a basic understanding of these fundamentals, we are now prepared to develop declarative UIs in JavaScript using React.

Conclusion

We are surrounded by user interfaces across a wide variety of devices. JavaScript and web technologies present an unparalleled opportunity to develop these interfaces across the multitude of platforms, using a single set of technologies. Meanwhile, React and other declarative view libraries allow us to build powerful, dynamic applications. The combination of these technologies enables developers to build amazing things without requiring specialized knowledge for each platform. In the coming chapters we'll put this into practice by utilizing a GraphQL API to build interfaces for web, desktop, and native mobile applications.

## CHAPTER 12

Building a Web Client with React

The original idea behind hypertext was to take related documents and link them together: if academic paper A references academic paper B let's make it easy to click something and navigate between them. In 1989, a software engineer at CERN named Tim Berners-Lee had the idea to combine hypertext with networked computers, making it easy for someone to make these connections regardless of the location of the documents. Every cat photo, news article, tweet, streaming video, job search site, and restaurant review is indebted to the simple idea of globally linking documents.

At its heart, the web remains a medium for linking documents together. Each page is HTML, rendered in a web browser, with CSS for styling and JavaScript for enhancements. Today, we use these technologies to build everything from personal blogs and small brochure sites to complex interactive applications. The underlying advantage is that the web provides universal access. All anyone needs is a web browser on a web-connected device, creating an inclusive-by-default environment.

What We're Building

In the upcoming chapters we'll build the web client for our social note application, Notedly. Users will be able to create and sign in to an account, write notes in Markdown, edit their notes, view a feed of other users' notes, and "favorite" other users' notes. To accomplish all of this, we'll be interacting with our GraphQL server API.

In our web application:

- Users will be able to create notes, as well as read, update, and delete the notes they've created.

- Users will be able to view a feed of notes created by other users, and read individual notes created by others, though they will not be able to update or delete them.

- Users will be able to create an account, log in, and log out.

- Users will be able to retrieve their profile information as well as the public profile information of other users.

- Users will be able to favorite the notes of other users as well as retrieve a list of their favorites.

These features will cover a lot of ground, but we'll be breaking them into small chunks throughout this portion of the book. Once you've learned to build a React application with all of these features, you'll be able to apply the tools and techniques toward building all sorts of rich web applications.

How We're Going to Build This

As you've probably guessed, to build this application we'll be using React as a client-side JavaScript library. Additionally, we'll be querying data from our GraphQL API. To aid in the querying, mutating, and caching of data, we'll make use of Apollo Client (*https://oreil.ly/hAG_X*). Apollo Client comprises a collection of open source tools for working with GraphQL. We'll be using the React version of the library, but the team at Apollo has also developed Angular, Vue, Scala.js, Native iOS, and Native Android integrations.

Other GraphQL Client Libraries

While we'll be using Apollo in this book, it is far from the only GraphQL client option available. Facebook's Relay (*https://relay.dev*) and Formiddable's urql (*https://oreil.ly/q_deu*) are two popular alternatives.

Additionally, we'll be using Parcel (*https://parceljs.org*) as our code bundler. A code bundler allows us to write JavaScript using features that may not be available in a web browser (e.g., newer language features, code modules, minificiation) and packages them for use in the browser environment. Parcel is a configuration-free alternative to application build tools like Webpack (*https://webpack.js.org*). It offers a lot of nice features such as code splitting and automatically updating the browser during development (aka *hot module replacement*), but without the need to set up a build chain. As you saw in the previous chapter, `create-react-app` (*https://oreil.ly/dMQyk*) also offers a zero-configuration initial setup, using Webpack behind the scenes, but Parcel allows us to build our application from the ground up, in a way that I find ideal for learning.

Getting Started

Before we can start development, we need to make a copy of the project starter files to our machine. The project's source code (*https://github.com/javascripteverywhere/web*) contains all of the scripts and references to third-party libraries that we will need to develop our application. To clone the code to your local machine, open the terminal, navigate to the directory where you keep your projects, and git clone the project repository. If you've worked through the API chapters, you may also have already create a *notedly* directory to keep the project code organized:

```
# change into the Projects directory
$ cd
$ cd Projects
$ # type the `mkdir notedly` command if you don't yet have a notedly directory
$ cd notedly
$ git clone git@github.com:javascripteverywhere/web.git
$ cd web
$ npm install
```

Installing Third-Party Dependencies

By making a copy of the book's starter code and running npm install in the directory, you avoid having to again run npm install for any of the individual third-party dependencies.

The code is structured as follows:

/src

This is the directory where you should perform your development as you follow along with the book.

/solutions

This directory contains the solutions for each chapter. If you get stuck, these are available for you to consult.

/final

This directory contains the final working project.

Now that you have the code on your local machine, you'll need to make a copy of the project's *.env* file. This file is a place to keep the variables unique to the environment we are working in. For example, when working locally we'll be pointing to a local instance of our API, but when we deploy our app we'll point to our remotely deployed API. To make a copy of the sample *.env* file, type the following into your terminal, from the *web* directory:

```
$ cp .env.example .env
```

You should now see an *.env* file in the directory. You don't yet need to do anything with this file, but we'll be adding information to it as we progress through the development of our API backend. The *.gitignore* file included with the project will ensure that you do not inadvertently commit your *.env* file.

Help, I Don't See the .env File!

By default, operating systems hide files that start with a period, as these are typically used by the system, not end users. If you don't see the *.env* file, try opening the directory in your text editor. The file should be visible in the file explorer of your editor. Alternately, typing `ls  -a` into your terminal window will list the files in the current working directory.

Building Out the Web Application

With our starter code cloned locally, we're ready to build out our React web application. Let's first take a look at our *src/index.html* file. This looks like a standard, yet completely empty, HTML file, but note the following two lines:

```
<div id="root"></div>
<script src="./App.js"></script>
```

These two lines are incredibly important to our React application. The `root` `<div>` will provide the container for our entire application. Meanwhile, the *App.js* file will be the entry point to our JavaScript application.

Now we can begin to develop our React application in our *src/App.js* file. If you followed along with the React introduction in the previous chapter, this may all feel familiar. In *src/App.js* we begin by importing the `react` and `react-dom` libraries:

```
import React from 'react';
import ReactDOM from 'react-dom';
```

Now we will create a function, named `App`, that will return the contents of our application. For now, this will simply be two lines of HTML contained within a `<div>` element:

```
const App = () => {
  return (
    <div>
      <h1>Hello Notedly!</h1>
      <p>Welcome to the Notedly application</p>
    </div>
  );
};
```

What's With All of the divs?

If you're just starting out with React, you may wonder about the tendency to surround components with <div> tags. React components must be contained with a parent element, which often is a <div> tag, but could also be any other appropriate HTML tag such as <section>, <header>, or <nav>. If a containing HTML tag feels extraneous, we can instead use <React.Fragment> or empty <> tags to contain the components in our JavaScript code.

Finally, we will instruct React to render our application within the element with an ID of root by adding the following:

```
ReactDOM.render(<App />, document.getElementById('root'));
```

The full content of our *src/App.js* file should now be:

```
import React from 'react';
import ReactDOM from 'react-dom';

const App = () => {
  return (
    <div>
      <h1>Hello Notedly!</h1>
      <p>Welcome to the Notedly application</p>
    </div>
  );
};

ReactDOM.render(<App />, document.getElementById('root'));
```

With this complete, let's take a look in our web browser. Start your local development server by typing **npm run dev** in your terminal application. Once the code is bundled, visit *http://localhost:1234* to view the page (Figure 12-1).

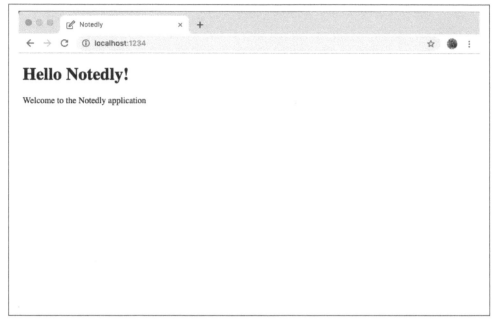

Figure 12-1. Our initial React application running in the browser

Routing

One of the defining features of the web is being able to link documents together. Similarly, for our application we'll want users to be able to navigate between screens or pages. In an HTML rendered application, this would involve creating multiple HTML documents. Whenever a user navigates to a new document, the entire document will reload, even if there are shared aspects, such as a header or footer, on the two pages.

In JavaScript applications we can make use of client-side routing. In many ways, this will be similar to HTML linking. A user will click a link, the URL will update, and they will navigate to a new screen. The difference is that our application will only update the page with the content that has changed. The experience will be smooth and "app-like," meaning that there will not be a visible refresh of the page.

In React, the most commonly used routing library is React Router (*https://oreil.ly/ MhQQR*). This library enables us to add routing capabilities to React web applications. To introduce routing to our application, let's first create a *src/pages* directory and add the following files:

- */src/pages/index.js*
- */src/pages/home.js*
- */src/pages/mynotes.js*

- */src/pages/favorites.js*

Our *home.js*, *mynotes.js*, and *favorites.js* files will be our individual page components. We can create each of them with some initial content and an `effect` hook, which will update the document title when a user navigates to the page.

In *src/pages/home.js*:

```
import React from 'react';

const Home = () => {
  return (
    <div>
      <h1>Notedly</h1>
      <p>This is the home page</p>
    </div>
  );
};

export default Home;
```

In *src/pages/mynotes.js*:

```
import React, { useEffect } from 'react';

const MyNotes = () => {
  useEffect(() => {
    // update the document title
    document.title = 'My Notes — Notedly';
  });

  return (
    <div>
      <h1>Notedly</h1>
      <p>These are my notes</p>
    </div>
  );
};

export default MyNotes;
```

In *src/pages/favorites.js*:

```
import React, { useEffect } from 'react';

const Favorites = () => {
  useEffect(() => {
    // update the document title
    document.title = 'Favorites — Notedly';
  });

  return (
    <div>
```

```
      <h1>Notedly</h1>
      <p>These are my favorites</p>
    </div>
  );
};

export default Favorites;
```

 useEffect

In the preceding examples we're using React's `useEffect` hook to set the title of the page. Effect hooks allow us to include side effects in our components, updating something that is not related to the component itself. If you are interested, React's documentation provides a deep dive into effect hooks (*https://oreil.ly/VkpTZ*).

Now, in *src/pages/index.js* we'll import React Router and the methods necessary for web browser routing with the `react-router-dom` package:

```
import React from 'react';
import { BrowserRouter as Router, Route } from 'react-router-dom';
```

Next, we'll import the page components that we just created:

```
import Home from './home';
import MyNotes from './mynotes';
import Favorites from './favorites';
```

Finally, we'll designate each of the page components that we created as routes with a specific URL. Note the use of **exact** for our "Home" route, which will ensure the home component is rendered only for the root URL:

```
const Pages = () => {
  return (
    <Router>
      <Route exact path="/" component={Home} />
      <Route path="/mynotes" component={MyNotes} />
      <Route path="/favorites" component={Favorites} />
    </Router>
  );
};

export default Pages;
```

Our complete *src/pages/index.js* file should now look as follows:

```
// import React and routing dependencies
import React from 'react';
import { BrowserRouter as Router, Route } from 'react-router-dom';

// import routes
import Home from './home';
```

```
import MyNotes from './mynotes';
import Favorites from './favorites';

// define routes
const Pages = () => {
  return (
    <Router>
      <Route exact path="/" component={Home} />
      <Route path="/mynotes" component={MyNotes} />
      <Route path="/favorites" component={Favorites} />
    </Router>
  );
};

export default Pages;
```

Finally, we can update the *src/App.js* file to use our routes by importing the routes and rendering the components:

```
import React from 'react';
import ReactDOM from 'react-dom';

// import routes
import Pages from '/pages';

const App = () => {
  return (
    <div>
      <Pages />
    </div>
  );
};

ReactDOM.render(<App />, document.getElementById('root'));
```

Now if you manually update the URL in your web browser, you should be able to view each component. For example, type **http://localhost:1234/favorites** to render the "favorites" page.

Linking

We've created our pages, but we're missing the key component of linking them together. So let's add some links to the other pages from our home page. To do so, we'll use React Router's Link component.

In *src/pages/home.js*:

```
import React from 'react';
// import the Link component from react-router
import { Link } from 'react-router-dom';

const Home = () => {
```

```
    return (
      <div>
        <h1>Notedly</h1>
        <p>This is the home page</p>
        { /* add a list of links */ }
        <ul>
          <li>
            <Link to="/mynotes">My Notes</Link>
          </li>
          <li>
            <Link to="/favorites">Favorites</Link>
          </li>
        </ul>
      </div>
    );
};

export default Home;
```

With this we're able to navigate our application. Clicking one of the links on the home page will navigate to the corresponding page component. Core browser navigation functions, such as the back and forward buttons, will continue to work as well.

UI Components

We've successfully created individual page components and can navigate between them. As we build out our pages, they will have several shared user interface elements, such as a header and sitewide navigation. Rewriting these each time they are used wouldn't be very efficient (and would get quite annoying). Instead, we can write reusable interface components and import them into our interface wherever we need them. In fact, thinking of our UI as composed of tiny components is one of the core tenants of React, and was my breakthrough in grasping the framework.

We'll start by creating header and navigation components for our application. First, let's create a new directory within our *src* directory called *components*. Within the *src/ components* directory, we'll create two new files called *Header.js* and *Navigation.js*. React components must be capitalized, so we'll follow the common convention of capitalizing the filename as well.

Let's begin by writing the header component in *src/components/Header.js*. To do so, we'll import our *logo.svg* file and add the corresponding markup for our component:

```
import React from 'react';
import logo from '../img/logo.svg';

const Header = () => {
  return (
    <header>
      <img src={logo} alt="Notedly Logo" height="40" />
```

```
        <h1>Notedly</h1>
      </header>
    );
};

export default Header;
```

For our navigation component we'll import React Router's `Link` functionality and mark up an unordered list of links. In *src/components/Navigation.js*:

```
import React from 'react';
import { Link } from 'react-router-dom';

const Navigation = () => {
  return (
    <nav>
      <ul>
        <li>
          <Link to="/">Home</Link>
        </li>
        <li>
          <Link to="/mynotes">My Notes</Link>
        </li>
        <li>
          <Link to="/favorites">Favorites</Link>
        </li>
      </ul>
    </nav>
  );
};

export default Navigation;
```

In screenshots you'll see that I've also included emoji characters as navigation icons. If you'd like to do the same, the accessible markup for including emoji characters is as follows:

```
<span aria-hidden="true" role="img">
  <!-- emoji character -->
</span>
```

With our header and navigation components complete, we can now use them within our application. Let's update our *src/pages/home.js* file to include the components. We will first import them and then include the component within our JSX markup.

Our *src/pages/home.js* will now look as follows (Figure 12-2):

```
import React from 'react';

import Header from '../components/Header';
import Navigation from '../components/Navigation';

const Home = () => {
```

```
    return (
      <div>
        <Header />
        <Navigation />
        <p>This is the home page</p>
      </div>
    );
};

export default Home;
```

Figure 12-2. With React components we're able to easily compose shareable UI features

This is everything we need in order to be able to create shareable components across our application. For more on using components within a UI, I highly recommend reading the React documentation page "Thinking in React" (*https://oreil.ly/n6o1Z*).

Conclusion

The web remains an unparalleled medium for distributing applications. It couples universal access with a developer's ability to deploy real-time updates. In this chapter we built out the foundation of our JavaScript web application in React. In the next chapter we will add layout and style to the app, using React components and CSS-in-JS.

## CHAPTER 13

Styling an Application

In his 1978 track "Lip Service," Elvis Costello sneers the line "don't act like you're above me, just look at your shoes." This kiss-off implies that the narrator can detect an attempt at elevated social status simply by seeing someone's shoes, no matter how finely pressed their suit or how elegant their dress. For better or worse, style is a major part of human culture, and we're all accustomed to picking up on these types of social cues. Archaeologists have even found that humans in the Upper Paleolithic era created necklaces and bracelets from bones, teeth, berries, and stone. Our clothes not only serve the functional purpose of protecting our bodies from the elements, but may also communicate to others information about our culture, social status, interests, and so much more.

A web application is functional without anything beyond the default styles of the web, but by applying CSS we are able to more clearly communicate with our users. In this chapter, we'll explore how we can use the CSS-in-JS Styled Components library to introduce layout and style to our application. This will allow us to make a more usable and aesthetically pleasing application within a maintainable, component-based, code structure.

Creating a Layout Component

Many, or in our case all, pages of an application will share a common layout. For example, all the pages of our application will have a header, a sidebar, and a content area (Figure 13-1). Rather than import the shared layout elements within each page component, we can instead create a component specifically for our layout and wrap each of our page components within it.

Figure 13-1. A wireframe of our page layout

To create our component, we'll begin by creating a new file at *src/components/ Layout.js*. Within this file we'll import our shared components and lay out our content. Our React component function will receive a property of `children`, which will allow us to specify where child content will appear in the layout. We'll also make use of the empty `<React.Fragment>` JSX element to help avoid extraneous markup.

Let's create our component in *src/components/Layout.js*:

```
import React from 'react';

import Header from './Header';
import Navigation from './Navigation';

const Layout = ({ children }) => {
  return (
    <React.Fragment>
      <Header />
      <div className="wrapper">
        <Navigation />
        <main>{children}</main>
      </div>
    </React.Fragment>
  );
};

export default Layout;
```

Now within our *src/pages/index.js* file, we can wrap our page components within the newly created `Layout` component to apply the shared layout to each page:

```
// import React and routing dependencies
import React from 'react';
import { BrowserRouter as Router, Route } from 'react-router-dom';

// import shared layout component
import Layout from '../components/Layout';

// import routes
import Home from './home';
import MyNotes from './mynotes';
import Favorites from './favorites';

// define routes
const Pages = () => {
  return (
    <Router>
      {/* Wrap our routes within the Layout component */}
      <Layout>
        <Route exact path="/" component={Home} />
        <Route path="/mynotes" component={MyNotes} />
        <Route path="/favorites" component={Favorites} />
      </Layout>
    </Router>
  );
};

export default Pages;
```

The final step is to remove any instances of `<Header>` or `<Navigation>` within our page components. For example, our *src/pages/Home.js* file will now have the following reduced code:

```
import React from 'react';

const Home = () => {
  return (
    <div>
      <p>This is the home page</p>
    </div>
  );
};

export default Home;
```

With this complete, you can view your application in your browser. As you navigate between the routes you'll see our header and navigation links appear on each page. For now, they are not styled and our page does not have a visual layout. Let's explore adding styles in the next section.

CSS

Cascading Style Sheets are precisely named: they are a set of rules that allow us to write styles for the web. The styles "cascade," meaning that the last or most specifically defined style will be rendered. For example:

```
p {
  color: green
}

p {
  color: red
}
```

This CSS will render all paragraphs red, making the `color: green` rule obsolete. This is such a simple idea, but it has resulted in dozens of patterns and techniques to aid in avoiding its pitfalls. CSS structural techniques such as BEM (block element modifier), OOCSS (object-oriented CSS), and Atomic CSS use prescriptive class naming to help scope styles. Preprocessors such as SASS (syntatically awesome stylesheets) and Less (leaner stylesheets) provide tooling that simplifies the CSS syntax and enables modular files. Though these each have their merits, CSS-in-JavaScript provides a compelling use case for developing React or other JavaScript-driven applications.

What About CSS Frameworks?

CSS and UI frameworks are a popular option for developing an application, with good reason. They present a solid style baseline and reduce the amount of code that a developer needs to write by providing styles and functionality for common application patterns. The tradeoffs are that applications using these frameworks may become visually similar and can increase the file bundle size. That tradeoff may be worthwhile to you, however. Some of my personal favorite UI frameworks for working with React are Ant Design (*https://ant.design*), Bootstrap (*https://oreil.ly/XJm-B*), Grommet (*https://v2.grommet.io*), and Rebass (*https://rebassjs.org*).

CSS-in-JS

When I first encountered CSS-in-JS, my initial reaction was one of horror. I spent the formative years of my web development career in the web standards era. I continue to advocate for accessibility and sensible progressive enhancement for web development. "Separation of concerns" has been a core tenant of my web practices for over a decade. So, if you're like me and simply reading "CSS-in-JS" makes you feel dirty, you're not alone. However, I was quickly won over once I gave it a proper (and judgment-free) try. CSS-in-JS makes it easy to think of our user interfaces as a series of components, something that I had been trying to do with a combination of structure techniques and CSS preprocessors for years.

In this book we'll be using Styled Components (*https://www.styled-components.com*) as our CSS-in-JS library. It is fast, flexible, under active development, and the most popular CSS-in-JS library. It's also used by companies such as Airbnb, Reddit, Patreon, Lego, BBC News, Atlassian, and many more.

The Styled Components library works by allowing us to define the styles of an element using JavaScript's template literal syntax. We create a JavaScript variable that will refer to an HTML element and its associated styles. Since that sounds fairly abstract, let's take a look at a simple example:

```
import React from 'react';
import styled from 'styled-components'

const AlertParagraph = styled.p`
  color: green;
`;

const ErrorParagraph = styled.p`
  color: red;
`;

const Example = () => {
  return (
    <div>
      <AlertParagraph>This is green.</AlertParagraph>
      <ErrorParagraph>This is red.</ErrorParagraph>
    </div>
  );
};

export default Example;
```

As you can see, we can easily scope styles. Additionally, we are scoping our style to that specific component. This helps us to avoid class name collisions across different parts of our application.

Creating a Button Component

Now that we have a basic understanding of styled components, let's integrate them into our application. To begin with, we'll write some styles for a <button> element, which will allow us to reuse the component throughout our application. In the previous example, we integrated our styles alongside our React/JSX code, but we can also write standalone styled components. To begin, create a new file at *src/components/Button.js*, import the styled library from styled-components, and set up the exportable component as a template literal like so:

```
import styled from 'styled-components';

const Button = styled.button`
  /* our styles will go here */
`;

export default Button;
```

With the component in place, we can fill it in with some styles. Add some baseline button styles as well as hover and active state styles as follows:

```
import styled from 'styled-components';

const Button = styled.button`
  display: block;
  padding: 10px;
  border: none;
  border-radius: 5px;
  font-size: 18px;
  color: #fff;
  background-color: #0077cc;
  cursor: pointer;

  :hover {
    opacity: 0.8;
  }

  :active {
    background-color: #005fa3;
  }
`;

export default Button;
```

Now we can use our button throughout our application. For example, to use it on the application's home page, we could import the component and use the `<Button>` element anywhere we would typically use `<button>`.

In *src/pages/home.js*:

```
import React from 'react';

import Button from '../components/Button';

const Home = () => {
  return (
    <div>
      <p>This is the home page</p>
      <Button>Click me!</Button>
    </div>
  );
};
```

```
export default Home;
```

With this, we've written a styled component that we can use anywhere in our application. This is great for maintainability, as we can easily find our styles and change them across our codebase. Additionally, we can couple styled components with markup, allowing us to create small, reusable, and maintainable components.

Adding Global Styles

Though many of our styles will be contained within individual components, every site or application also has a set of global styles (things like CSS resets, fonts, and baseline colors). We can create a *GlobalStyle.js* component to house these styles.

This will look a bit different from our previous example, as we'll be creating a style-sheet rather than styles attached to a specific HTML element. To accomplish this, we'll import the `createGlobalStyle` module from `styled-components`. We'll also import the `normalize.css` library (*https://oreil.ly/i4lyd*) to ensure consistent rendering of HTML elements across browsers. Finally, we'll add some global rules for the HTML body of our application and default link styles.

In *src/components/GlobalStyle.js*:

```
// import createGlobalStyle and normalize
import { createGlobalStyle } from 'styled-components';
import normalize from 'normalize.css';

// we can write our CSS as a JS template literal
export default createGlobalStyle`
  ${normalize}

  *, *:before, *:after {
    box-sizing: border-box;
  }

  body,
  html {
    height: 100%;
    margin: 0;
  }

  body {
    font-family: -apple-system, BlinkMacSystemFont, 'Segoe UI', Roboto,
      Oxygen-Sans, Ubuntu, Cantarell, 'Helvetica Neue', sans-serif;
    background-color: #fff;
    line-height: 1.4;
  }

  a:link,
  a:visited {
```

```
  color: #0077cc;
}

a:hover,
a:focus {
  color: #004499;
}

code,
pre {
  max-width: 100%;
}
`;
```

To apply these styles, we'll import them into our *App.js* file and add a <Global Style /> element to our application:

```
import React from 'react';
import ReactDOM from 'react-dom';

// import global styles
import GlobalStyle from '/components/GlobalStyle';
// import routes
import Pages from '/pages';

const App = () => {
  return (
    <div>
      <GlobalStyle />
      <Pages />
    </div>
  );
};

ReactDOM.render(<App />, document.getElementById('root'));
```

With this, our global styles will be applied to the application. When you preview the app in the browser, you'll see that the typeface has changed, the links have a new style, and the margins have been removed (Figure 13-2).

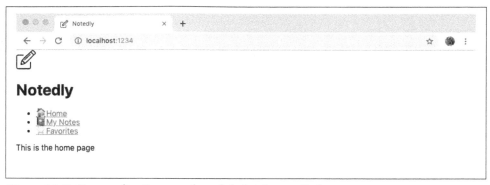

Figure 13-2. Our application now has global styles applied

Component Styles

Now that we've applied some global styles to our application, we can begin styling the individual components. In doing this we'll also introduce the overall layout of our application. For each component we style, we'll first import the `styled` library from `styled-components`. We'll then define some element styles as variables. Lastly, we'll use those elements within the JSX of our React component.

Styled Component Naming

To avoid collisions with HTML elements, it's mandatory to capitalize the names of our styled components.

We can begin in *src/components/Layout.js*, where we'll add style to the structural `<div>` and `<main>` tags for the application's layout.

```
import React from 'react';
import styled from 'styled-components';

import Header from './Header';
import Navigation from './Navigation';

// component styles
const Wrapper = styled.div`
  /* We can apply media query styles within the styled component */
  /* This will only apply the layout for screens above 700px wide */
  @media (min-width: 700px) {
    display: flex;
    top: 64px;
    position: relative;
    height: calc(100% - 64px);
    width: 100%;
    flex: auto;
    flex-direction: column;
```

```
  }
`;

const Main = styled.main`
  position: fixed;
  height: calc(100% - 185px);
  width: 100%;
  padding: 1em;
  overflow-y: scroll;
  /* Again apply media query styles to screens above 700px */
  @media (min-width: 700px) {
    flex: 1;
    margin-left: 220px;
    height: calc(100% - 64px);
    width: calc(100% - 220px);
  }
`;

const Layout = ({ children }) => {
  return (
    <React.Fragment>
      <Header />
      <Wrapper>
        <Navigation />
        <Main>{children}</Main>
      </Wrapper>
    </React.Fragment>
  );
};

export default Layout;
```

With our *Layout.js* component complete, we can add some styles to our *Header.js* and *Navigation.js* files:

In *src/components/Header.js*:

```
import React from 'react';
import styled from 'styled-components';
import logo from '../img/logo.svg';

const HeaderBar = styled.header`
  width: 100%;
  padding: 0.5em 1em;
  display: flex;
  height: 64px;
  position: fixed;
  align-items: center;
  background-color: #fff;
  box-shadow: 0 0 5px 0 rgba(0, 0, 0, 0.25);
  z-index: 1;
`;
```

```
const LogoText = styled.h1`
  margin: 0;
  padding: 0;
  display: inline;
`;

const Header = () => {
  return (
    <HeaderBar>
      <img src={logo} alt="Notedly Logo" height="40" />
      <LogoText>Notedly</LogoText>
    </HeaderBar>
  );
};

export default Header;
```

Finally, in *src/components/Navigation.js*:

```
import React from 'react';
import { Link } from 'react-router-dom';
import styled from 'styled-components';

const Nav = styled.nav`
  padding: 1em;
  background: #f5f4f0;

  @media (max-width: 700px) {
    padding-top: 64px;
  }

  @media (min-width: 700px) {
    position: fixed;
    width: 220px;
    height: calc(100% - 64px);
    overflow-y: scroll;
  }
`;

const NavList = styled.ul`
  margin: 0;
  padding: 0;
  list-style: none;
  line-height: 2;

  /* We can nest styles in styled-components */
  /* The following styles will apply to links within the NavList component */
  a {
    text-decoration: none;
    font-weight: bold;
    font-size: 1.1em;
    color: #333;
  }
```

```
  a:visited {
    color: #333;
  }

  a:hover,
  a:focus {
    color: #0077cc;
  }
`;

const Navigation = () => {
  return (
    <Nav>
      <NavList>
        <li>
          <Link to="/">Home</Link>
        </li>
        <li>
          <Link to="/mynotes">My Notes</Link>
        </li>
        <li>
          <Link to="/favorites">Favorites</Link>
        </li>
      </NavList>
    </Nav>
  );
};

export default Navigation;
```

With these styles applied, we now have a fully styled application (Figure 13-3). Going forward, we can apply styles as we create individual components.

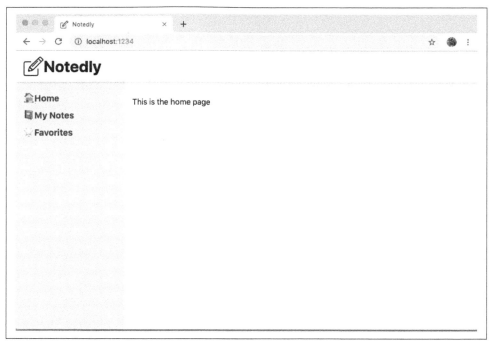

Figure 13-3. Our application with styles applied

Conclusion

In this chapter we introduced layout and style to our application. Using the CSS-in-JS library Styled Components allows us to write concise and properly scoped CSS styles. These styles can then be applied to individual components or globally across our application. In the next chapter, we'll work toward a fully featured application by implementing our GraphQL client and making calls to our API.

## CHAPTER 14

Working with Apollo Client

I remember my first internet connection vividly. My computer's modem would dial in to a local number connected to my internet service provider (ISP), setting me free on the web. As magical as this felt at the time, it is a far cry from the instant, always-on connections that we use today. Here's what the process looked like:

1. Sit down at my computer and open the ISP software.
2. Click Connect, and wait for the modem to dial the number.
3. If the connection is successful, hear the glorious "modem sounds." If not, such as during peak hours when the lines may be overloaded and busy, try again.
4. Once connected, receive a success notification and browse the web in all of its GIF-filled 90s glory.

This cycle may seem arduous, but it still represents the way in which services speak to each other: they request a connection, make that connection, send a request, and get something back in return. Our client applications will work in the same manner. We will first make a connection to our server API application and, if successful, make requests to that server.

In this chapter, we'll use Apollo Client to connect to our API. Once we've connected, we'll write a GraphQL query, which will be used to display data on a page. We'll also introduce pagination, both within an API query and in our interface components.

Running the API Locally

The development of our web client application will require access to a local instance of our API. If you've been following along with the book, you may already have the Notedly API and its database up and running on your machine. If not, I've added instructions to Appendix A on how to get a copy of the API up and running along with some sample data. If you already have the API running, but would like some additional data to work with, run `npm run seed` from the root of the API project directory.

Setting Up Apollo Client

Much like Apollo Server, Apollo Client offers a number of helpful features to simplify working with GraphQL within JavaScript UI applications. Apollo Client provides libraries for connecting a web client to an API, local caching, GraphQL syntax, local state management, and more. We'll also be using Apollo Client with a React application, but Apollo also offers libraries for Vue, Angular, Meteor, Ember, and Web Components.

First, we'll want to ensure that our *.env* file contains a reference to our local API URI. This will allow us to use our local API instance in development, while pointing to our product API when we release our application to a public web server. In our *.env* file, we should have a `API_URI` variable with our local API server's address:

```
API_URI=http://localhost:4000/api
```

Our code bundler, Parcel, is configured to automatically work with *.env* files. Any time we want to reference an *.env* variable in our code, we can use `process.env.VARIABLE_NAME`. This will allow us to use unique values in local development, production, and any other environment that we may need (such as staging or continuous integration).

With the address stored in an environment variable, we are ready to connect our web client to our API server. Working in our *src/App.js* file, first we need to import the Apollo packages that we'll be using:

```
// import Apollo Client libraries
import { ApolloClient, ApolloProvider, InMemoryCache } from '@apollo/client';
```

With these imported, we can configure a new Apollo Client instance, passing it the API URI, initiating the cache, and enabling the use of the local Apollo developer tools:

```
// configure our API URI & cache
const uri = process.env.API_URI;
const cache = new InMemoryCache();
```

```
// configure Apollo Client
const client = new ApolloClient({
  uri,
  cache,
  connectToDevTools: true
});
```

Finally, we can connect our React application to our Apollo Client by wrapping it in an ApolloProvider. We'll replace our empty <div> tags with <ApolloProvider> and include our client as a connection:

```
const App = () => {
  return (
    <ApolloProvider client={client}>
      <GlobalStyle />
      <Pages />
    </ApolloProvider>
  );
};
```

Overall, our *src/App.js* file will now look as follows:

```
import React from 'react';
import ReactDOM from 'react-dom';

// import Apollo Client libraries
import { ApolloClient, ApolloProvider, InMemoryCache } from '@apollo/client';

// global styles
import GlobalStyle from '/components/GlobalStyle';
// import our routes
import Pages from '/pages';

// configure our API URI & cache
const uri = process.env.API_URI;
const cache = new InMemoryCache();

// configure Apollo Client
const client = new ApolloClient({
  uri,
  cache,
  connectToDevTools: true
});

const App = () => (
  <ApolloProvider client={client}>
    <GlobalStyle />
    <Pages />
  </ApolloProvider>
);

ReactDOM.render(<App />, document.getElementById('root'));
```

With our client connected to our API server, we can now integrate GraphQL queries and mutations into our application.

Querying an API

When we query an API, we are requesting data. In a UI client, we want to be able to query that data and display it to the user. Apollo enables us to compose queries to fetch data. We can then update React components to display the data to the end user. We can explore the use of queries by writing a `noteFeed` query, which will return a feed of the latest notes to the user and display it on the application's home page.

When I am first writing a query, I find the following process useful:

1. Consider what data the query needs to return.
2. Write the query in the GraphQL Playground.
3. Integrate the query into the client application.

Let's follow this process in drafting our query. If you followed along in the API portion of the book, you may recall that the `noteFeed` query returns a list of 10 notes along with a `cursor`, which indicates the position of the last note returned, and a `has NextPage` boolean, which allows us to determine if there are additional notes to load. We can view our schema within the GraphQL Playground, allowing us to see all of the data options available. For our query, we'll most likely require the following information:

```
{
  cursor
  hasNextPage
  notes {
    id
    createdAt
    content
    favoriteCount
    author {
      id
      username
      avatar
      }
    }
}
```

Now, in our GraphQL Playground we can flesh this out into a GraphQL query. We'll be writing this a bit more verbosely than the queries from a server chapter, by naming the query and providing an optional variable named `cursor`. To use the GraphQL Playground, first ensure that the API server is running, and then visit *http://localhost: 4000/api*. In the GraphQL Playground, add the following query:

```
query noteFeed($cursor: String) {
  noteFeed(cursor: $cursor) {
    cursor
    hasNextPage
    notes {
      id
      createdAt
      content
      favoriteCount
      author {
        username
        id
        avatar
      }
    }
  }
}
```

In the GraphQL Playground, also add a "query variable" to test out the use of the variable:

```
{
  "cursor": ""
}
```

To test out this variable, replace the empty string with the ID value of any of the notes in our database (Figure 14-1).

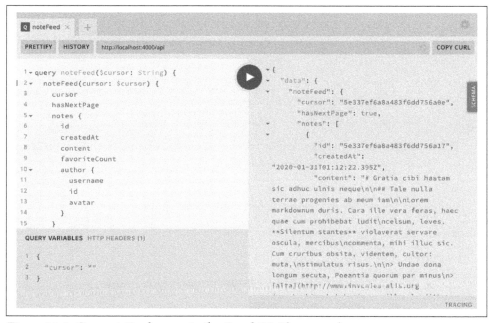

Figure 14-1. Our noteFeed query in the GraphQL Playground

Now that we know that our query is properly written, we can confidently integrate it into our web application. In the *src/pages/home.js* file, import the `useQuery` library as well as the GraphQL syntax via the `gql` library from `@apollo/client`:

```
// import the required libraries
import { useQuery, gql } from '@apollo/client';

// our GraphQL query, stored as a variable
const GET_NOTES = gql`
  query NoteFeed($cursor: String) {
    noteFeed(cursor: $cursor) {
      cursor
      hasNextPage
      notes {
        id
        createdAt
        content
        favoriteCount
        author {
          username
          id
          avatar
        }
      }
    }
  }
`;
```

Now we can integrate the query into our React application. To do this, we'll pass our GraphQL query string to Apollo's `useQuery` React hook. Our hook will return an object containing one of the following values:

`data`
> The data returned by the query, if successful.

`loading`
> The loading state, which is set to `true` when the data is being fetched. This allows us to display a loading indicator to our users.

`error`
> If our data fails to fetch, an error is returned to our application.

We can update our `Home` component to include our query:

```
const Home = () => {
  // query hook
  const { data, loading, error, fetchMore } = useQuery(GET_NOTES);

  // if the data is loading, display a loading message
  if (loading) return <p>Loading...</p>;
  // if there is an error fetching the data, display an error message
```

```
    if (error) return <p>Error!</p>;

    // if the data is successful, display the data in our UI
    return (
      <div>
        {console.log(data)}
        The data loaded!
      </div>
    );
  };

  export default Home;
```

If you've done everything successfully, you should see a "The data loaded!" message on the home page of our application (Figure 14-2). We've also included a `console.log` statement, which will print our data to the browser console. Taking a look at the structure of data results can be a helpful guidepost when integrating the data into the application.

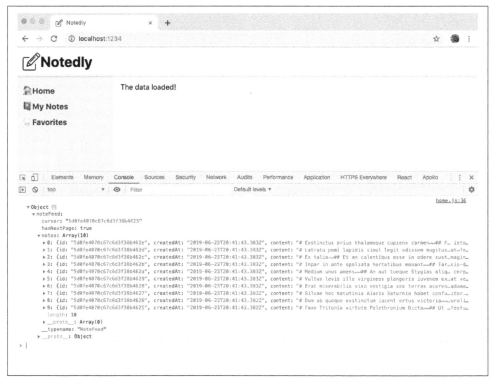

Figure 14-2. If our data has been successfully fetched, our component will display a "The data loaded!" message and the data will print to the console

Now, let's integrate the data we receive into the application. To do this, we will map over the array of notes returned within our data. React requires that each result be assigned a unique key, for which we'll use the individual note's ID. To begin, we'll display the username of the author for each note:

```
const Home = () => {
  // query hook
  const { data, loading, error, fetchMore } = useQuery(GET_NOTES);

  // if the data is loading, display a loading message
  if (loading) return <p>Loading...</p>;
  // if there is an error fetching the data, display an error message
  if (error) return <p>Error!</p>;

  // if the data is successful, display the data in our UI
  return (
    <div>
      {data.noteFeed.notes.map(note => (
        <div key={note.id}>{note.author.username}</div>
      ))}
    </div>
  );
};
```

Using JavaScript's map() Method

If you haven't worked with JavaScript's map() method before, the syntax can seem a bit intimidating at first. The map() method allows you to perform an action for items within an array. This can be incredibly useful when you're working with data returned from an API, allowing you to perform actions such as displaying each item in a certain way within the template. To learn more about map(), I recommend reading the MDN Web Docs guide (*https://oreil.ly/Oca3y*).

If there is data in our database, you should now see a list of usernames on the page (Figure 14-3).

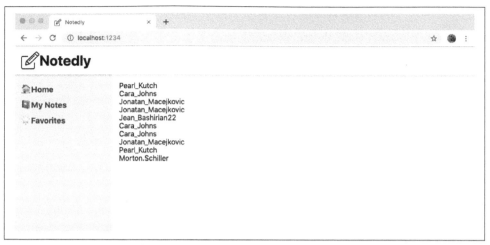

Figure 14-3. Usernames from our data, printed to the screen

Now that we have successfully mapped over our data, we can write the rest of our component. Since our notes are written in Markdown, let's import a library that will allow us to render Markdown to the page.

In *src/pages/home.js*:

```
import ReactMarkdown from 'react-markdown';
```

Now we can update our UI to include the author's avatar, the author's username, the date the note was created, the number of favorites that a note has, and finally the content of the note itself. In *src/pages/home.js*:

```
// if the data is successful, display the data in our UI
return (
  <div>
    {data.noteFeed.notes.map(note => (
      <article key={note.id}>
      <img
          src={note.author.avatar}
          alt={`${note.author.username} avatar`}
          height="50px"
        />{' '}
        {note.author.username} {note.createdAt} {note.favoriteCount}{' '}
        <ReactMarkdown source={note.content} />
      </article>
    ))}
  </div>
);
```

Whitespace in React

React strips the whitespace between elements on new lines. Using
{' '} in our markup is a way of manually adding whitespace.

You should now see a complete list of notes in your browser. Before we move on to styling them, however, there is an opportunity for a small refactor. This is our first page displaying notes, but we know that we will be making several more. On other pages we will need to display individual notes, as well as feeds of other note types (such as "my notes" and "favorites"). Let's go ahead and create two new components: *src/components/Note.js* and *src/components/NoteFeed.js*.

In *src/components/Note.js*, we'll include the markup for an individual note. To accomplish this, we'll pass each of our component functions a property containing the appropriate content.

```
import React from 'react';
import ReactMarkdown from 'react-markdown';

const Note = ({ note }) => {
  return (
    <article>
      <img
        src={note.author.avatar}
        alt="{note.author.username} avatar"
        height="50px"
      />{' '}
      {note.author.username} {note.createdAt} {note.favoriteCount}{' '}
      <ReactMarkdown source={note.content} />
    </article>
  );
};

export default Note;
```

Now for the *src/components/NoteFeed.js* component:

```
import React from 'react';
import Note from './Note';

const NoteFeed = ({ notes }) => {
  return (
    <div>
      {notes.map(note => (
        <div key={note.id}>
          <Note note={note} />
        </div>
      ))}
    </div>
  );
```

```
  };

  export default NoteFeed;
```

Finally, we can update the *src/pages/home.js* component to reference our NoteFeed:

```
  import React from 'react';
  import { useQuery, gql } from '@apollo/client';

  import Button from '../components/Button';
  import NoteFeed from '../components/NoteFeed';

  const GET_NOTES = gql`
    query NoteFeed($cursor: String) {
      noteFeed(cursor: $cursor) {
        cursor
        hasNextPage
        notes {
          id
          createdAt
          content
          favoriteCount
          author {
            username
            id
            avatar
          }
        }
      }
    }
  `;

  const Home = () => {
    // query hook
   const { data, loading, error, fetchMore } = useQuery(GET_NOTES);

   // if the data is loading, display a loading message
   if (loading) return <p>Loading...</p>;
   // if there is an error fetching the data, display an error message
   if (error) return <p>Error!</p>;

   // if the data is successful, display the data in our UI
    return <NoteFeed notes={data.noteFeed.notes} />;
  };

  export default Home;
```

With this refactor, we'll now be able to easily re-create note and note feed instances across our application.

Some Style

Now that we have written our components and can view our data, we can add some style. One of the most obvious opportunities for improvement is in the way that our "created at" date displays. To address this, we'll use the `date-fns` library (*https://date-fns.org*), which provides small components for working with dates in JavaScript. In *src/components/Note.js*, import the library and update the date markups to apply the conversion as follows:

```
// import the format utility from `date-fns`
import { format } from 'date-fns';

// update the date markup to format it as Month, Day, and Year
{format(note.createdAt, 'MMM Do YYYY')} Favorites:{' '}
```

With our date formatted, we can use the Styled Components library to update the note layout:

```
import React from 'react';
import ReactMarkdown from 'react-markdown';
import { format } from 'date-fns';
import styled from 'styled-components';

// Keep notes from extending wider than 800px
const StyledNote = styled.article`
  max-width: 800px;
  margin: 0 auto;
`;

// Style the note metadata
const MetaData = styled.div`
  @media (min-width: 500px) {
    display: flex;
    align-items: top;
  }
`;

// add some space between the avatar and meta info
const MetaInfo = styled.div`
  padding-right: 1em;
`;

// align 'UserActions' to the right on large screens
const UserActions = styled.div`
  margin-left: auto;
`;

const Note = ({ note }) => {
  return (
    <StyledNote>
      <MetaData>
        <MetaInfo>
```

```
          <img
            src={note.author.avatar}
            alt="{note.author.username} avatar"
            height="50px"
          />
        </MetaInfo>
        <MetaInfo>
          <em>by</em> {note.author.username} <br />
          {format(note.createdAt, 'MMM Do YYYY')}
        </MetaInfo>
        <UserActions>
          <em>Favorites:</em> {note.favoriteCount}
        </UserActions>
      </MetaData>
      <ReactMarkdown source={note.content} />
    </StyledNote>
  );
};

export default Note;
```

We would also be well served to add some space and a light border between the notes in our *NoteFeed.js* component:

```
import React from 'react';
import styled from 'styled-components';

const NoteWrapper = styled.div`
  max-width: 800px;
  margin: 0 auto;
  margin-bottom: 2em;
  padding-bottom: 2em;
  border-bottom: 1px solid #f5f4f0;
`;

import Note from './Note';

const NoteFeed = ({ notes }) => {
  return (
    <div>
      {notes.map(note => (
        <NoteWrapper key={note.id}>
          <Note note={note} />
        </NoteWrapper>
      ))}
    </div>
  );
};

export default NoteFeed;
```

With these updates, we've introduced layout styles to our application.

Dynamic Queries

Currently our application consists of three routes, each of which is static. These routes are located at a static URL and will always make the same data request. However, applications commonly need dynamic routes and queries based upon those routes. As an example, every tweet on Twitter.com is assigned a unique URL at *twitter.com/<username>/status/<tweet_id>*. This allows users to link and share individual tweets both within the Twitter ecosystem as well as anywhere on the web.

Currently, in our application notes can only be accessed within a feed, but we want to allow users to view and link to individual notes. To accomplish this we'll set up dynamic routing in our React application as well as an individual note GraphQL query. Our goal is for users to be able to access routes at *note/<note_id>*.

To begin, we'll create a new page component at *src/pages/note.js*. We will pass our `props` (property) object to the component, which includes the `match` property via React Router. This property contains information about how the route path matches the URL. This will give us access to the URL parameters through `match.params`.

```
import React from 'react';

const NotePage = props => {
  return (
    <div>
      <p>ID: {props.match.params.id}</p>
    </div>
  );
};

export default NotePage;
```

Now we can add a corresponding route to our *src/pages/index.js* file. This route will include an ID parameter indicated with `:id`:

```
// import React and routing dependencies
import React from 'react';
import { BrowserRouter as Router, Route } from 'react-router-dom';

// import shared layout component
import Layout from '../components/Layout';

// import routes
import Home from './home';
import MyNotes from './mynotes';
import Favorites from './favorites';
import NotePage from './note';

// define routes
const Pages = () => {
  return (
```

```
    <Router>
      <Layout>
        <Route exact path="/" component={Home} />
        <Route path="/mynotes" component={MyNotes} />
        <Route path="/favorites" component={Favorites} />
        <Route path="/note/:id" component={NotePage} />
      </Layout>
    </Router>
  );
};

export default Pages;
```

Now, visiting *http://localhost:1234/note/123* will print ID: 123 to our page. To test it out, replace the ID parameter with anything of your choosing, such as */note/pizza* or */note/GONNAPARTYLIKE1999*. This is pretty cool, but not very useful. Let's update our *src/pages/note.js* component to make a GraphQL query for the note with the ID found in the URL. To do this, we'll use the note query from our API as well as our Note React component:

```
import React from 'react';
// import GraphQL dependencies
import { useQuery, gql } from '@apollo/client';

// import the Note component
import Note from '../components/Note';

// the note query, which accepts an ID variable
const GET_NOTE = gql`
  query note($id: ID!) {
    note(id: $id) {
      id
      createdAt
      content
      favoriteCount
      author {
        username
        id
        avatar
      }
    }
  }
`;

const NotePage = props => {
  // store the id found in the url as a variable
  const id = props.match.params.id;

  // query hook, passing the id value as a variable
  const { loading, error, data } = useQuery(GET_NOTE, { variables: { id } });

  // if the data is loading, display a loading message
```

```
    if (loading) return <p>Loading...</p>;
    // if there is an error fetching the data, display an error message
    if (error) return <p>Error! Note not found</p>;

    // if the data is successful, display the data in our UI
    return <Note note={data.note} />;
};

export default NotePage;
```

Now, navigating to a URL with an ID parameter will render either the corresponding note or an error message. Finally, let's update our *src/components/NoteFeed.js* component to display a link to the individual note in the UI.

First, at the top of the file, import {Link} from React Router:

```
import { Link } from 'react-router-dom';
```

Then, update the JSX to include a link to the note page as follows:

```
<NoteWrapper key={note.id}>
  <Note note={note} />
  <Link to={`note/${note.id}`}>Permalink</Link>
</NoteWrapper>
```

With this, we are using dynamic routes in our application and enabling users to view individual notes.

Pagination

Currently we are only retrieving the 10 most recent notes within our application's home page. If we want to display additional notes, we need to enable pagination. You may recall from the beginning of this chapter and the development of our API server that our API returns a cursor, which is the ID of the last note returned in a page of results. Additionally, the API returns the hasNextPage boolean, which is true if there are additional notes found in our database. When making a request to our API, we can pass it a cursor argument, which will return the next 10 items.

In other words, if we have a list of 25 objects (with corresponding IDs of 1–25), when we make an initial request it will return items 1–10 as well as a cursor value of 10 and a hasNextPage value of true. If we make a request, passing a cursor value of 10, we will receive items 11–20, with a cursor value of 20 and a hasNextPage value of true. Finally, if we make a third request, passing it a cursor of 20, we will receive items 21–25, with a cursor value of 25 and a hasNextPage value of false. This is exactly the logic we'll be implementing within our noteFeed query.

To do this, let's update our *src/pages/home.js* file to make paginated queries. In our UI, when a user clicks a See More button, the next 10 notes should load on the page. We'll want this to happen without any page refreshes. To do this we need to include the fetchMore argument within our query component and display the Button component only when hasNextPage is true. For now we'll write this directly into our home page component, but it could easily be isolated into its own component or become part of the NoteFeed component.

```
// if the data is successful, display the data in our UI
return (
  // add a <React.Fragment> element to provide a parent element
  <React.Fragment>
    <NoteFeed notes={data.noteFeed.notes} />
    {/* Only display the Load More button if hasNextPage is true */}
    {data.noteFeed.hasNextPage && (
      <Button>Load more</Button>
    )}
  </React.Fragment>
);
```

Conditionals in React

In the previous example we are conditionally displaying the "Load more" button using an inline if statement with the && operator. If hasNextPage is true, the button is displayed. You can read more about conditional rendering in the official React documentation (*https://oreil.ly/a_F5s*).

Now we can update the <Button> component to use an onClick handler. When a user clicks the button, we'll want to use the fetchMore method to make an additional query and append the returned data to our page.

```
{data.noteFeed.hasNextPage && (
  //  onClick peform a query, passing the current cursor as a variable
  <Button
    onClick={() =>
      fetchMore({
        variables: {
          cursor: data.noteFeed.cursor
        },
        updateQuery: (previousResult, { fetchMoreResult }) => {
          return {
            noteFeed: {
              cursor: fetchMoreResult.noteFeed.cursor,
              hasNextPage: fetchMoreResult.noteFeed.hasNextPage,
              // combine the new results and the old
              notes: [
                ...previousResult.noteFeed.notes,
                ...fetchMoreResult.noteFeed.notes
              ],
              __typename: 'noteFeed'
            }
          };
```

```
        }
      })
    }
  >
    Load more
  </Button>
)}
```

The previous code might look a little gnarly, so let's break it down. Our `<Button>` component includes an `onClick` handler. When the button is clicked, a new query is executed using the `fetchMore` method, passing the `cursor` value returned in the previous query. Once returned, `updateQuery` is executed, which updates our `cursor` and `hasNextPage` values and combines the results into a single array. The `__typename` is the name of the query, which is included in Apollo's results.

With this change, we are able to view all of the notes from our note feed. Try it out yourself by scrolling to the bottom of your note feed. If your database contains more than 10 notes, the button will be visible. Clicking "Load more" will add the next `note Feed` result to the page.

Conclusion

We've covered a lot of ground in this chapter. We've set up Apollo Client to work with our React application and integrated multiple GraphQL queries into our UI. The power of GraphQL is demonstrated in the ability to write single queries that return precisely the data that a UI requires. In the next chapter we'll integrate user authentication into our application, allowing users to log in and view their notes and favorites.

## CHAPTER 15

Web Authentication and State

My family and I recently moved. After filling out and signing several forms (my hand is *still* tired), we were handed the keys to the front door. Each time we come back home, we are able to use those keys to unlock the door and enter. I'm grateful that I don't need to complete the form each time that I come home, but also appreciate having a lock so that we don't have any unexpected guests.

Client-side web authentication works in much the same way. Our users will fill out a form and will be handed a key to the website, in the form of a password alongside a token stored in their browser. When they return to the site they will either be automatically authenticated with the token, or be able to sign back in using their password.

In this chapter, we'll build out a web authentication system with our GraphQL API. To do this, we'll be building forms, storing JWTs in the browser, sending tokens with each request, and keeping track of our application's state.

Creating a Sign-up Form

To get started with our application's client authentication, we can create a user sign-up React component. Before doing so, let's map out how the component will work.

First, a user will navigate to the */signup* route within our application. On this page they will be presented with a form where they can enter their email address, desired username, and password. Submitting the form will perform our API's signUp mutation. If the mutation is successful, a new user account will be created and the API will return a JWT. If there is an error, we can inform the user. We'll be displaying a generic error message, but we could update our API to return specific error messages, such as a pre-existing username or a duplicate email address.

Let's get started by creating our new route. First, we'll create a new React component at *src/pages/signup.js*:

```
import React, { useEffect } from 'react';

// include the props passed to the component for later use
const SignUp = props => {
  useEffect(() => {
    // update the document title
    document.title = 'Sign Up — Notedly';
  });

  return (
    <div>
      <p>Sign Up</p>
    </div>
  );
};

export default SignUp;
```

Now we'll update our route list in *src/pages/index.js* to include the `signup` route:

```
// import the signup route
import SignUp from './signup';

// within the Pages component add the route
<Route path="/signup" component={SignUp} />
```

By adding the route, we will be able to navigate to *http://localhost:1234/signup* to see the (mostly empty) sign-up page. Now, let's add the markup for our form:

```
import React, { useEffect } from 'react';

const SignUp = props => {
  useEffect(() => {
    // update the document title
    document.title = 'Sign Up — Notedly';
  });

  return (
    <div>
      <form>
        <label htmlFor="username">Username:</label>
        <input
          required
          type="text"
          id="username"
          name="username"
          placeholder="username"
        />
        <label htmlFor="email">Email:</label>
        <input
```

```
      required
      type="email"
      id="email"
      name="email"
      placeholder="Email"
    />
    <label htmlFor="password">Password:</label>
    <input
      required
      type="password"
      id="password"
      name="password"
      placeholder="Password"
    />
    <button type="submit">Submit</button>
  </form>
</div>
);
};

export default SignUp;
```

htmlFor

If you're just learning React, one of the common gotchas are JSX attributes that differ from their HTML counterparts. In this case we are using the JSX htmlFor in place of HTML's for attribute to avoid any JavaScript collisions. You can see a full, though short, list of these attributes in the React DOM Elements documentation (*https://oreil.ly/Kn5Ke*).

Now we can add some style by importing our Button component and styling the form as a styled component:

```
import React, { useEffect } from 'react';
import styled from 'styled-components';

import Button from '../components/Button';

const Wrapper = styled.div`
  border: 1px solid #f5f4f0;
  max-width: 500px;
  padding: 1em;
  margin: 0 auto;
`;

const Form = styled.form`
  label,
  input {
    display: block;
    line-height: 2em;
```

```
  }

  input {
    width: 100%;
    margin-bottom: 1em;
  }
`;

const SignUp = props => {
  useEffect(() => {
    // update the document title
    document.title = 'Sign Up — Notedly';
  });

  return (
    <Wrapper>
      <h2>Sign Up</h2>
      <Form>
        <label htmlFor="username">Username:</label>
        <input
          required
          type="text"
          id="username"
          name="username"
          placeholder="username"
        />
        <label htmlFor="email">Email:</label>
        <input
          required
          type="email"
          id="email"
          name="email"
          placeholder="Email"
        />
        <label htmlFor="password">Password:</label>
        <input
          required
          type="password"
          id="password"
          name="password"
          placeholder="Password"
        />
        <Button type="submit">Submit</Button>
      </Form>
    </Wrapper>
  );
};

export default SignUp;
```

React Forms and State

In an application, things change. Data is entered into a form, a user toggles a slider open, a message is sent. In React, we can track these changes at the component level by assigning *state*. In our form, we'll need to track the state of each form element, so that it can be submitted.

React Hooks

In this book we're using functional components and React's newer Hooks API. If you've used other learning resources that make use of React's class components, this may look a little different. You can read more about Hooks in the React documentation (*https://oreil.ly/Tz9Hg*).

To get started with state, we'll first update the React import at the top of our *src/pages/signup.js* file to include useState:

```
import React, { useEffect, useState } from 'react';
```

Next, within our SignUp component we'll set the default form value state:

```
const SignUp = props => {
  // set the default state of the form
  const [values, setValues] = useState();

// rest of component goes here
};
```

Now we'll update our component to change the state when a form field is entered and perform an operation when a user submits the form. First, we'll create an onChange function, which will update our component's state whenever the form is updated. We'll also update the markup of each form element to call this function when a user makes a change, using the onChange property. Then we'll update our form element to include an onSubmit handler. For now, we'll simply log our form data to the console.

In */src/pages/sigunp.js*:

```
const SignUp = () => {
  // set the default state of the form
  const [values, setValues] = useState();

  // update the state when a user types in the form
  const onChange = event => {
    setValues({
      ...values,
      [event.target.name]: event.target.value
    });
  };
};
```

```
useEffect(() => {
  // update the document title
  document.title = 'Sign Up — Notedly';
});

return (
  <Wrapper>
    <h2>Sign Up</h2>
    <Form
      onSubmit={event => {
        event.preventDefault();
        console.log(values);
      }}
    >
      <label htmlFor="username">Username:</label>
      <input
        required
        type="text"
        name="username"
        placeholder="username"
        onChange={onChange}
      />
      <label htmlFor="email">Email:</label>
      <input
        required
        type="email"
        name="email"
        placeholder="Email"
        onChange={onChange}
      />
      <label htmlFor="password">Password:</label>
      <input
        required
        type="password"
        name="password"
        placeholder="Password"
        onChange={onChange}
      />
      <Button type="submit">Submit</Button>
    </Form>
  </Wrapper>
);
};
```

With this form markup in place, we're ready to request data with a GraphQL mutation.

signUp Mutation

To sign up a user, we'll be using our API's `signUp` mutation. This mutation will accept an email, username, and password as variables and return a JWT if the signup is successful. Let's write our mutation and integrate it into our sign-up form.

First, we'll need to import our Apollo libraries. We'll be making using of the `useMutation` and `useApolloClient` hooks, as well as the `gql` syntax, from Apollo Client. In *src/pages/signUp*, add the following alongside the other library import statements:

```
import { useMutation, useApolloClient, gql } from '@apollo/client';
```

Now write the GraphQL mutation as follows:

```
const SIGNUP_USER = gql`
  mutation signUp($email: String!, $username: String!, $password: String!) {
    signUp(email: $email, username: $username, password: $password)
  }
`;
```

With the mutation written, we can update our React component markup to perform the mutation when a user submits the form, passing the form elements as variables. For now, we'll log our response (which, if successful, should be a JWT) to the console:

```
const SignUp = props => {
  // useState, onChange, and useEffect all remain the same here

  //add the mutation hook
  const [signUp, { loading, error }] = useMutation(SIGNUP_USER, {
   onCompleted: data => {
     // console.log the JSON Web Token when the mutation is complete
     console.log(data.signUp);
   }
});

  // render our form
  return (
    <Wrapper>
      <h2>Sign Up</h2>
      {/* pass the form data to the mutation when a user submits the form */}
      <Form
        onSubmit={event => {
          event.preventDefault();
          signUp({
            variables: {
              ...values
            }
          });
        }}
      >
        {/* ... the rest of the form remains unchanged ... */}
      </Form>
```

```
        </Wrapper>
    );
};
```

Now if you complete and submit the form, you should see a JWT logged to your console (Figure 15-1). Additionally, if you perform a `users` query in the GraphQL Playground (*http://localhost:4000/api*), you'll see the new account (Figure 15-2).

Figure 15-1. If successful, a JSON Web Token will print to our console when we submit the form

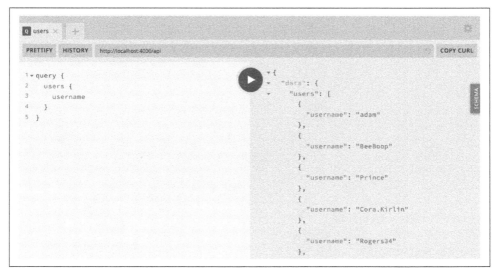

Figure 15-2. We can also see a list of users by performing a users query in the GraphQL Playground

With our mutation in place and returning the expected data, next we want to store the response that we receive.

JSON Web Tokens and Local Storage

When our `signUp` mutation is successful, it returns a JSON Web Token (JWT). You may recall from the API portion of the book that a JWT (*https://jwt.io*) allows us to securely store a user's ID on the user's device. To achieve this in our user's web browser, we'll store the token in the browser's `localStorage`. `localStorage` is a simple key-value store that persists across browser sessions until the storage is updated or cleared. Let's update our mutation to store the token in `localStorage`.

In *src/pages/signup.js*, update the `useMutation` hook to store the token in `localStorage` (see Figure 15-3):

```
const [signUp, { loading, error }] = useMutation(SIGNUP_USER, {
  onCompleted: data => {
    // store the JWT in localStorage
    localStorage.setItem('token', data.signUp);
  }
});
```

Figure 15-3. Our web token is now stored in the browser's localStorage

JWTs and Security

When a token is stored in `localStorage`, any JavaScript that can be run on the page has access to the token, making it susceptible to cross-site scripting (XSS) attacks. For this reason, when using `localStorage` to store token credentials, you need to take extra care to limit (or avoid) CDN hosted scripts. If a third-party script is compromised, it would have access to the JWT.

With our JWT stored locally, we're prepared to use it in our GraphQL mutations and queries.

Redirects

Currently when a user completes the sign-up form, the form re-renders as an empty form. This doesn't leave the user with much of a visual cue that their account registration was successful. Instead, let's redirect the user to the home page of our application. Another option would be to create a "Success" page that thanks the user for registering and onboards them to the application.

As you may recall from earlier in the chapter, we're passing the properties into the component. We can redirect a route using React Router's `history`, which will be available to us through `props.history.push`. To implement this, we'll update our mutation's `onCompleted` event to include a redirect like so:

```
const [signUp, { loading, error }] = useMutation(SIGNUP_USER, {
    onCompleted: data => {
      // store the token
      localStorage.setItem('token', data.signUp);
      // redirect the user to the homepage
      props.history.push('/');
    }
});
```

With this change, users will now be redirected to our application's home page after registering for an account.

Attaching Headers to Requests

Though we are storing our token in `localStorage`, our API does not yet have access to it. This means that even if a user has created an account, the API has no way of identifying the user. If you recall from our API development, each API call receives a token in the header of the request. We'll modify our client to send the JWT as a header with each request.

In *src/App.js* we'll update our dependencies to include `createHttpLink` from Apollo Client as well as `setContext` from Apollo's Link Context package. We'll then update Apollo's configuration to send the token in the header of each request:

```
// import the Apollo dependencies
import {
  ApolloClient,
  ApolloProvider,
  createHttpLink,
  InMemoryCache
} from '@apollo/client';
import { setContext } from 'apollo-link-context';

// configure our API URI & cache
const uri = process.env.API_URI;
```

```
const httpLink = createHttpLink({ uri });
const cache = new InMemoryCache();

// check for a token and return the headers to the context
const authLink = setContext((_, { headers }) => {
  return {
    headers: {
      ...headers,
      authorization: localStorage.getItem('token') || ''
    }
  };
});

// create the Apollo client
const client = new ApolloClient({
  link: authLink.concat(httpLink),
  cache,
  resolvers: {},
  connectToDevTools: true
});
```

With this change, we'll now be able to pass the information of the logged-in user to our API.

Local State Management

We've looked at managing state within a component, but what about across our application? There are times where it's useful to have some information shared among many components. We could pass props from a base component across our application, but as soon as we get past a couple of levels of subcomponents, this can get messy. Libraries such as Redux (*https://redux.js.org*) and MobX (*https://mobx.js.org*) have sought to solve the challenges of state management and have proven useful for many developers and teams. In our case, we're already making use of the Apollo Client library, which includes the ability to use GraphQL queries for local state management. Rather than introducing another dependency, let's implement a local state property that will store whether the user is logged in.

The Apollo React library puts the ApolloClient instance within React's context, but at times we may need to access it directly. We can do so with the useApolloClient hook, which will allow us to perform actions such as directly updating or resetting the cache store or writing local data.

Currently, we have two ways to determine if a user is logged in to our application. First, we know they are a current user if they've successfully submitted the sign-up form. Second, we know that if a visitor accesses the site with a token stored in local Storage, then they are already logged in. Let's begin by adding to our state when a user completes the sign-up form. To achieve this, we'll write directly to our Apollo Client's local store, using `client.writeData` and the `useApolloClient` hook.

In *src/pages/signup.js* we first need to update the `@apollo/client` library import to include `useApolloClient`:

```
import { useMutation, useApolloClient } from '@apollo/client';
```

In *src/pages/signup.js* we'll call the `useApolloClient` function and update the mutation to add to the local store, using `writeData`, when it is complete:

```
// Apollo Client
const client = useApolloClient();
// Mutation Hook
const [signUp, { loading, error }] = useMutation(SIGNUP_USER, {
  onCompleted: data => {
    // store the token
    localStorage.setItem('token', data.signUp);
    // update the local cache
    client.writeData({ data: { isLoggedIn: true } });
    // redirect the user to the homepage
    props.history.push('/');
  }
});
```

Now, let's update our application to check for a pre-existing token when the page loads and update the state when a token is found. In `src/App.js`, first update the `ApolloClient` configuration to an empty `resolvers` object. This will allow us to perform GraphQL queries on our local cache.

```
// create the Apollo client
const client = new ApolloClient({
  link: authLink.concat(httpLink),
  cache,
  resolvers: {},
  connectToDevTools: true
});
```

Next, we can perform the check on the initial page load of our application:

```
// check for a local token
const data = {
  isLoggedIn: !!localStorage.getItem('token')
};

// write the cache data on initial load
cache.writeData({ data });
```

Here comes the cool part: we can now access `isLoggedIn` as a GraphQL query anywhere within our application by using the `@client` directive. To demonstrate this, let's update the header of our application to display a "Sign Up" and "Sign In" link if `isLoggedIn` is `false` and a "Log Out" link if `isLoggedIn` is `true`.

In *src/components/Header.js*, import the necessary dependencies and write the query like so:

```
// new dependencies
import { useQuery, gql } from '@apollo/client';
import { Link } from 'react-router-dom';

// local query
const IS_LOGGED_IN = gql`
  {
    isLoggedIn @client
  }
`;
```

Now, within our React component we can include a simple query to retrieve the state along with a tertiary operator that displays options either to log out or sign in:

```
const UserState = styled.div`
  margin-left: auto;
`;

const Header = props => {
  // query hook for user logged in state
  const { data } = useQuery(IS_LOGGED_IN);

  return (
    <HeaderBar>
      <img src={logo} alt="Notedly Logo" height="40" />
      <LogoText>Notedly</LogoText>
      {/* If logged in display a logout link, else display sign-in options */}
      <UserState>
        {data.isLoggedIn ? (
          <p>Log Out</p>
        ) : (
          <p>
            <Link to={'/signin'}>Sign In</Link> or{' '}
            <Link to={'/signup'}>Sign Up</Link>
          </p>
        )}
      </UserState>
    </HeaderBar>
  );
};
```

With this, when a user is logged in they'll see a "Log Out" option: otherwise, they'll be presented with options to sign up or in, all thanks to local state. We're not limited to simple boolean logic, either. Apollo enables us to write local resolvers and type definitions, allowing us to take advantage of everything GraphQL has to offer within our local state.

Logging Out

Currently once a user is signed in, they have no way to log out of our application. Let's turn the "Log Out" language in our header into a button that, when clicked, will log out the user. To do this, when the button is clicked we will remove the token that has been stored in localStorage. We'll use a <button> element for its built-in accessibility, as it both serves as a semantic representation of a user action and receives focus, like a link, when a user is navigating the application with their keyboard.

Before writing our code, let's write a styled component that will render a button like a link. Create a new file at *src/Components/ButtonAsLink.js* and add the following:

```
import styled from 'styled-components';

const ButtonAsLink = styled.button`
  background: none;
  color: #0077cc;
  border: none;
  padding: 0;
  font: inherit;
  text-decoration: underline;
  cursor: pointer;

  :hover,
  :active {
    color: #004499;
  }
`;

export default ButtonAsLink;
```

Now in *src/components/Header.js* we can implement our logout functionality. We need to use React Router's withRouter higher-order component to handle the redirect since our *Header.js* file is a UI component and not a defined route. Let's begin by importing the ButtonAsLink component as well as withRouter:

```
// import both Link and withRouter from React Router
import { Link, withRouter } from 'react-router-dom';
// import the ButtonAsLink component
import ButtonAsLink from './ButtonAsLink';
```

Now, within our JSX we'll update our component to include the props parameter and update the logout markup to be a button:

```
const Header = props => {
  // query hook for user logged-in state,
  // including the client for referencing the Apollo store
  const { data, client } = useQuery(IS_LOGGED_IN);

  return (
    <HeaderBar>
```

```
        <img src={logo} alt="Notedly Logo" height="40" />
        <LogoText>Notedly</LogoText>
        {/* If logged in display a logout link, else display sign-in options */}
        <UserState>
          {data.isLoggedIn ? (
            <ButtonAsLink>
              Logout
            </ButtonAsLink>
          ) : (
            <p>
              <Link to={'/signin'}>Sign In</Link> or{' '}
              <Link to={'/signup'}>Sign Up</Link>
            </p>
          )}
        </UserState>
      </HeaderBar>
    );
};

// we wrap our component in the withRouter higher-order component
export default withRouter(Header);
```

withRouter

When we want to include routing in a component that is not itself directly routable, we need to use React Router's `withRouter` higher-order component.

When a user logs out of our application, we want to reset the cache store to prevent any unwanted data from appearing outside of the session. Apollo offers the ability to call the `resetStore` function, which will fully clear the cache. Let's add an `onClick` handler to our component's button to remove the user's token, reset the Apollo Store, update the local state, and redirect the user to the home page. To accomplish this, we'll update our `useQuery` hook to include a reference to the client and wrap our component in the `withRouter` higher-order component in our `export` statement.

```
const Header = props => {
  // query hook for user logged in state
  const { data, client } = useQuery(IS_LOGGED_IN);

  return (
    <HeaderBar>
      <img src={logo} alt="Notedly Logo" height="40" />
      <LogoText>Notedly</LogoText>
      {/* If logged in display a logout link, else display sign-in options */}
      <UserState>
        {data.isLoggedIn ? (
          <ButtonAsLink
            onClick={() => {
              // remove the token
```

```
              localStorage.removeItem('token');
              // clear the application's cache
              client.resetStore();
              // update local state
              client.writeData({ data: { isLoggedIn: false } });
              // redirect the user to the home page
              props.history.push('/');
            }}
          >
            Logout
          </ButtonAsLink>
        ) : (
          <p>
            <Link to={'/signin'}>Sign In</Link> or{' '}
            <Link to={'/signup'}>Sign Up</Link>
          </p>
        )}
      </UserState>
    </HeaderBar>
  );
};

export default withRouter(Header);
```

Finally, we will need Apollo to add the user state back to our cached state when the store is reset. In *src/App.js* update the cache settings to include `onResetStore`:

```
// check for a local token
const data = {
  isLoggedIn: !!localStorage.getItem('token')
};

// write the cache data on initial load
cache.writeData({ data });
// write the cache data after cache is reset
client.onResetStore(() => cache.writeData({ data }));
```

With this, logged-in users are able to easily log out of our application. We've integrated this functionality directly into our `Header` component, but in the future we could refactor it into a standalone component.

Creating a Sign-In Form

Currently our users are able to sign up and log out of our application, but they have no way to sign back in. Let's create a sign-in form and do a bit of refactoring along the way so that we can reuse much of the code found in our signup component.

Our first step will be to create a new page component that will live at */signin*. In a new file at *src/pages/signin.js*, add the following:

```
import React, { useEffect } from 'react';

const SignIn = props => {
  useEffect(() => {
    // update the document title
    document.title = 'Sign In — Notedly';
  });

  return (
    <div>
      <p>Sign up page</p>
    </div>
  );
};

export default SignIn;
```

Now we can make our page routable, so that users can navigate to it. In *src/pages/ index.js* import the route page and add a new route path:

```
// import the sign-in page component
import SignIn from './signin';

const Pages = () => {
  return (
    <Router>
      <Layout>
        // ... our other routes
        // add a signin route to our routes list
        <Route path="/signin" component={SignIn} />
      </Layout>
    </Router>
  );
};
```

Let's pause here, before we implement our sign-in form, to consider our options. We could reimplement a form, much like we wrote for our Sign Up page, but that feels tedious and would require us to maintain two similar forms. When one changes, we would need to be sure to update the other. Another option is to isolate the form into its own component, which would allow us to reuse common code and make updates in a single location. Let's go forward with the shared form component approach.

We'll first create a new component at *src/components/UserForm.js*, bringing over our <form> markup and styles. We will be making a few minor, but notable, changes to this form to use the properties that it receives from the parent component. First, we'll rename our onSubmit mutation to props.action, which will allow us to pass the mutation to our form through the component's properties. Second, we'll add some conditional statements where we know that our two forms will differ. We'll make use of a second property named formType, which we'll pass a string. We can change our template's rendering based on the value of the string.

We'll write these either as an inline `if` statement with a logical && operator or as a conditional ternary operator:

```
import React, { useState } from 'react';
import styled from 'styled-components';

import Button from './Button';

const Wrapper = styled.div`
  border: 1px solid #f5f4f0;
  max-width: 500px;
  padding: 1em;
  margin: 0 auto;
`;

const Form = styled.form`
  label,
  input {
    display: block;
    line-height: 2em;
  }

  input {
    width: 100%;
    margin-bottom: 1em;
  }
`;

const UserForm = props => {
  // set the default state of the form
  const [values, setValues] = useState();

  // update the state when a user types in the form
  const onChange = event => {
    setValues({
      ...values,
      [event.target.name]: event.target.value
    });
  };

  return (
    <Wrapper>
      {/* Display the appropriate form header */}
      {props.formType === 'signup' ? <h2>Sign Up</h2> : <h2>Sign In</h2>}
      {/* perform the mutation when a user submits the form */}
      <Form
        onSubmit={e => {
          e.preventDefault();
          props.action({
            variables: {
              ...values
            }
```

```
          });
        }}
    >
      {props.formType === 'signup' && (
        <React.Fragment>
          <label htmlFor="username">Username:</label>
          <input
            required
            type="text"
            id="username"
            name="username"
            placeholder="username"
            onChange={onChange}
          />
        </React.Fragment>
      )}
      <label htmlFor="email">Email:</label>
      <input
        required
        type="email"
        id="email"
        name="email"
        placeholder="Email"
        onChange={onChange}
      />
      <label htmlFor="password">Password:</label>
      <input
        required
        type="password"
        id="password"
        name="password"
        placeholder="Password"
        onChange={onChange}
      />
      <Button type="submit">Submit</Button>
    </Form>
  </Wrapper>
);
};

export default UserForm;
```

Now we can simplify our *src/pages/signup.js* component to make use of the shared form component:

```
import React, { useEffect } from 'react';
import { useMutation, useApolloClient, gql } from '@apollo/client';

import UserForm from '../components/UserForm';

const SIGNUP_USER = gql`
  mutation signUp($email: String!, $username: String!, $password: String!) {
    signUp(email: $email, username: $username, password: $password)
```

```
    }
`;

const SignUp = props => {
  useEffect(() => {
    // update the document title
    document.title = 'Sign Up – Notedly';
  });

  const client = useApolloClient();
  const [signUp, { loading, error }] = useMutation(SIGNUP_USER, {
    onCompleted: data => {
      // store the token
      localStorage.setItem('token', data.signUp);
      // update the local cache
      client.writeData({ data: { isLoggedIn: true } });
      // redirect the user to the homepage
      props.history.push('/');
    }
  });

  return (
    <React.Fragment>
      <UserForm action={signUp} formType="signup" />
      {/* if the data is loading, display a loading message*/}
      {loading && <p>Loading...</p>}
      {/* if there is an error, display a error message*/}
      {error && <p>Error creating an account!</p>}
    </React.Fragment>
  );
};

export default SignUp;
```

Finally, we can write our SignIn component, making use of our signIn mutation and
UserForm component. In *src/pages/signin.js*:

```
import React, { useEffect } from 'react';
import { useMutation, useApolloClient, gql } from '@apollo/client';

import UserForm from '../components/UserForm';

const SIGNIN_USER = gql`
  mutation signIn($email: String, $password: String!) {
    signIn(email: $email, password: $password)
  }
`;

const SignIn = props => {
  useEffect(() => {
    // update the document title
    document.title = 'Sign In – Notedly';
  });
```

```
const client = useApolloClient();
const [signIn, { loading, error }] = useMutation(SIGNIN_USER, {
  onCompleted: data => {
    // store the token
    localStorage.setItem('token', data.signIn);
    // update the local cache
    client.writeData({ data: { isLoggedIn: true } });
    // redirect the user to the homepage
    props.history.push('/');
  }
});

return (
  <React.Fragment>
    <UserForm action={signIn} formType="signIn" />
    {/* if the data is loading, display a loading message*/}
    {loading && <p>Loading...</p>}
    {/* if there is an error, display a error message*/}
    {error && <p>Error signing in!</p>}
  </React.Fragment>
);
};

export default SignIn;
```

With this, we now have a manageable form component and have enabled users to both sign up and sign in to our application.

Protected Routes

A common application pattern is to limit access to specific pages or portions of the site to authenticated users. In our case, nonauthenticated users would have no use for the My Notes or Favorites pages. We can implement this pattern in our router, automatically routing unauthenticated users to the application's Sign In page when they attempt to visit those routes.

In *src/pages/index.js* we'll start by importing the necessary dependencies and adding our isLoggedIn query:

```
import { useQuery, gql } from '@apollo/client';

const IS_LOGGED_IN = gql`
  {
    isLoggedIn @client
  }
`;
```

Now we'll import React Router's Redirect library and write a PrivateRoute component, which will redirect the user if they are not logged in:

```
// update our react-router import to include Redirect
import { BrowserRouter as Router, Route, Redirect } from 'react-router-dom';

// add the PrivateRoute component below our `Pages` component
const PrivateRoute = ({ component: Component, ...rest }) => {
  const { loading, error, data } = useQuery(IS_LOGGED_IN);
  // if the data is loading, display a loading message
  if (loading) return <p>Loading...</p>;
  // if there is an error fetching the data, display an error message
  if (error) return <p>Error!</p>;
  // if the user is logged in, route them to the requested component
  // else redirect them to the sign-in page
  return (
    <Route
      {...rest}
      render={props =>
        data.isLoggedIn === true ? (
          <Component {...props} />
        ) : (
          <Redirect
            to={{
              pathname: '/signin',
              state: { from: props.location }
            }}
          />
        )
      }
    />
  );
};

export default Pages;
```

Finally, we can update any of our routes intended for logged-in users to use the PrivateRoute component:

```
const Pages = () => {
  return (
    <Router>
      <Layout>
        <Route exact path="/" component={Home} />
        <PrivateRoute path="/mynotes" component={MyNotes} />
        <PrivateRoute path="/favorites" component={Favorites} />
        <Route path="/note/:id" component={Note} />
        <Route path="/signup" component={SignUp} />
        <Route path="/signin" component={SignIn} />
      </Layout>
    </Router>
  );
};
```

Redirect State

When we redirect a private route, we are also storing the referring URL as state. This allows us to redirect users back to the page they were originally attempting to navigate to. We could update our redirect on the Sign In page to optionally use `props.state.location.from` to enable this feature.

Now when a user attempts to navigate to a page intended for logged-in users, they will be redirected to our Sign In page.

Conclusion

In this chapter we've covered two critical concepts for building client-side JavaScript applications: authentication and state. By building a full authentication flow, you've gained insight into how user accounts work with a client application. From here, I would encourage you to explore alternate options such as OAuth and authentication services such as Auth0, Okta, and Firebase. Additionally, you've learned to manage state in an application, both at the component level, using the React Hooks API, as well as across the application, using Apollo's local state. With these key concepts behind you, you can now build robust user interface applications.

## CHAPTER 16

Create, Read, Update, and Delete Operations

I love paper notebooks and keep one with me at nearly all times. Usually they are relatively inexpensive and I quickly fill them with half-formed thoughts. Not long ago I purchased a pricier hardback notebook, with a lovely cover and fancy paper stock. At the time of purchase, I had grand ambitions of the types of sketches and planning that would happen within that notebook, but it sat completely empty on my desk for months. Eventually, I put it on a shelf and went back to my standard notebook brand.

Much like my fancy notebook, our app is useful only if our users are able to interact with it. You may recall from our API development that the Notedly application is a "CRUD" (create, read, update, and delete) application. An authenticated user can create new notes, read notes, update the content of a note or a note's status as a favorite, and delete a note. In this chapter, we'll implement all of this functionality within our web user interface. To accomplish these tasks, we'll be writing GraphQL mutations and queries.

Creating New Notes

Currently we have the means to view notes, but not a way to create them. This is akin to having a notebook without a pen. Let's add the ability for users to create new notes. We'll do this by creating a `textarea` form in which users can write the note. When the user submits the form, we'll perform a GraphQL mutation to create the note in our database.

To begin, let's create the `NewNote` component at *src/pages/new.js*:

```
import React, { useEffect } from 'react';
import { useMutation, gql } from '@apollo/client';
```

```
const NewNote = props => {
  useEffect(() => {
    // update the document title
    document.title = 'New Note — Notedly';
  });

  return <div>New note</div>;
};

export default NewNote;
```

Next, let's set up the new route in our *src/pages/index.js* file:

```
// import the NewNote route component
import NewNote from './new';

// add a private route to our list of routes, within the
<PrivateRoute path="/new" component={NewNote} />
```

We know that we'll be both creating new notes as well as updating existing notes. To accommodate this behavior, let's create a new component called `NoteForm`, which will serve as the markup and React state for note form editing.

We'll create a new file at *src/components/NoteForm.js*. The component will consist of a form element containing a text area along with some minimal styles. The functionality will be much like our `UserForm` component:

```
import React, { useState } from 'react';
import styled from 'styled-components';

import Button from './Button';

const Wrapper = styled.div`
  height: 100%;
`;

const Form = styled.form`
  height: 100%;
`;

const TextArea = styled.textarea`
  width: 100%;
  height: 90%;
`;

const NoteForm = props => {
  // set the default state of the form
  const [value, setValue] = useState({ content: props.content || '' });

  // update the state when a user types in the form
  const onChange = event => {
    setValue({
```

```
      ...value,
      [event.target.name]: event.target.value
    });
  };

  return (
    <Wrapper>
      <Form
        onSubmit={e => {
          e.preventDefault();
          props.action({
            variables: {
              ...values
            }
          });
        }}
      >
        <TextArea
          required
          type="text"
          name="content"
          placeholder="Note content"
          value={value.content}
          onChange={onChange}
        />
        <Button type="submit">Save</Button>
      </Form>
    </Wrapper>
  );
};

export default NoteForm;
```

Next, we will need to reference our `NoteForm` component in our `NewNote` page component. In *src/pages/new.js*:

```
import React, { useEffect } from 'react';
import { useMutation, gql } from '@apollo/client';
// import the NoteForm component
import NoteForm from '../components/NoteForm';

const NewNote = props => {
  useEffect(() => {
    // update the document title
    document.title = 'New Note — Notedly';
  });

  return <NoteForm />;
];
export default NewNote;
```

With these updates, navigating to *http://localhost:1234/new* will display our form (Figure 16-1).

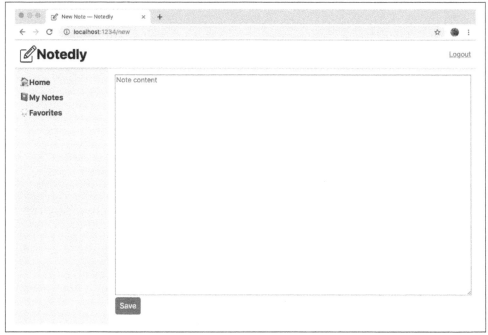

Figure 16-1. Our NewNote component presents the user with a large text area and Save button

With the form complete, we can go about writing our mutation to create the new note. In *src/pages/new.js*:

```
import React, { useEffect } from 'react';
import { useMutation, gql } from '@apollo/client';

import NoteForm from '../components/NoteForm';

// our new note query
const NEW_NOTE = gql`
  mutation newNote($content: String!) {
    newNote(content: $content) {
      id
      content
      createdAt
      favoriteCount
      favoritedBy {
        id
        username
      }
      author {
```

```
      username
      id
    }
  }
}
`;

const NewNote = props => {
  useEffect(() => {
    // update the document title
    document.title = 'New Note — Notedly';
  });

  const [data, { loading, error }] = useMutation(NEW_NOTE, {
    onCompleted: data => {
      // when complete, redirect the user to the note page
      props.history.push(`note/${data.newNote.id}`);
    }
  });

  return (
    <React.Fragment>
      {/* as the mutation is loading, display a loading message*/}
      {loading && <p>Loading...</p>}
      {/* if there is an error, display a error message*/}
      {error && <p>Error saving the note</p>}
      {/* the form component, passing the mutation data as a prop */}
      <NoteForm action={data} />
    </React.Fragment>
  );
};

export default NewNote;
```

In the previous code we are performing a newNote mutation when the form is submitted. If the mutation is successful, the user is redirected to the individual note page. You may notice that the newNote mutation requests quite a bit of data. This matches the data requested by the note mutation, ideally updating Apollo's cache for quick navigation to the individual note component.

As mentioned earlier, Apollo aggressively caches our queries, which is helpful for speeding up our application's navigation. Unfortunately, this also means a user could visit a page and not see an update they've just made. We can manually update Apollo's cache, but an easier way to accomplish this is to use Apollo's refetchQueries feature to intentionally update the cache when performing a mutation. To do this, we'll need access to our prewritten queries. Up until now, we've been including them at the top of a component file, but let's move them to their own *query.js* file. Create a new file at */src/gql/query.js* and add each of our note queries as well as our IS_LOGGED_IN query:

```
import { gql } from '@apollo/client';

const GET_NOTES = gql`
  query noteFeed($cursor: String) {
    noteFeed(cursor: $cursor) {
      cursor
      hasNextPage
      notes {
        id
        createdAt
        content
        favoriteCount
        author {
          username
          id
          avatar
        }
      }
    }
  }
`;

const GET_NOTE = gql`
  query note($id: ID!) {
    note(id: $id) {
      id
      createdAt
      content
      favoriteCount
      author {
        username
        id
        avatar
      }
    }
  }
`;

const IS_LOGGED_IN = gql`
  {
    isLoggedIn @client
  }
`;

export { GET_NOTES, GET_NOTE, IS_LOGGED_IN };
```

Reusable Queries and Mutations

Moving forward, we will keep all of our queries and mutations separate from our components This will allow us to easily reuse them
in our application and is also useful for mocking (*https://oreil.ly/
qo9uE*) during testing.

Now in *src/pages/new.js* we can request that our mutation refetch the `GET_NOTES` query by importing the query and adding the `refetchQueries` option:

```
// import the query
import { GET_NOTES } from '../gql/query';

// within the NewNote component update the mutation
//everything else stays the same

const NewNote = props => {
  useEffect(() => {
    // update the document title
    document.title = 'New Note — Notedly';
  });

  const [data, { loading, error }] = useMutation(NEW_NOTE, {
    // refetch the GET_NOTES query to update the cache
    refetchQueries: [{ query: GET_NOTES }],
    onCompleted: data => {
      // when complete, redirect the user to the note page
      props.history.push(`note/${data.newNote.id}`);
    }
  });

  return (
    <React.Fragment>
      {/* as the mutation is loading, display a loading message*/}
      {loading && <p>Loading...</p>}
      {/* if there is an error, display a error message*/}
      {error && <p>Error saving the note</p>}
      {/* the form component, passing the mutation data as a prop */}
      <NoteForm action={data} />
    </React.Fragment>
  );
};
```

Our final step will be to add a link to our */new* page, so that users can easily navigate to it. In the *src/components/Navigation.js* file, add a new link item as follows:

```
<li>
  <Link to="/new">New</Link>
</li>
```

With this, our users are able to navigate to the new note page, type a note, and save the note to the database.

Reading User Notes

Our application is currently capable of reading our note feed as well as individual notes, but we are not yet querying the notes of authenticated users. Let's write two GraphQL queries to create a feed of notes by the user as well as their favorites.

In *src/gql/query.js*, add a GET_MY_NOTES query and update the exports like so:

```
// add the GET_MY_NOTES query
const GET_MY_NOTES = gql`
  query me {
    me {
      id
      username
      notes {
        id
        createdAt
        content
        favoriteCount
        author {
          username
          id
          avatar
        }
      }
    }
  }
`;

// update to include GET_MY_NOTES
export { GET_NOTES, GET_NOTE, IS_LOGGED_IN, GET_MY_NOTES };
```

Now in *src/pages/mynotes.js*, import the query and display the notes using the Note Feed component:

```
import React, { useEffect } from 'react';
import { useQuery, gql } from '@apollo/client';

import NoteFeed from '../components/NoteFeed';
import { GET_MY_NOTES } from '../gql/query';

const MyNotes = () => {
  useEffect(() => {
    // update the document title
    document.title = 'My Notes — Notedly';
  });

  const { loading, error, data } = useQuery(GET_MY_NOTES);

  // if the data is loading, our app will display a loading message
  if (loading) return 'Loading...';
  // if there is an error fetching the data, display an error message
  if (error) return `Error! ${error.message}`;
  // if the query is successful and there are notes, return the feed of notes
  // else if the query is successful and there aren't notes, display a message
  if (data.me.notes.length !== 0) {
    return <NoteFeed notes={data.me.notes} />;
  } else {
    return <p>No notes yet</p>;
```

```
      }
    };

    export default MyNotes;
```

We can repeat this process to make the "favorites" page. First, in *src/gql/query.js*:

```
    // add the GET_MY_FAVORITES query
    const GET_MY_FAVORITES = gql`
      query me {
        me {
          id
          username
          favorites {
            id
            createdAt
            content
            favoriteCount
            author {
              username
              id
              avatar
            }
          }
        }
      }
    `;

    // update to include GET_MY_FAVORITES
    export { GET_NOTES, GET_NOTE, IS_LOGGED_IN, GET_MY_NOTES, GET_MY_FAVORITES };
```

Now, in *src/pages/favorites.js*:

```
    import React, { useEffect } from 'react';
    import { useQuery, gql } from '@apollo/client';

    import NoteFeed from '../components/NoteFeed';
    // import the query
    import { GET_MY_FAVORITES } from '../gql/query';

    const Favorites = () => {
      useEffect(() => {
        // update the document title
        document.title = 'Favorites — Notedly';
      });

      const { loading, error, data } = useQuery(GET_MY_FAVORITES);

      // if the data is loading, our app will display a loading message
      if (loading) return 'Loading...';
      // if there is an error fetching the data, display an error message
      if (error) return `Error! ${error.message}`;
      // if the query is successful and there are notes, return the feed of notes
      // else if the query is successful and there aren't notes, display a message
```

```
      if (data.me.favorites.length !== 0) {
        return <NoteFeed notes={data.me.favorites} />;
      } else {
        return <p>No favorites yet</p>;
      }
    };

    export default Favorites;
```

Finally, let's update our *src/pages/new.js* file to refetch the `GET_MY_NOTES` query, to ensure that a cached list of user notes is updated when the note is created. In *src/pages/new.js*, first update the GraphQL query import statement:

```
    import { GET_MY_NOTES, GET_NOTES } from '../gql/query';
```

And then update the mutation:

```
    const [data, { loading, error }] = useMutation(NEW_NOTE, {
      // refetch the GET_NOTES and GET_MY_NOTES queries to update the cache
      refetchQueries: [{ query: GET_MY_NOTES }, { query: GET_NOTES }],
      onCompleted: data => {
        // when complete, redirect the user to the note page
        props.history.push(`note/${data.newNote.id}`);
      }
    });
```

With these changes, we now can perform all of the read operations within our application.

Updating Notes

Currently once a user writes a note, they have no way to make an update to it. To address this, we want to enable note editing in our application. Our GraphQL API has an `updateNote` mutation, which accepts a note ID and content as parameters. If the note exists in the database, the mutation will update the stored content with the content sent in the mutation.

In our application, we can create a route at */edit/NOTE_ID* that will place the existing note content in a form `textarea`. When a user clicks Save, we'll submit the form and perform the `updateNote` mutation.

Let's create a new route where our notes will be edited. To begin, we can make a duplicate of our *src/pages/note.js* page and name it *edit.js*. For now, this page will simply display the note.

At *src/pages/edit.js*:

```
    import React from 'react';
    import { useQuery, useMutation, gql } from '@apollo/client';

    // import the Note component
```

```
import Note from '../components/Note';
// import the GET_NOTE query
import { GET_NOTE } from '../gql/query';

const EditNote = props => {
  // store the id found in the url as a variable
  const id = props.match.params.id;
  // define our note query
  const { loading, error, data } = useQuery(GET_NOTE, { variables: { id } });

  // if the data is loading, display a loading message
  if (loading) return 'Loading...';
  // if there is an error fetching the data, display an error message
  if (error) return <p>Error! Note not found</p>;
  // if successful, pass the data to the note component
  return <Note note={data.note} />;
};

export default EditNote;
```

Now, we can make the page navigable by adding it to our routes in *src/pages/index.js*:

```
// import the edit page component
import EditNote from './edit';

// add a new private route that accepts an :id parameter
<PrivateRoute path="/edit/:id" component={EditNote} />
```

With this, if you navigate to a note page at */note/ID* and swap it for */edit/ID* you'll see a render of the note itself. Let's change this so that it instead displays the note content presented in a form's textarea.

In *src/pages/edit.js*, remove the import statement of the Note component and replace it with the NoteForm component:

```
// import the NoteForm component
import NoteForm from '../components/NoteForm';
```

Now we can update our EditNote component to use our editing form. We can pass the content of the note to our form component by using the content property. Though our GraphQL mutation will accept updates only from the original author, we can also limit displaying the form to the note's author, to avoid confusing other users.

First, add a new query to the *src/gql/query.js* file to get the current user, their user ID, and a list of favorited note IDs:

```
// add GET_ME to our queries
const GET_ME = gql`
  query me {
    me {
      id
      favorites {
        id
```

```
        }
      }
    }
  `;

// update to include GET_ME
export {
  GET_NOTES,
  GET_NOTE,
  GET_MY_NOTES,
  GET_MY_FAVORITES,
  GET_ME,
  IS_LOGGED_IN
};
```

In *src/pages/edit.js*, import the GET_ME query and include a user check:

```
import React from 'react';
import { useMutation, useQuery } from '@apollo/client';

// import the NoteForm component
import NoteForm from '../components/NoteForm';
import { GET_NOTE, GET_ME } from '../gql/query';
import { EDIT_NOTE } from '../gql/mutation';

const EditNote = props => {
  // store the id found in the url as a variable
  const id = props.match.params.id;
  // define our note query
  const { loading, error, data } = useQuery(GET_NOTE, { variables: { id } });
  // fetch the current user's data
  const { data: userdata } = useQuery(GET_ME);
  // if the data is loading, display a loading message
  if (loading) return 'Loading...';
  // if there is an error fetching the data, display an error message
  if (error) return <p>Error! Note not found</p>;
  // if the current user and the author of the note do not match
  if (userdata.me.id !== data.note.author.id) {
    return <p>You do not have access to edit this note</p>;
  }
  // pass the data to the form component
  return <NoteForm content={data.note.content} />;
};
```

We are now able to edit a note in the form, but clicking the button does not yet save our changes. Let's write our GraphQL updateNote mutation. Similar to our file of queries, let's create a file to hold our mutations. In *src/gql/mutation*, add the following:

```
import { gql } from '@apollo/client';

const EDIT_NOTE = gql`
  mutation updateNote($id: ID!, $content: String!) {
    updateNote(id: $id, content: $content) {
```

```
        id
        content
        createdAt
        favoriteCount
        favoritedBy {
          id
          username
        }
        author {
          username
          id
        }
      }
    }
  }
`;
```

```
export { EDIT_NOTE };
```

With our mutation written, we can import it and update our component code to call
the mutation when the button is clicked. To do this, we will add a useMutation hook.
When the mutation is complete, we'll redirect the user to the note page.

```
// import the mutation
import { EDIT_NOTE } from '../gql/mutation';

const EditNote = props => {
  // store the id found in the url as a variable
  const id = props.match.params.id;
  // define our note query
  const { loading, error, data } = useQuery(GET_NOTE, { variables: { id } });
  // fetch the current user's data
  const { data: userdata } = useQuery(GET_ME);
  // define our mutation
  const [editNote] = useMutation(EDIT_NOTE, {
    variables: {
      id
    },
    onCompleted: () => {
      props.history.push(`/note/${id}`);
    }
  });

  // if the data is loading, display a loading message
  if (loading) return 'Loading...';
  // if there is an error fetching the data, display an error message
  if (error) return <p>Error!</p>;
  // if the current user and the author of the note do not match
  if (userdata.me.id !== data.note.author.id) {
    return <p>You do not have access to edit this note</p>;
  }

  // pass the data and mutation to the form component
```

```
    return <NoteForm content={data.note.content} action={editNote} />;
};

export default EditNote;
```

Finally, we'll want to display an "Edit" link to users, but only if they are the author of the note. In our application, we will need to check to ensure that the ID of the current user matches the ID of the note author. To implement this behavior, we'll be touching several components.

Now we could implement our functionality directly within the Note component, but let's instead create a component specifically for logged-in user interactions at *src/components/NoteUser.js*. In this React component we will perform a GraphQL query for the current user ID and provide a routable link to the edit page. With this information, we can begin by including our required libraries and setting up a new React component. Within the React component, we will include an edit link, which will route the user to the edit page for the note. For now, the user will see this link regardless of who owns the note.

Update *src/components/NoteUser.js* as follows:

```
import React from 'react';
import { useQuery, gql } from '@apollo/client';
import { Link } from 'react-router-dom';

const NoteUser = props => {
  return <Link to={`/edit/${props.note.id}`}>Edit</Link>;
};

export default NoteUser;
```

Next, we will update our Note component to perform a local isLoggedIn state query. We can then conditionally render our NoteUser component based on the logged-in state of the user.

Let's first import the GraphQL libraries to perform the query along with our Note User component. In *src/components/Note.js*, add the following at the top of the file:

```
import { useQuery } from '@apollo/client';

// import logged in user UI components
import NoteUser from './NoteUser';
// import the IS_LOGGED_IN local query
import { IS_LOGGED_IN } from '../gql/query';
```

Now, we can update our JSX component to check the logged-in state. If the user is logged in, we'll display the NoteUser component; otherwise, we'll display the favorite count.

```
const Note = ({ note }) => {
  const { loading, error, data } = useQuery(IS_LOGGED_IN);
```

```
// if the data is loading, display a loading message
if (loading) return <p>Loading...</p>;
// if there is an error fetching the data, display an error message
if (error) return <p>Error!</p>;

return (
  <StyledNote>
    <MetaData>
      <MetaInfo>
        <img
          src={note.author.avatar}
          alt={`${note.author.username} avatar`}
          height="50px"
        />
      </MetaInfo>
      <MetaInfo>
        <em>by</em> {note.author.username} <br />
        {format(note.createdAt, 'MMM Do YYYY')}
      </MetaInfo>
      {data.isLoggedIn ? (
        <UserActions>
          <NoteUser note={note} />
        </UserActions>
      ) : (
        <UserActions>
          <em>Favorites:</em> {note.favoriteCount}
        </UserActions>
      )}
    </MetaData>
    <ReactMarkdown source={note.content} />
  </StyledNote>
);
};
```

Unauthenticated Edits

Though we will be hiding the edit link in the UI, users could still navigate to a note's edit screen without being the note owner. Thankfully, our GraphQL API is designed to prevent anyone but the note owner from editing the note's content. Though we won't be doing it in this book, a good additional step would be to update the *src/pages/edit.js* component to redirect a user if they are not the note owner.

With this change, logged-in users are able to see an edit link at the top of each note. Clicking the link will navigate to an edit form, regardless of who is the owner of the note. Let's address this by updating our `NoteUser` component to query for the current user's ID and display the edit link only if it matches the ID of the note author.

First in *src/components/NoteUser.js*, add the following:

```
import React from 'react';
import { useQuery } from '@apollo/client';
import { Link } from 'react-router-dom';

// import our GET_ME query
import { GET_ME } from '../gql/query';

const NoteUser = props => {
  const { loading, error, data } = useQuery(GET_ME);
  // if the data is loading, display a loading message
  if (loading) return <p>Loading...</p>;
  // if there is an error fetching the data, display an error message
  if (error) return <p>Error!</p>;
  return (
    <React.Fragment>
      Favorites: {props.note.favoriteCount}
      <br />
      {data.me.id === props.note.author.id && (
        <React.Fragment>
          <Link to={`/edit/${props.note.id}`}>Edit</Link>
        </React.Fragment>
      )}
    </React.Fragment>
  );
};

export default NoteUser;
```

With this change, only the note's original author will see the edit link in the UI (Figure 16-2).

Figure 16-2. Only the note's author will see the edit link

Deleting Notes

Our CRUD application is still missing the ability to delete a note. We can write a button UI component that, when clicked, will perform a GraphQL mutation, deleting the note. Let's start by creating a new component at *src/components/DeleteNote.js*. Since we will be performing a redirect within a nonroutable component, we will use React Router's `withRouter` higher-order component:

```
import React from 'react';
import { useMutation } from '@apollo/client';
import { withRouter } from 'react-router-dom';

import ButtonAsLink from './ButtonAsLink';

const DeleteNote = props => {
  return <ButtonAsLink>Delete Note</ButtonAsLink>;
};

export default withRouter(DeleteNote);
```

Now, we can write our mutation. Our GraphQL API has a `deleteNote` mutation, which returns a boolean of `true` if the note is deleted. When the mutation completes, we'll redirect the user to the */mynotes* page of our application.

First, in *src/gql/mutation.js*, write the mutation as follows:

```
const DELETE_NOTE = gql`
  mutation deleteNote($id: ID!) {
    deleteNote(id: $id)
  }
`;

// update to include DELETE_NOTE
export { EDIT_NOTE, DELETE_NOTE };
```

Now in *src/components/DeleteNote*, add the following:

```
import React from 'react';
import { useMutation } from '@apollo/client';
import { withRouter } from 'react-router-dom';

import ButtonAsLink from './ButtonAsLink';
// import the DELETE_NOTE mutation
import { DELETE_NOTE } from '../gql/mutation';
// import queries to refetch after note deletion
import { GET_MY_NOTES, GET_NOTES } from '../gql/query';

const DeleteNote = props => {
  const [deleteNote] = useMutation(DELETE_NOTE, {
    variables: {
      id: props.noteId
    },
```

```
    // refetch the note list queries to update the cache
    refetchQueries: [{ query: GET_MY_NOTES, GET_NOTES }],
    onCompleted: data => {
      // redirect the user to the "my notes" page
      props.history.push('/mynotes');
    }
  });

  return <ButtonAsLink onClick={deleteNote}>Delete Note</ButtonAsLink>;
};

export default withRouter(DeleteNote);
```

Now, we can import the new `DeleteNote` component within our *src/components/ NoteUser.js* file, displaying it only to a note's author:

```
import React from 'react';
import { useQuery } from '@apollo/client';
import { Link } from 'react-router-dom';

import { GET_ME } from '../gql/query';
// import the DeleteNote component
import DeleteNote from './DeleteNote';

const NoteUser = props => {
  const { loading, error, data } = useQuery(GET_ME);
  // if the data is loading, display a loading message
  if (loading) return <p>Loading...</p>;
  // if there is an error fetching the data, display an error message
  if (error) return <p>Error!</p>;

  return (
    <React.Fragment>
      Favorites: {props.note.favoriteCount} <br />
      {data.me.id === props.note.author.id && (
        <React.Fragment>
          <Link to={`/edit/${props.note.id}`}>Edit</Link> <br />
          <DeleteNote noteId={props.note.id} />
        </React.Fragment>
      )}
    </React.Fragment>
  );
};

export default NoteUser;
```

With this mutation written, logged-in users are now able to delete a note with the click of a button.

Toggling Favorites

The last piece of user functionality missing from our application is the ability to add and remove "favorite" notes. Let's follow our pattern of creating a component for this feature and integrating it into our application. First, create a new component at *src/components/FavoriteNote.js*:

```
import React, { useState } from 'react';
import { useMutation } from '@apollo/client';

import ButtonAsLink from './ButtonAsLink';

const FavoriteNote = props => {
  return <ButtonAsLink>Add to favorites</ButtonAsLink>;
};

export default FavoriteNote;
```

Before we add any functionality, let's go ahead and incorporate this component into our *src/components/NoteUser.js* component. First, import the component:

```
import FavoriteNote from './FavoriteNote';
```

Now, within our JSX, include a reference to the component. You may recall that when we wrote our GET_ME query, we included a list of favorited note IDs, which we'll make use of here:

```
return (
  <React.Fragment>
    <FavoriteNote
      me={data.me}
      noteId={props.note.id}
      favoriteCount={props.note.favoriteCount}
    />
    <br />
    {data.me.id === props.note.author.id && (
      <React.Fragment>
        <Link to={`/edit/${props.note.id}`}>Edit</Link> <br />
        <DeleteNote noteId={props.note.id} />
      </React.Fragment>
    )}
  </React.Fragment>
);
```

You'll notice that we're passing three properties to our FavoriteNote component. First is our me data, which will include the current user's ID as well as a list of notes favorited by that user. Second, the noteID of the current note. And finally is the favor iteCount, which is the current total number of user favorites.

Now we can return to our *src/components/FavoriteNote.js* file. In this file, we'll store the current number of favorites as state and check to see if the current note ID is in the existing list of user favorites. We'll change the text that the user sees based on the state of the user's favorite. When the user clicks the button, it will call our `toggleFa vorite` mutation, which will either add or remove the favorite from the user's list. Let's begin by updating the component to use state to control the click functionality.

```
const FavoriteNote = props => {
  // store the note's favorite count as state
  const [count, setCount] = useState(props.favoriteCount);

  // store if the user has favorited the note as state
  const [favorited, setFavorited] = useState(
    // check if the note exists in the user favorites list
    props.me.favorites.filter(note => note.id === props.noteId).length > 0
  );

  return (
    <React.Fragment>
      {favorited ? (
        <ButtonAsLink
          onClick={() => {
            setFavorited(false);
            setCount(count - 1);
          }}
        >
          Remove Favorite
        </ButtonAsLink>
      ) : (
        <ButtonAsLink
          onClick={() => {
            setFavorited(true);
            setCount(count + 1);
          }}
        >
          Add Favorite
        </ButtonAsLink>
      )}
      : {count}
    </React.Fragment>
  );
};
```

With the preceding changes we're updating the state when a user clicks, but we're not yet calling our GraphQL mutation. Let's complete this component by writing the mutation and adding it to the component. The result is shown in Figure 16-3.

In *src/gql/mutation.js*:

```
// add the TOGGLE_FAVORITE mutation
const TOGGLE_FAVORITE = gql`
  mutation toggleFavorite($id: ID!) {
    toggleFavorite(id: $id) {
      id
```

```
      favoriteCount
    }
  }
`;

// update to include TOGGLE_FAVORITE
export { EDIT_NOTE, DELETE_NOTE, TOGGLE_FAVORITE };
```

In *src/components/FavoriteNote.js*:

```
import React, { useState } from 'react';
import { useMutation } from '@apollo/client';

import ButtonAsLink from './ButtonAsLink';
// the TOGGLE_FAVORITE mutation
import { TOGGLE_FAVORITE } from '../gql/mutation';
// add the GET_MY_FAVORITES query to refetch
import { GET_MY_FAVORITES } from '../gql/query';

const FavoriteNote = props => {
  // store the note's favorite count as state
  const [count, setCount] = useState(props.favoriteCount);

  // store if the user has favorited the note as state
  const [favorited, setFavorited] = useState(
    // check if the note exists in the user favorites list
    props.me.favorites.filter(note => note.id === props.noteId).length > 0
  );

  // toggleFavorite mutation hook
  const [toggleFavorite] = useMutation(TOGGLE_FAVORITE, {
    variables: {
      id: props.noteId
    },
    // refetch the GET_MY_FAVORITES query to update the cache
    refetchQueries: [{ query: GET_MY_FAVORITES }]
  });

  // if the user has favorited the note, display the option to remove the favorite
  // else, display the option to add as a favorite
  return (
    <React.Fragment>
      {favorited ? (
        <ButtonAsLink
          onClick={() => {
            toggleFavorite();
            setFavorited(false);
            setCount(count - 1);
          }]
        >
          Remove Favorite
        </ButtonAsLink>
      ) : (
```

```
      <ButtonAsLink
        onClick={() => {
          toggleFavorite();
          setFavorited(true);
          setCount(count + 1);
        }}
      >
        Add Favorite
      </ButtonAsLink>
    )}
    : {count}
  </React.Fragment>
  );
};

export default FavoriteNote;
```

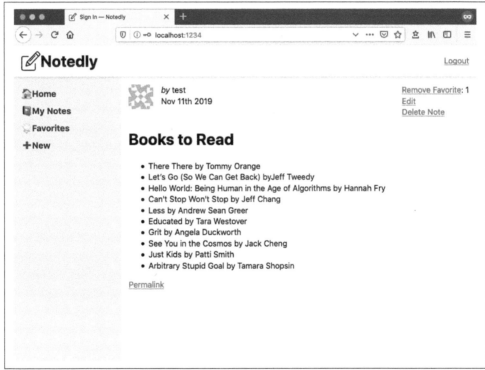

Figure 16-3. A logged-in user will be able to create, read, update, and delete notes

Conclusion

In this chapter we've turned our site into a fully functioning CRUD (create, read, update, delete) application. We are now able to implement GraphQL queries and mutations based on the state of a signed-in user. The ability to build user interfaces that integrate CRUD user interactions will provide a solid foundation for building all sorts of web applications. With this functionality, we've completed the MVP (minimum viable product) of our app. In the next chapter, we'll deploy the application to a web server.

## CHAPTER 17

Deploying a Web Application

When I first began doing web development professionally, a "deployment" meant uploading files from my local machine to a web server through an FTP client. There weren't any build steps or pipelines, meaning that the raw files on my machine were the same as those on my web server. If something went wrong, I would either frantically try to fix the issue or roll back the change by replacing it with copies of the old files. This wild west approach worked OK at the time, but also led to a lot of site downtime and unexpected issues.

In today's world of web development, the needs of our local development environment and our web servers are quite different. On my local machine, I want to see instant changes when I update a file and have uncompressed files for debugging. On my web server, I only expect to see changes when I deploy them and value small file sizes. In this chapter, we'll look at one way that we can deploy a static application to the web.

Static Websites

A web browser parses HTML, CSS, and JavaScript to generate the web pages that we interact with. Unlike frameworks such as Express, Rails, and Django, which generate the markup for a page server-side at the time of the request, static websites are simply a collection of HTML, CSS, and JavaScript stored on a server. This can range in complexity from a single HTML file containing markup to complicated frontend build processes that compile templating languages, multiple JavaScript files, and CSS preprocessors. In the end, however, static websites are a collection of those three file types.

Our application, Notedly, is a static web app. It contains some markup, CSS, and Java-Script. Our build tool, Parcel (*https://parceljs.org*), compiles the components that we write into files usable by the browser. In local development, we run a web server and these files are updated on the fly using Parcel's hot module replacement feature. If we look at our *package.json* file, you'll see that I've included two `deploy` scripts:

```
"scripts": {
  "deploy:src": "parcel build src/index.html --public-url ./",
  "deploy:final": "parcel build final/index.html --public-url ./"
}
```

To build the application, open your terminal application, **cd** into the root of your *web* directory, which contains the project, and then run the **build** command:

```
# if you're not already in the web directory, be sure to cd into it
$ cd Projects/notedly/web
# build the files from the src directory
$ npm run deploy:src
```

If you've been following along with the book and developing your web application in the *src* directory, running `npm run deploy:src` in the terminal, as just described, will generate the built application from your code. If you would prefer to use the final version of the application that is bundled with the sample code, using `npm run deploy:final` will build the code from the *final* application directory.

In the rest of the chapter, I'll demonstrate one way to deploy a statically built application, but these files could be hosted anywhere that can serve HTML—from a web hosting provider to a Raspberry Pi left running on your desk. While there are many tangible benefits to the type of process we'll be working through, your deploy could be as simple as updating the *.env* file to point to the remote API, running the build script, and uploading the files.

 Server-Side Rendered React

Though we're building our React application as a static web application, it is also possible to render JSX on the server. This technique is often referred to as "universal JavaScript" and can have many benefits, including performance gains, client-side JavaScript fallbacks, and SEO improvements. Frameworks such as Next.js (*https://nextjs.org*) have sought to simplify this setup. Though we're not covering server-side rendered JavaScript applications in this book, I highly recommend exploring this approach once you're comfortable with client-side JavaScript application development.

Our Deployment Pipeline

For our application's deployment, we'll make use of a simple pipeline, which will allow us to automatically deploy changes to our codebase. For our pipeline we'll be using two services. The first will be our source code repository, GitHub (*https://github.com*). The second will be our web host, Netlify (*https://www.netlify.com*). I've chosen Netlify for its extensive, but easy-to-use, feature set for deployments as well as its focus on static and serverless applications.

Our goal is for any commit to the `master` branch of our application to be automatically deployed to our web host. We could visualize that process as shown in Figure 17-1.

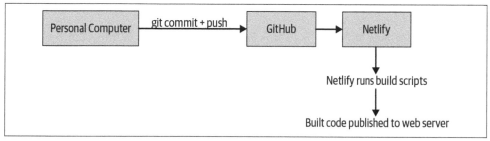

Figure 17-1. Our deployment process

Hosting Source Code with Git

The first step in our deployment process is to set up our source code repository. You may have already done this, in which case feel free to skip ahead. As noted before we'll be using GitHub (*https://github.com*), but this process could be configured with other public Git hosts, such as GitLab (*https://about.gitlab.com*) or Bitbucket (*https://bitbucket.org*).

GitHub Repositories

We'll be creating a new GitHub repository, but if you prefer, you can use the official code sample at *https://github.com/javascript everywhere/web* by creating a fork to your GitHub account.

First, navigate to GitHub and create an account or sign in to your existing account. Then click the New Repository button. Provide a name and click the Create Repository button (Figure 17-2).

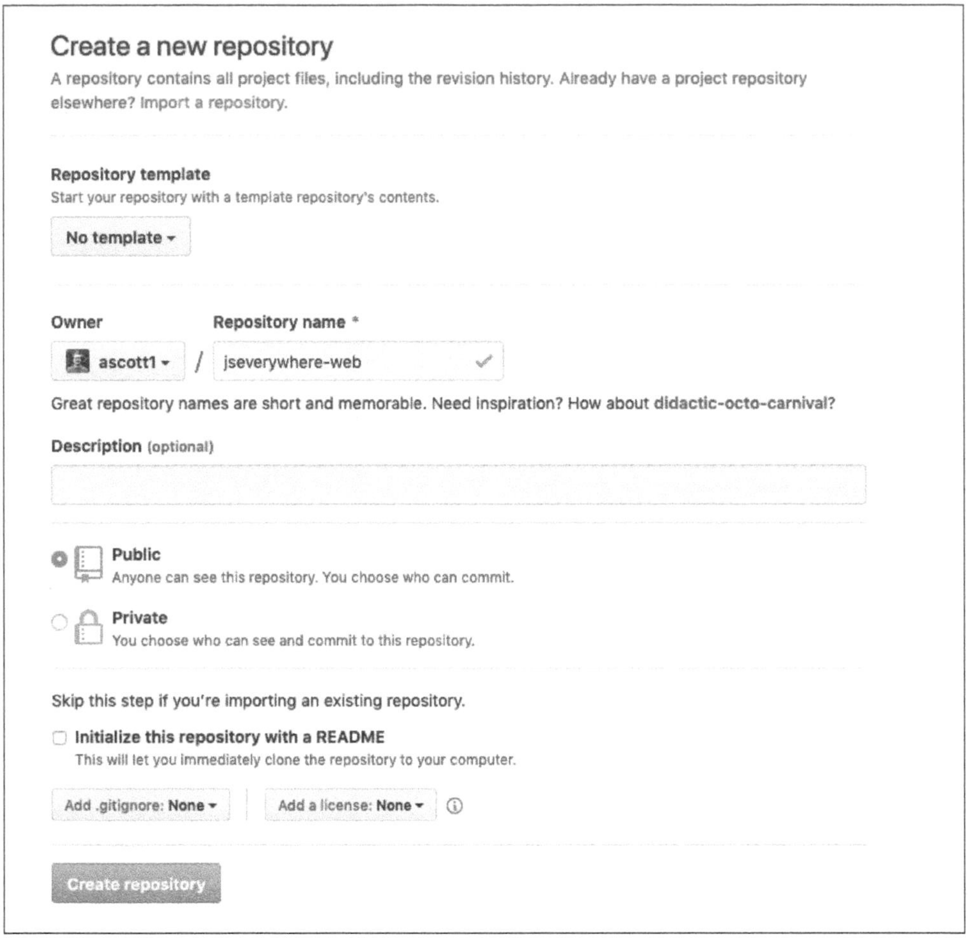

Figure 17-2. GitHub's new repository page

Now, in your terminal application, navigate to your web application's directory, set the Git origin to the new GitHub repository, and push the code. Because we are updating an existing Git repo, our instructions will differ slightly from GitHub's:

```
# first navigate to the directory if you're not already there
cd Projects/notedly/web
# update the GitHub remote origin to match your repository
git remote set-url origin git://YOUR.GIT.URL
# push the code to the new GitHub repository
git push -u origin master
```

Now, if you navigate to *https://github.com/<your_username>/<your_repo_name>*, you will see the source code of the application.

Deploy with Netlify

With our source code in a remote Git repository, we can now configure our web host, Netlify, to build and deploy our code. First, go to *netlify.com* and register for an account. Once you've created an account, click the "New site from Git" button. This will walk you through setting up your site deployment:

1. Choose your Git provider by selecting GitHub, which will connect and authorize your GitHub account.

2. Next, select the repository that contains the source code.

3. Finally, set up your build settings.

For our build settings, add the following (Figure 17-3):

1. Build command: `npm run deploy:src` (or `npm run deploy:final`, if deploying the final example code).

2. Publish directory: `dist`.

3. Under "Advanced settings," click "New variable" and add a variable name of `API_URI` with a variable value of *https://<your_api_name>.herokuapp.com/api* (this will be the URL of the API application, which we deployed to Heroku).

Once you've configured the application, click the "Deploy site" button. After a few minutes your application will be running at the Netlify-supplied URL. Now, anytime we push a change to our GitHub repo, our site will be automatically deployed.

Slow Initial Load

Our deployed web application will be loading data from our deployed Heroku API. With Heroku's free plan, application containers sleep after one hour of inactivity. If you haven't used your API in a while, the initial data load will be slow while the container spins back up.

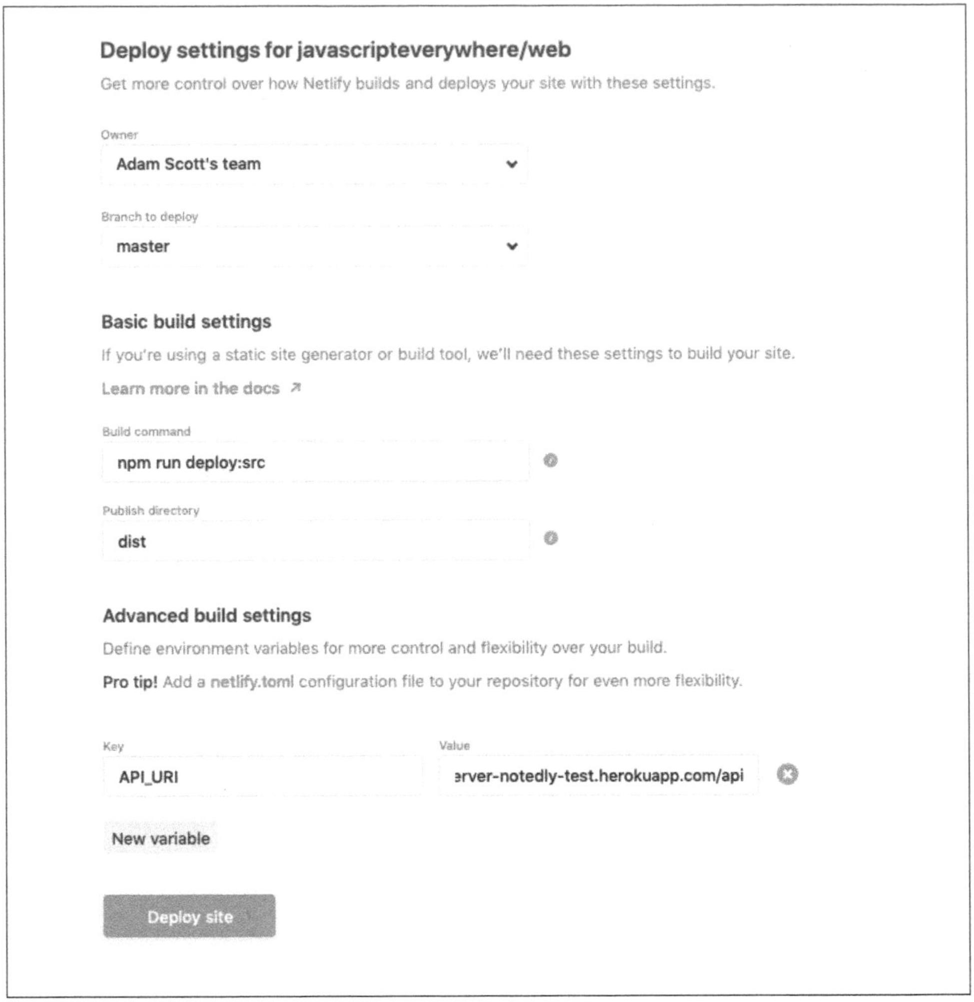

Figure 17-3. With Netlify we can configure our build process and environment variables

Conclusion

In this chapter we've deployed a static web application. To do this, we've used Netlify's deployment pipeline features to watch for changes to our Git repository, run our build processes, and store environment variables. With this foundation, we have everything we need to publicly release web applications.

## CHAPTER 18

Desktop Applications with Electron

My introduction to personal computers was in a school lab full of Apple II machines. Once a week, my classmates and I were ushered into the room, handed some floppy disks, and given a rough set of instructions on how to load an application (typically *Oregon Trail*). I don't remember much from these sessions other than feeling completely *locked in* to the little world I was now able to control. Personal computers have come a long way since the mid-1980s, but we still rely on desktop applications to perform many tasks.

On a typical day, I may access an email client, a text editor, a chat client, spreadsheet software, a music streaming service, and several more desktop applications. Oftentimes, these have a web application equivalent, but the convenience and integration of a desktop application can provide several user experience benefits. However, for years the ability to create these applications felt out of reach. Thankfully, today we are able to use web technologies to build fully featured desktop applications with a small learning curve.

What We're Building

Over the next few chapters we'll build a desktop client for our social note application, Notedly. Our goal is to use JavaScript and web technologies to develop a desktop application that a user can download and install on their computer. For now, this application will be a simple implementation that wraps our web application within a desktop application shell. Developing our app in this way will allow us to quickly ship a desktop app to those users who are interested, while providing us the flexibility to introduce a custom application for desktop users at a later date.

How We're Going To Build This

To build our application, we'll be using Electron (*https://electronjs.org*), an open source framework for building cross-platform desktop applications with web technologies. It works by utilizing Node.js and Chrome's underlying browser engine, Chromium. This means that as developers we have access to the world of the browser, Node.js, and operating system–specific abilities, which are typically unavailable in a web environment. Electron was originally developed by GitHub for the Atom text editor (*https://atom.io*), but has since been used as a platform for applications both big and small, including Slack, VS Code, Discord, and WordPress Desktop.

Getting Started

Before we can start development, we need to make a copy of the project starter files to our machine. The project's source code (*https://github.com/javascripteverywhere/desktop*) contains all of the scripts and references to third-party libraries that we will need to develop your application. To clone the code to our local machine, open the terminal, navigate to the directory where you keep your projects, and **git clone** the project repository. If you've worked through the API and web chapters, you may also have already created a *notedly* directory to keep the project code organized:

```
$ cd Projects
$ # type the `mkdir notedly` command if you don't yet have a notedly directory
$ cd notedly
$ git clone git@github.com:javascripteverywhere/desktop.git
$ cd desktop
$ npm install
```

 Installing Third-Party Dependencies

By making a copy of the book's starter code and running `npm install` in the directory, you avoid having to again run `npm install` for any of the individual third-party dependencies.

The code is structured as follows:

/src
> This is the directory where you should perform your development as you follow along with the book.

/solutions
> This directory contains the solutions for each chapter. If you get stuck, these are available for you to consult.

/final
> This directory contains the final working project.

With our project directory created and dependencies installed, we are ready to begin our development.

Our First Electron App

With our repository cloned to our machine, let's develop our first Electron app. If you look within your *src* directory, you'll see that there are a few files. The *index.html* file contains bare-bones HTML markup. For now, this file will serve as Electron's "renderer process," meaning that it will be the web page displayed as a window by our Electron application.

```
<!DOCTYPE html>
<html>
  <head>
    <meta charset="UTF-8">
    <title>Notedly Desktop</title>
  </head>
  <body>
    <h1>Hello World!</h1>
  </body>
</html>
```

The *index.js* file is where we will set up our Electron application. In our application, this file will contain what Electron calls the "main process," which defines the application shell. The main process works by creating a `BrowserWindow` instance in Electron, which serves as the application shell.

index.js Versus main.js

Though I've named the file *index.js* to follow the pattern found in the rest of our sample applications, it is common in Electron development to name the "main process" file *main.js*.

Let's set up our main process to display a browser window containing our HTML page. First, import Electron's `app` and `browserWindow` functionality in *src/index.js*:

```
const { app, BrowserWindow } = require('electron');
```

Now we can define our application's `browserWindow` and define the file that our application will load. In *src/index.js*, add the following:

```
const { app, BrowserWindow } = require('electron');

// to avoid garbage collection, declare the window as a variable
let window;

// specify the details of the browser window
function createWindow() {
  window = new BrowserWindow({
```

```
    width: 800,
    height: 600,
    webPreferences: {
      nodeIntegration: true
    }
  });

  // load the HTML file
  window.loadFile('index.html');

  // when the window is closed, reset the window object
  window.on('closed', () => {
    window = null;
  });
}

// when electron is ready, create the application window
app.on('ready', createWindow);
```

With this in place, we are ready to run our desktop application locally. In your terminal application, from your project's directory, run the following:

```
$ npm start
```

This command will run `electron src/index.js`, launching a development environment version of our application (see Figure 18-1).

Figure 18-1. Running the start command will launch our "Hello World" Electron application

macOS Application Window Details

macOS handles application windows differently from Windows. When a user clicks the "close window" button, the application window closes, but the application itself does not quit. Clicking the application's icon in the macOS dock will reopen the application window. Electron allows us to implement this functionality. Add the following to the bottom of the *src/index.js* file:

```
// quit when all windows are closed.
app.on('window-all-closed', () => {
  // On macOS only quit when a user explicitly quits the application
  if (process.platform !== 'darwin') {
    app.quit();
  }
});

app.on('activate', () => {
  // on macOS, re-create the window when the icon is clicked in the dock
  if (window === null) {
    createWindow();
  }
});
```

With this added, you can see these changes by quitting the application and rerunning it with the `npm start` command. Now, if a user is accessing our application with macOS, they will see the expected behavior when closing a window.

Developer Tools

Since Electron is based on the Chromium browser engine (the engine behind Chrome, Microsoft Edge, Opera, and many other browsers (*https://oreil.ly/iz_GY*)), it also gives us access to Chromium's Developer Tools. This allows us to perform all of the same JavaScript debugging that we might do in a browser environment. Let's check if our application is in development mode and, if so, automatically open dev tools when our app launches.

To perform this check, we'll use the `electron-util` library (*https://oreil.ly/JAf2Q*). This is a small collection of utilities that will allow us to easily check system conditions and simplifies boilerplate code for common Electron patterns. For now, we'll be making use of the `is` module, which will allow us to check if our application is in development mode.

At the top of our *src/index.js* file, import the module:

```
const { is } = require('electron-util');
```

Now, in our application code, we can add the following on the line below `window.loadFile(index.html)` where we load our HTML file, which will open the development tools when the application is in a development environment (Figure 18-2):

```
// if in development mode, open the browser dev tools
if (is.development) {
  window.webContents.openDevTools();
}
```

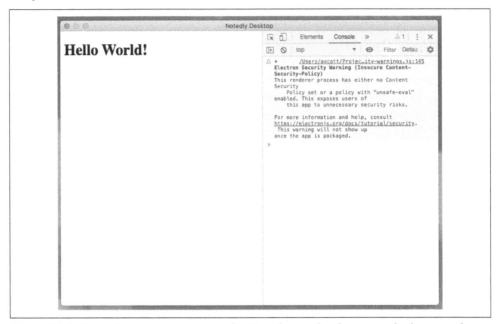

Figure 18-2. Now when we open our application during development, the browser dev tools will automatically open

Electron Security Warning

You may notice that our Electron app currently displays a security warning related to an insecure Content Security Policy (CSP). We will address this warning in the next chapter.

With easy access to the browser dev tools, we are well prepared to develop a client application.

The Electron API

One of the advantages of desktop development is that, through the Electron API, we gain access to operating system-level features that are rightfully unavailable in a web browser environment, including:

- Notifications
- Native file drag and drop
- macOS Dark Mode
- Custom menus
- Robust keyboard shortcuts
- System dialogs
- The application tray
- System information

As you can imagine, these options allow us to add some unique features and improved user experiences to our desktop clients. We won't be using these in our simple sample application, but it is worth familiarizing yourself with them. Electron's documentation (*https://electronjs.org/docs*) provides detailed examples of each of Electron's APIs. Additionally, the Electron team has created `electron-api-demos` (*https://oreil.ly/Xo7NM*), a fully functioning Electron application that demonstrates many of the unique features of the Electron API.

Conclusion

In this chapter we've explored the basics of using Electron to build desktop applications with web technologies. The Electron environment offers us, as developers, an opportunity to provide a cross-platform desktop experience to users without learning the intricacies of multiple programming languages and operating systems. Armed with the simple setup we've explored in this chapter and knowledge of web development, we are well prepared to build robust desktop applications. In the next chapter, we'll look at how we can incorporate an existing web app into an Electron shell.

## CHAPTER 19

Integrating an Existing Web Application with Electron

I tend to accumulate web browser tabs like a child at the beach collects shells. I don't necessarily set out to collect them, but by the end of the day, I have dozens of tabs open across a few browser windows. I'm not proud of this, but I suspect that I'm not alone. As a result, I use desktop versions of some of my most commonly used web applications. Often, these applications offer no advantage over the web, but the convenience of an independent app makes them easy to access, find, and switch to throughout the day.

In this chapter, we'll look at how we can take an existing web application and wrap it in an Electron shell. Before proceeding, you will need a local copy of our example API and web applications. If you haven't been following along through the whole book, visit Appendixes A and B to run these.

Integrating Our Web Application

In the previous chapter, we set up our Electron application to load an *index.html* file. Alternately, we can load a specific URL. In our case, we'll begin by loading the URL of our locally running web application. First, be sure that your web application and API are running locally. Then we can update our *src/index.js* file, first by updating the `nodeIntegration` setting in the `BrowserWindow` to `false`. This will avoid the security risks of a locally running node application accessing an external site.

```
webPreferences: {
  nodeIntegration: false
},
```

Now, replace the `window.loadFile('index.html');` line with the following:

```
window.loadURL('http://localhost:1234');
```

Running the Web Application

A local instance of your web application will need to be running on the 1234 port. If you've been following along with the book, run **npm start** from the root of your web application's directory to start the development server.

This will instruct Electron to load a URL, rather than a file. Now if you run the app with npm start, you'll see it loaded in an Electron window, with some caveats.

Warnings and Errors

The Electron browser developer tools and our terminal currently display a large number of warnings and errors. Let's look at each of these (see Figure 19-1).

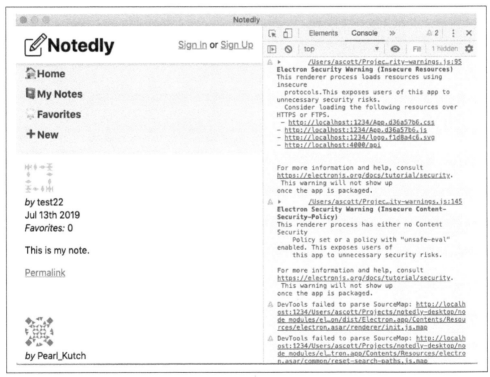

Figure 19-1. Our application is running, but displays a large number of errors and warnings

First, our terminal displays a large number of `SyntaxError: Unexpected Token` errors. Additionally, our developer tools show several corresponding warnings stating `DevTools failed to parse SourceMap`. These two errors are related to the way in which Parcel generates source maps and Electron reads them. Unfortunately, with the combination of technologies that we are using, there does not seem to be a reasonable fix for this issue. Our best option is to disable JavaScript source maps. In the application window's developer tools, click "Settings" and then uncheck "Enable JavaScript source maps" (see Figure 19-2).

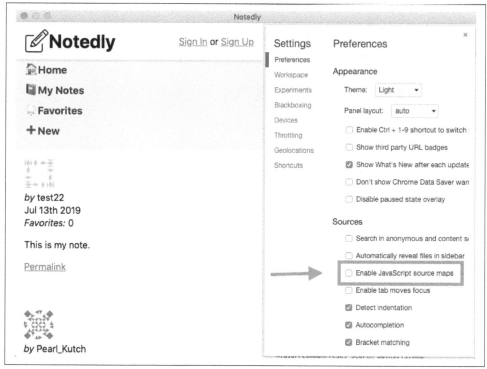

Figure 19-2. Disabling source maps will reduce the number of errors and warnings

Now, if you quit and restart the application you'll no longer see the source map–related issues. This does come with the tradeoff that debugging our client-side JavaScript within Electron may be more difficult, but thankfully we can still access this feature and our application in our web browser.

The final two warnings are related to Electron's security. We will address these before bundling our application for production, but it's worth exploring now what these warnings are.

Electron Security Warning (Insecure Resources)
This warning notifies us that we are loading web resources over an *http* connection. In production, we should always load resources over *https* to ensure privacy and security. In development, loading our localhost over *http* is not a problem, as we will be referencing our hosted website, which uses *https* in the bundled application.

Electron Security Warning (Insecure Content-Security-Policy)
This warning informs us that we have not yet set a Content Security Policy (CSP). A CSP allows us to specify which domains our application is permitted to load resources from, greatly reducing the risk of a cross-site scripting (XSS) attack. Again, this is not a concern during local development, but it's important in production. We'll be implementing a CSP later in the chapter.

With our errors addressed, we're ready to set up our application's configuration file.

Configuration

When developing locally, we want to be able to run the local version of our web application, but when bundling the app to be used by others, we want it to reference the publicly available URL. We can set up a simple configuration file to handle this.

In our *./src* directory, we will add a *config.js* file where we can store application-specific properties. I've included a *config.example.js* file, which you can easily copy from the terminal:

```
cp src/config.example.js src/config.js
```

Now we can fill in the properties of our application:

```
const config = {
  LOCAL_WEB_URL: 'http://localhost:1234/',
  PRODUCTION_WEB_URL: 'https://YOUR_DEPLOYED_WEB_APP_URL',
  PRODUCTION_API_URL: 'https://YOUR_DEPLOYED_API_URL'
};

module.exports = config;
```

Why Not .env?

In our previous environments, we've used *.env* files to manage environment-specific settings. In this instance, we're using a Java-Script configuration file because of the way that Electron apps bundle their dependencies.

Now in our Electron application's main process, we can use the configuration file to specify which URL we would like to load in development and production. In *src/index.js*, first import the *config.js* file:

```
const config = require('./config');
```

Now, we can update the `loadURL` functionality to load different URLs for each environment:

```
// load the URL
if (is.development) {
  window.loadURL(config.LOCAL_WEB_URL);
} else {
  window.loadURL(config.PRODUCTION_WEB_URL);
}
```

By using a configuration file, we can easily provide Electron with environment-specific settings.

Content Security Policy

As stated earlier in the chapter, a CSP allows us to limit the domains that our application has permission to load resources from. This helps to limit potential XSS and data injection attacks. In Electron, we can specify our CSP settings to help improve the security of the application. To learn more about CSP for both your Electron and web applications, I recommend the MDN article (*https://oreil.ly/VZS1H*) on the subject.

Electron provides a built-in API for CSP, but the `electron-util` library offers a simpler and cleaner syntax. At the top of our *src/index.js* file, update the `electron-util` import statement to include `setContentSecurityPolicy`:

```
const { is, setContentSecurityPolicy } = require('electron-util');
```

Now we can set our CSP for the production version of the application:

```
// set the CSP in production mode
if (!is.development) {
  setContentSecurityPolicy(`
  default-src 'none';
  script-src 'self';
  img-src 'self' https://www.gravatar.com;
  style-src 'self' 'unsafe-inline';
  font-src 'self';
  connect-src 'self' ${config.PRODUCTION_API_URL};
  base-uri 'none';
  form-action 'none';
  frame-ancestors 'none';
  `);
}
```

With our CSP written, we can check for errors using the CSP Evaluator (*https://oreil.ly/1xNK1*) tool. If we are intentionally accessing resources at additional URLs, we could add them to our CSP rule set.

Our final *src/index.js* file will read as follows:

```
const { app, BrowserWindow } = require('electron');
const { is, setContentSecurityPolicy } = require('electron-util');
const config = require('./config');

// to avoid garbage collection, declare the window as a variable
let window;

// specify the details of the browser window
function createWindow() {
  window = new BrowserWindow({
    width: 800,
    height: 600,
    webPreferences: {
      nodeIntegration: false
    }
  });

  // load the URL
  if (is.development) {
    window.loadURL(config.LOCAL_WEB_URL);
  } else {
    window.loadURL(config.PRODUCTION_WEB_URL);
  }

  // if in development mode, open the browser dev tools
  if (is.development) {
    window.webContents.openDevTools();
  }

  // set the CSP in production mode
  if (!is.development) {
    setContentSecurityPolicy(`
    default-src 'none';
    script-src 'self';
    img-src 'self' https://www.gravatar.com;
    style-src 'self' 'unsafe-inline';
    font-src 'self';
    connect-src 'self' ${config.PRODUCTION_API_URL};
    base-uri 'none';
    form-action 'none';
    frame-ancestors 'none';
    `);
  }

  // when the window is closed, dereference the window object
  window.on('closed', () => {
```

```
    window = null;
  });
}

// when electron is ready, create the application window
app.on('ready', createWindow);

// quit when all windows are closed.
app.on('window-all-closed', () => {
  // On macOS only quit when a user explicitly quits the application
  if (process.platform !== 'darwin') {
    app.quit();
  }
});

app.on('activate', () => {
  // on macOS, re-create the window when the icon is clicked in the dock
  if (window === null) {
    createWindow();
  }
});
```

With this, we have a working implementation of our web application running within an Electron shell (shown in Figure 19-3).

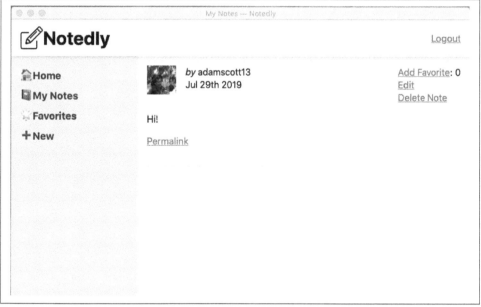

Figure 19-3. Our web application running within an Electron application shell

Conclusion

In this chapter we integrated an existing web app into an Electron desktop application, which enables us to get a desktop application to market quickly. It's worth noting that there are tradeoffs to this approach, however, as it offers limited desktop-specific benefits and requires an internet connection to access the full features of the application. For those of us looking to get a desktop application to market soon, these downsides may be worthwhile. In the next chapter, we'll look at how we can build and distribute an Electron app.

## CHAPTER 20

Electron Deployment

The first time I taught a programming course, I came up with the clever idea of introducing the course topics through a text adventure game. Students would come into the lab, sit down at a desk, and walk through a series of hilarious (to me) prompts and instructions. This was met with mixed reactions, not because of the jokes (well, maybe because of the jokes), but because students had not interacted with a "program" in this way. The students were accustomed to a GUI (graphic user interface), and interacting with a program through text prompts felt *wrong* to many of them.

Presently, to run our application we need to type a prompt in our terminal application to start the Electron process. In this chapter, we'll look at how we can bundle our application for distribution. To achieve this, we'll be using the popular Electron Builder (*https://www.electron.build*) library, which will help us package and distribute our application to our users.

Electron Builder

Electron Builder is a library designed to simplify the packaging and distribution of Electron and Proton Native (*https://proton-native.js.org*) applications. While there are other packaging solutions, Electron Builder simplifies a number of pain points associated with application distribution, including:

- Code signing
- Multiplatform distribution targets
- Autoupdates
- Distribution

It offers a great balance between flexibility and features. Additionally, though we won't be making use of them, there are several Electron Builder boilerplates for Webpack (*https://oreil.ly/faYta*), React (*https://oreil.ly/qli_e*), Vue (*https://oreil.ly/9QY2W*), and Vanilla JavaScript (*https://oreil.ly/uJo7e*).

Electron Builder Versus Electron Forge

Electron Forge (*https://www.electronforge.io*) is another popular library that offers many similar features to Electron Builder. A primary advantage of Electron Forge is that it is based on official Electron libraries, while Electron Builder is an independent build tool. This means that users benefit from the growth of the Electron ecosystem. The downside is that Electron Forge is based on a much more rigid application setup. For the purposes of this book, Electron Builder provides the right balance of features and learning opportunities, but I encourage you to take a close look at Electron Forge as well.

Configuring Electron Builder

All of the configuration of Electron Builder will take place in our application's *package.json* file. In that file we can see that `electron-builder` is already listed as a development dependency. Within the *package.json* file we can include a key, called `"build"`, which will contain all of the instructions to Electron Builder for packaging our app. To begin, we will include two fields:

appId

This is a unique identifier for our application. macOS calls the concept `CFBundle Identifier` (*https://oreil.ly/OOg1O*) and Windows terms it the `AppUserModelID` (*https://oreil.ly/mr9si*). The standard is to use the reverse DNS format. For example, if we run a company with a domain of *jseverywhere.io* and build an application named Notedly, the ID would be `io.jseverywhere.notedly`.

productName

This is the human-readable version of our product's name, as the `package.json` `name` field requires hyphenated or single-word names.

All together, our beginning build configuration will appear as follows:

```
"build": {
  "appId": "io.jseverywhere.notedly",
  "productName": "Notedly"
},
```

Electron Builder provides us with many configuration options, several of which we'll be exploring throughout this chapter. For the complete list, visit the Electron Builder docs (*https://oreil.ly/ESAx-*).

Build for Our Current Platform

With our minimal configuration in place, we can create our first application build. By default, Electron Builder will produce a build for the system we are developing on. For example, since I am writing this on a MacBook, my build will default to macOS.

Let's first add two scripts to our *package.json* file, which will be responsible for application builds. First, a `pack` script will generate a package directory, without fully packaging the app. This can be useful for testing purposes. Second, a `dist` script will package the application in distributable format, such as a macOS DMG, Windows installer, or DEB package.

```
"scripts": {
  // add the pack and dist scripts to the existing npm scripts list
  "pack": "electron-builder --dir",
  "dist": "electron-builder"
}
```

With this change, you can run `npm run dist` in your terminal application, which will package the application in the project's *dist/* directory. Navigating to the *dist/* directory, you can see that Electron Builder has packaged the application for distribution for your operating system.

App Icons

One thing that you have likely noticed is that our application is using the default Electron app icon. This is fine for local development, but for a production application we will want to use our own branding. In our project's */resources* folder, I have included some application icons for both macOS and Windows. To generate these icons from a PNG file, I used the iConvert Icons application (*https://iconverticons.com*), which is available for both macOS and Windows.

In our */resources* folder you will see the following files:

- *icon.icns*, the macOS application icon
- *icon.ico*, the Windows application icon
- An *icons* directory with a series of different-sized *.png* files, used by Linux

Optionally, we could also include background images for the macOS DMG by adding icons with the names of *background.png* and *background@2x.png*, for retina screens.

Now within our *package.json* file, we update the build object to specify the name of the build resource directory:

```
"build": {
  "appId": "io.jseverywhere.notedly",
  "productName": "Notedly",
  "directories": {
    "buildResources": "resources"
  }
},
```

Now, when we build the application, Electron Builder will package it with our custom application icons (see Figure 20-1).

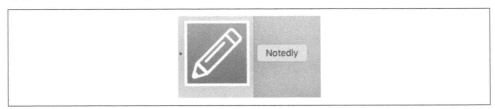

Figure 20-1. Our custom application icon in the macOS dock

Building for Multiple Platforms

Currently, we're only building our application for the operating system that matches our development platform. One of the great advantages of Electron as a platform is that it allows us to use the same code to target multiple platforms, by updating our `dist` script. To achieve this, Electron Builder makes use of the free and open source `electron-build-service` (*https://oreil.ly/IEIfW*). We'll be using the public instance of this service, but it is possible to self-host it for organizations seeking additional security and privacy.

In our `package.json` update the `dist` script to:

```
"dist": "electron-builder -mwl"
```

This will result in a build that targets macOS, Windows, and Linux. From here we can distribute our application by uploading it as a release to GitHub or anywhere that we can distribute files, such as Amazon S3 or our web server.

Code Signing

Both macOS and Windows include the concept of *code signing*. Code signing is a boost for the security and trust of users, as it helps signify the trustworthiness of the app. I won't be walking through the code-signing process, as it is operating system specific and comes at a cost to developers. The Electron Builder documentation offers a comprehensive article (*https://oreil.ly/g6wEz*) on code signing for various platforms.

Additionally, the Electron documentation (*https://oreil.ly/Yb4JF*) offers several resources and links. If you are building a production application, I encourage you to further research the code-signing options for macOS and Windows.

Conclusion

We've covered the tip of the iceberg for deploying an Electron application. In this chapter we used Electron Builder to build our applications. We can then easily upload and distribute them through any web host. Once we have outgrown these needs, we can use Electron Builder to integrate builds into a continuous delivery pipeline; automatically push releases to GitHub, S3, or other distribution platforms; and integrate automatic updates into the application. If you are interested in further exploring the topics of Electron development and app distribution, these are fantastic next steps to take.

## CHAPTER 21

Mobile Applications with React Native

One day in the late 1980s I was shopping with my parents when I spotted a small portable television. It was a battery-powered square box, with an antenna, small speaker, and a tiny black-and-white screen. I was blown away by the possibility of watching Saturday morning cartoons *in my backyard*. Though I'd never own one, just knowing that such a device existed made me feel like I was living in a science-fiction future world. Little did I know that as an adult, I'd carry a device in my pocket that would allow me to not only watch *Masters of the Universe*, but also to access infinite information, listen to music, play games, take notes, take photos, summon a car, buy things, check the weather, and complete an infinite number of other tasks.

In 2007 Steve Jobs introduced the iPhone, saying "every once in a while a revolutionary product comes along that changes everything." Sure, smartphones existed before 2007, but it wasn't until the rise of the iPhone (and subsequent rise of Android) that they were truly smart. In the intervening years, smartphone applications have evolved past the initial "anything goes" gold rush phase to be something that users demand quality from and have high expectations for. Today's applications have high standards of functionality, interaction, and design. To add to the challenge, modern mobile application development is splintered across the Apple iOS and Android platforms, each using a different programming language and toolchain.

You've probably already guessed it (it *is* in the book title), but JavaScript enables us as developers to write cross-platform mobile applications. In this chapter I'll introduce the library that enables this, React Native, as well as the Expo tool chain. We'll also clone the sample project code, which we'll be building upon over the next few chapters.

What We're Building

Over the next few chapters we'll build a mobile client for our social note application, Notedly. The goal is to use JavaScript and web technologies to develop an application a user can install on their mobile device. We'll be implementing a subset of features so as to avoid too much repetition from the web application chapters. Specifically, our application will:

- Work on both iOS and Android operating systems
- Load a note feed and individual user notes from our GraphQL API
- Use CSS and styled components for styling
- Perform standard and dynamic routing

These features will provide a solid overview of the core concepts of developing a mobile application with React Native. Before we get started, let's take a closer look at the technologies we will be using.

How We're Going To Build This

React Native is the core technology that we will be using to develop our application. React Native allows us to write applications in JavaScript, using React, and render them for the native mobile platform. This means that to users, there is no discernible difference between a React Native application and one written in the platform's programming language. This is React Native's key advantage over other popular web technology–based mobile frameworks, which traditionally wrapped a web view within an application shell. React Native has been used to develop apps by Facebook, Instagram, Bloomberg, Tesla, Skype, Walmart, Pinterest, and many others.

The second key piece of our application development workflow is Expo, a set of tools and services that simplify React Native development through really useful features such as on-device previews, application builds, and extending the core React Native library. Before getting started with our development, I recommend that you do the following:

1. Visit *expo.io* and create an Expo account.

2. Install the Expo command-line tools by typing `npm install expo-cli --global` into your terminal application.

3. Sign in to your Expo account locally by typing `expo login` in your terminal application.

4. Install the Expo Client application for your mobile device. Links to the Expo Client iOS and Android app can be found at *expo.io/tools*.

5. Sign in to your account in the Expo Client application.

Finally, we'll again use Apollo Client (*https://oreil.ly/xR62T*) to interact with data from our GraphQL API. Apollo Client comprises a collection of open source tools for working with GraphQL.

Getting Started

Before we can start development, you'll need to make a copy of the project starter files to your machine. The project's source code (*https://github.com/javascripteverywhere/mobile*) contains all of the scripts and references to third-party libraries that we will need to develop our application. To clone the code to your local machine, open the terminal, navigate to the directory where you keep your projects, and **git clone** the project repository. If you've worked through the API, web, and/or desktop chapters, you may also have already created a *notedly* directory to keep the project code organized:

```
$ cd Projects
$ # type the `mkdir notedly` command if you don't yet have a notedly directory
$ cd notedly
$ git clone git@github.com:javascripteverywhere/mobile.git
$ cd mobile
$ npm install
```

Installing Third-Party Dependencies

By making a copy of the book's starter code and running npm install in the directory, you avoid having to again run npm install for any of the individual third-party dependencies.

The code is structured as follows:

/src

This is the directory where you should perform your development as you follow along with the book.

/solutions

This directory contains the solutions for each chapter. If you get stuck, these are available for you to consult.

/final

This directory contains the final working project.

The remaining files and project setup match the standard output of the expo-cli React Native generator, which you can run by typing **expo init** in your terminal.

App.js?

Because of the way that Expo's build chain works, the *App.js* file in the root of the project directory is typically the application's point of entry. To standardize our mobile project with the code found in the rest of the book, the *App.js* file is used only as a reference to a */src/Main.js* file.

Now that we have the code on our local machines and our dependencies installed, let's run the app. To start the application, in your terminal application, type the following:

```
$ npm start
```

This will open Expo's "Metro Bundler" web application on a local port in our browser. From here, you can launch a local device simulator by clicking one of the "Run on…" links. You can also launch the application on any physical device with the Expo Client by scanning the QR code (Figure 21-1).

Figure 21-1. Expo's Metro Bundler after launching our application

Installing Device Simulators

To run an iOS device simulator, you will need to download and install Xcode (*https://oreil.ly/bgde4*) (macOS only). For Android, download Android Studio (*https://oreil.ly/bjqkn*) and follow Expo's guide (*https://oreil.ly/cUGsr*) on setting up a device simulator. (See Figure 21-2 for a comparison.) However, if you're just getting started with mobile application development, I recommend starting with your own physical device.

Figure 21-2. Our application running side by side on iOS and Android device simulators

If you've signed in to Expo from your computer's terminal application as well as within the Expo Client application on your mobile device, you can open the application simply by opening the Expo Client application and clicking the Projects tab (Figure 21-3).

Figure 21-3. With Expo Client, we can preview our application on a physical device

With the code cloned to your local machine and the ability to preview the application with Expo Client, you have everything in place to develop a mobile application.

Conclusion

This chapter introduced React Native and Expo. We cloned the sample project code, ran it locally, and previewed it on a physical device or simulator. React Native empowers web and JavaScript developers to build fully featured native mobile applications, using the skills and tools they are familiar with. Expo simplifies the toolchain and lowers the barrier to entry for native mobile development. With these two tools, novices can easily get started with mobile development and web-savvy teams can quickly introduce a mobile application development skillset. In the next chapter we'll take a closer look at React Native's capabilities and introduce both routes and styles to our app.

Mobile Application Shell

My wife is a photographer, which means that much of her life is based around composing images within a rectangular frame. In photography there are many variables—subject, light, angle—but the proportions of the image remain consistent. With that limitation, incredible things happen, shaping the way that we see and remember the world around us. Mobile application development presents a similar opportunity. Within the constraints of a small rectangular screen, we can build incredibly powerful applications with immersive user experiences.

In this chapter, we'll begin to build out a shell for our application. To do this, we'll first take a closer look at some of the key building blocks of React Native components. From there we'll look at how to apply styles to our application, both with React Native's built-in style support as well as with our CSS-in-JS library of choice, Styled Components. Once we've covered how to apply styles, we'll take a look at how to integrate routing into our application. Finally, we'll explore how to easily enhance our app interfaces with icons.

React Native Building Blocks

Let's begin by taking a look at the basic building blocks of a React Native application. You may have already guessed that a React Native application consists of React components written in JSX. But without an HTML page's DOM (document object model), what exactly goes within those components? We can start by looking at the "Hello World" component at *src/Main.js*. For now, I've removed the styles:

```
import React from 'react';
import { Text, View } from 'react-native';

const Main = () => {
  return (
    <View>
```

```
    <Text>Hello world!</Text>
  </View>
);
};

export default Main;
```

In this markup there are two notable JSX tags: `<View>` and `<Text>`. If you're coming from a web background, a `<View>` tag serves much of the same purpose as a `<div>` tag. It is a container for the content of our applications. On their own they don't do much, but they contain all of our app's content, can be nested within one another, and are used to apply styles. Each of our components will be contained within a `<View>`. In React Native, you can use a `<View>` anywhere that you might use a `<div>` or `<span>` tag on the web. The `<Text>` tag, unsurprisingly, is used to contain any text in our app. Unlike on the web, however, this single tag is used for all text.

As you can imagine, we can also add images to our applications, by using the `<Image>` JSX element. Let's update our *src/Main.js* file to include an image. To do so, we import the `Image` component from React Native and use an `<Image>` tag with a `src` attribute (see Figure 22-1):

```
import React from 'react';
import { Text, View, Image } from 'react-native';

const Main = () => {
  return (
    <View style={{ flex: 1, justifyContent: 'center', alignItems: 'center' }}>
      <Text>Hello world!</Text>
      <Image source={require('../assets/images/hello-world.jpg')} />
    </View>
  );
};

export default Main;
```

The preceding code renders some text and image within a view. You may notice that our `<View>` and `<Image>` JSX tags are passed properties that allow us to control specific behavior (in this case the style of the view and the source of the image). Passing properties to an element allows us to extend the element with all sorts of additional features. React Native's API documentation (*https://oreil.ly/3fACI*) catalogs the properties that are made available to each element.

Figure 22-1. Using the <Image> tag we can add images to our application (photo by Windell Oskay (https://oreil.ly/lkW3F))

Our app doesn't do much yet, but in the next section we'll explore how we can improve the look and feel using React Native's built-in style support and Styled Components.

Style and Styled Components

As app developers and designers, we want to be able to style our applications to have a precise look, feel, and user experience. There are a number of UI component libraries, such as NativeBase (*https://nativebase.io*) or React Native Elements (*https://oreil.ly/-M8EE*), which offer a wide range of predefined and often customizable components. These are well worth a look, but for our purposes let's explore how we might compose our own styles and application layouts.

As we've already seen, React Native provides a `style` property that allows us to apply custom styles to any JSX element in our application. The style names and values match those of CSS, except that the names are written in camelCase, such as `line Height` and `backgroundColor`. Let's update our */src/Main.js* file to include some styles for the `<Text>` element (see Figure 22-2):

```
const Main = () => {
  return (
    <View style={{ flex: 1, justifyContent: 'center', alignItems: 'center' }}>
      <Text style={{ color: '#0077cc', fontSize: 48, fontWeight: 'bold' }}>
        Hello world!
      </Text>
      <Image source={require('../assets/images/hello-world.jpg')} />
    </View>
  );
};
```

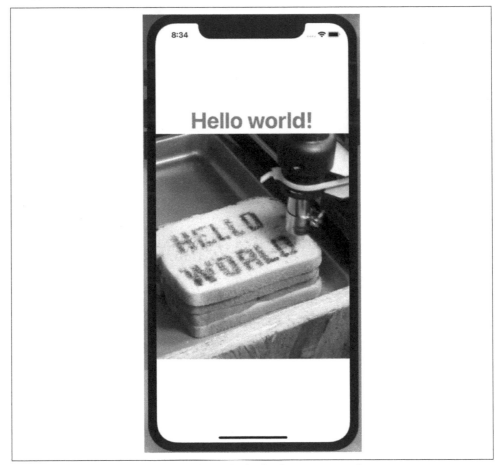

Figure 22-2. Using styles we can adjust the look of our <Text> element

You may be thinking, rightfully, that applying styles at the element level would quickly become an unmaintainable mess. We can use React Native's `StyleSheet` library to help organize and reuse our styles.

First, we need to add `StyleSheet` to our list of imports (Figure 22-3):

```
import { Text, View, Image, StyleSheet } from 'react-native';
```

Now we can abstract our styles:

```
const Main = () => {
  return (
    <View style={styles.container}>
      <Text style={styles.h1}>Hello world!</Text>
      <Text style={styles.paragraph}>This is my app</Text>
      <Image source={require('../assets/images/hello-world.jpg')} />
    </View>
  );
};

const styles = StyleSheet.create({
  container: {
    flex: 1,
    justifyContent: 'center'
  },
  h1: {
    fontSize: 48,
    fontWeight: 'bold'
  },
  paragraph: {
    marginTop: 24,
    marginBottom: 24,
    fontSize: 18
  }
});
```

Flexbox

React Native uses the CSS flexbox algorithm to define layout styles. We won't be covering flexbox in depth, but React Native offers documentation (*https://oreil.ly/owhZK*) that clearly explains flexbox and its use cases for arranging elements on the screen.

Figure 22-3. By using stylesheets we can scale the styles of our application

Styled Components

While React Native's built-in `style` properties and `StyleSheets` may offer everything that we need out of the box, they are far from our only options for styling our applications. We can also make use of popular web CSS-in-JS solutions, such as Styled Components (*https://www.styled-components.com*) and Emotion (*https://emotion.sh*). These offer, in my opinion, a cleaner syntax, are more closely aligned to CSS, and limit the amount of context switching needed between the web and mobile application codebases. Using these web-enabled CSS-in-JS libraries also creates the opportunity to share styles or components across platforms.

For our purposes, let's look at how we can adapt the previous example to use the Styled Components library. First, in *src/Main.js* we will import the `native` version of the library:

```
import styled from 'styled-components/native'
```

From here we can migrate our styles to the Styled Components syntax. If you followed along in Chapter 13, this syntax should look very familiar. The final code of our *src/Main.js* file becomes:

```
import React from 'react';
import { Text, View, Image } from 'react-native';
import styled from 'styled-components/native';

const StyledView = styled.View`
  flex: 1;
  justify-content: center;
`;

const H1 = styled.Text`
  font-size: 48px;
  font-weight: bold;
`;

const P = styled.Text`
  margin: 24px 0;
  font-size: 18px;
`;

const Main = () => {
  return (
    <StyledView>
      <H1>Hello world!</H1>
      <P>This is my app.</P>
      <Image source={require('../assets/images/hello-world.jpg')} />
    </StyledView>
  );
};

export default Main;
```

Styled Components Capitalization

In the Styled Components library, the element names must always be capitalized.

With this we're now able to apply custom styling to our applications, with the option of using React Native's built-in style system or Styled Components library.

Routing

On the web we can use HTML anchor links to link from one HTML document to any other, including those on our own site. For JavaScript-driven applications we use routing to link together JavaScript-rendered templates. What about native mobile applications? For these, we will route our users between screens. In this section we'll explore two common routing types: tab-based navigation and stack navigation.

Tabbed Routing with React Navigation

To perform our routing we'll make use of the React Navigation library (*https://reactnavigation.org*), which is the routing solution recommended by both the React Native and Expo teams. Most importantly, it makes it very straightforward to implement common routing patterns with a platform-specific look and feel.

To get started, let's first create a new directory within our *src* directory named *screens*. Within the *screens* directory, let's create three new files, each containing a very basic React component.

Add the following in *src/screens/favorites.js*:

```
import React from 'react';
import { Text, View } from 'react-native';

const Favorites = () => {
  return (
    <View style={{ flex: 1, justifyContent: 'center', alignItems: 'center' }}>
      <Text>Favorites</Text>
    </View>
  );
};

export default Favorites;
```

Add this in *src/screens/feed.js*:

```
import React from 'react';
import { Text, View } from 'react-native';

const Feed = () => {
  return (
    <View style={{ flex: 1, justifyContent: 'center', alignItems: 'center' }}>
      <Text>Feed</Text>
    </View>
  );
};

export default Feed;
```

Finally, add this in *src/screens/mynotes.js*:

```
import React from 'react';
import { Text, View } from 'react-native';

const MyNotes = () => {
  return (
    <View style={{ flex: 1, justifyContent: 'center', alignItems: 'center' }}>
      <Text>My Notes</Text>
    </View>
  );
};

export default MyNotes;
```

We can then create a new file at *src/screens/index.js* to be used as the root of our application's routing. We'll begin by importing our initial `react` and `react-navigation` dependencies:

```
import React from 'react';
import { createAppContainer } from 'react-navigation';
import { createBottomTabNavigator } from 'react-navigation-tabs';

// import screen components
import Feed from './feed';
import Favorites from './favorites';
import MyNotes from './mynotes';
```

With these dependencies imported, we can create a tab navigator between these three screens using React Navigation's `createBottomTabNavigator` to define which React component screens should appear in our navigation:

```
const TabNavigator = createBottomTabNavigator({
  FeedScreen: {
    screen: Feed,
    navigationOptions: {
      tabBarLabel: 'Feed',
    }
  },
  MyNoteScreen: {
    screen: MyNotes,
    navigationOptions: {
      tabBarLabel: 'My Notes',
    }
  },
  FavoriteScreen: {
    screen: Favorites,
    navigationOptions: {
      tabBarLabel: 'Favorites',
    }
  }
});
```

```
// create the app container
export default createAppContainer(TabNavigator);
```

Finally, let's update our *src/Main.js* file to do nothing but import our router. It should now be simplified to read as follows:

```
import React from 'react';
import Screens from './screens';

const Main = () => {
  return <Screens />;
};

export default Main;
```

Be sure that your application is running by entering the **npm start** command in your terminal. You should now see tab navigation at the bottom of the screen, where tapping a tab will route you to the appropriate screen (Figure 22-4).

Figure 22-4. We can now navigate between screens with tabbed navigation

Stack Navigation

A second kind of routing type is stack navigation, in which screens are conceptually "stacked" on top of one another, allowing users to navigate deeper into and backward through the stack. Consider a news application where a user views a feed of articles. The user can tap a news article title and navigate deeper in the stack to the article contents. They can then click a back button, navigating back to the article feed, or perhaps a different article title, navigating deeper into the stack.

In our application we want users to be able to navigate from a feed of notes to the notes themselves and back. Let's look at how we might implement a stack navigation for each of our screens.

First, let's create a new `NoteScreen` component, which will contain the second screen in our stack. Create a new file at *src/screens/note.js* with a minimal React Native component:

```
import React from 'react';
import { Text, View } from 'react-native';

const NoteScreen = () => {
  return (
    <View style={{ padding: 10 }}>
      <Text>This is a note!</Text>
    </View>
  );
};

export default NoteScreen;
```

Next, we will make the changes to our router to enable stacked navigation for the `NoteScreen` component. To do so, we'll import `createStackNavigator` from `react-navigation-stack` as well as our new *note.js* component. In *src/screens/index.js* update the imports to look as follows:

```
import React from 'react';
import { Text, View, ScrollView, Button } from 'react-native';
import { createAppContainer } from 'react-navigation';
import { createBottomTabNavigator } from 'react-navigation-tabs';
// add import for createStackNavigator
import { createStackNavigator } from 'react-navigation-stack';

// import screen components, including note.js
import Feed from './feed';
import Favorites from './favorites';
import MyNotes from './mynotes';
import NoteScreen from './note';
```

With our libraries and files imported, we can implement the stack navigation capability. In our router file we must tell React Navigation which screens are "stackable." For each of our tabbed routes, we'll want a user to be able to navigate to a `Note` screen. Go ahead and define those stacks as follows:

```
const FeedStack = createStackNavigator({
  Feed: Feed,
  Note: NoteScreen
});

const MyStack = createStackNavigator({
  MyNotes: MyNotes,
  Note: NoteScreen
});

const FavStack = createStackNavigator({
  Favorites: Favorites,
  Note: NoteScreen
});
```

Now we can update our `TabNavigator` to reference the stack, rather than an individual screen. To do this, update the `screen` property in each `TabNavigator` object:

```
const TabNavigator = createBottomTabNavigator({
  FeedScreen: {
    screen: FeedStack,
    navigationOptions: {
      tabBarLabel: 'Feed'
    }
  },
  MyNoteScreen: {
    screen: MyStack,
    navigationOptions: {
      tabBarLabel: 'My Notes'
    }
  },
  FavoriteScreen: {
    screen: FavStack,
    navigationOptions: {
      tabBarLabel: 'Favorites'
    }
  }
});
```

All together, our *src/screens/index.js* file should appear as follows:

```
import React from 'react';
import { Text, View, ScrollView, Button } from 'react-native';
import { createAppContainer } from 'react-navigation';
import { createBottomTabNavigator } from 'react-navigation-tabs';
import { createStackNavigator } from 'react-navigation-stack';

// import screen components
import Feed from './feed';
import Favorites from './favorites';
```

```
import MyNotes from './mynotes';
import NoteScreen from './note';

// navigation stack
const FeedStack = createStackNavigator({
  Feed: Feed,
  Note: NoteScreen
});

const MyStack = createStackNavigator({
  MyNotes: MyNotes,
  Note: NoteScreen
});

const FavStack = createStackNavigator({
  Favorites: Favorites,
  Note: NoteScreen
});

// navigation tabs
const TabNavigator = createBottomTabNavigator({
  FeedScreen: {
    screen: FeedStack,
    navigationOptions: {
      tabBarLabel: 'Feed'
    }
  },
  MyNoteScreen: {
    screen: MyStack,
    navigationOptions: {
      tabBarLabel: 'My Notes'
    }
  },
  FavoriteScreen: {
    screen: FavStack,
    navigationOptions: {
      tabBarLabel: 'Favorites'
    }
  }
});

// create the app container
export default createAppContainer(TabNavigator);
```

If we open our application in a simulator or the Expo app on our device, we should see no discernible difference. This is because we have yet to add a link to our stacked navigation. Let's update our *src/screens/feed.js* component to include a stacked navigation link.

To do so, first include the `Button` dependency from React Native:

```
import { Text, View, Button } from 'react-native';
```

Now we can include a button that, on press, will navigate to the content of our *note.js* component. We will pass the component `props`, which will contain the navigation information, and add a `<Button>` that will include the `title` and `onPress` props:

```
const Feed = props => {
  return (
    <View style={{ flex: 1, justifyContent: 'center', alignItems: 'center' }}>
      <Text>Note Feed</Text>
      <Button
        title="Keep reading"
        onPress={() => props.navigation.navigate('Note')}
      />
    </View>
  );
};
```

With this, we should be able to navigate between our screens. Click the button from the Feed screen to navigate to the Note screen, and click the arrow to return (Figure 22-5).

Figure 22-5. Clicking the button link will navigate to the new screen, while clicking the arrow will return the user to the previous screen

Adding Screen Titles

Adding the stack navigator automatically adds a title bar to the top of our app. We can style or even remove that top bar. For now let's add a title to each screen at the top of our stack. To do this, we will set the component navigationOptions outside of the component itself. In *src/screens/feed.js*:

```
import React from 'react';
import { Text, View, Button } from 'react-native';

const Feed = props => {
// component code
};

Feed.navigationOptions = {
```

```
    title: 'Feed'
};

export default Feed;
```

We can repeat this process for our other screen components.

In *src/screens/favorites.js*:

```
Favorites.navigationOptions = {
    title: 'Favorites'
};
```

In *src/screens/mynotes.js*:

```
MyNotes.navigationOptions = {
    title: 'My Notes'
};
```

Now each of our screens will include a title in the top navigation bar (Figure 22-6).

Figure 22-6. Setting the title in navigationOptions will add it to the top nav bar

Icons

Right now our navigation is functionally complete, but lacks a visual component to make it easier for users. Thankfully, Expo makes it incredibly easy to include icons in our application. We can search all of the icons that Expo makes available by visiting *expo.github.io/vector-icons*. A number of icon sets are included, such as Ant Design, Ionicons, Font Awesome, Entypo, Foundation, Material Icons, and Material Community Icons. This provides us with a tremendous amount of variety out of the box.

Let's add some icons to our tabbed navigation. First, we must import the icon sets that we'd like to use. In our case, we'll make use of the Material Community Icons by adding the following in *src/screens/index.js*:

```
import { MaterialCommunityIcons } from '@expo/vector-icons';
```

Now anywhere we want to use an icon in a component, we can include it as JSX, including setting properties such as `size` and `color`:

```
<MaterialCommunityIcons name="star" size={24} color={'blue'} />
```

We'll be adding our icons to our tab navigation. React Navigation includes a property called the `tabBarIcon` property, which allows us to set the icon. We can pass this as a function, which enables us to set the `tintColor`, so that active tab icons have a different color than those that are inactive:

```
const TabNavigator = createBottomTabNavigator({
  FeedScreen: {
    screen: FeedStack,
    navigationOptions: {
      tabBarLabel: 'Feed',
      tabBarIcon: ({ tintColor }) => (
        <MaterialCommunityIcons name="home" size={24} color={tintColor} />
      )
    }
  },
  MyNoteScreen: {
    screen: MyStack,
    navigationOptions: {
      tabBarLabel: 'My Notes',
      tabBarIcon: ({ tintColor }) => (
        <MaterialCommunityIcons name="notebook" size={24} color={tintColor} />
      )
    }
  },
  FavoriteScreen: {
    screen: FavStack,
    navigationOptions: {
      tabBarLabel: 'Favorites',
      tabBarIcon: ({ tintColor }) => (
        <MaterialCommunityIcons name="star" size={24} color={tintColor} />
      )
    }
  }
});
```

With this, our tabbed navigation will display icons (Figure 22-7).

Figure 22-7. Our application's navigation now includes icons

Conclusion

In this chapter we covered how to build the basic components of a React Native application. You're now able to create components, add styles to them, and navigate between them. Hopefully with this basic setup, you can see the incredible potential of React Native. With minimal new technologies, you are already able to build the beginnings of an impressive and professional mobile application. In the next chapter, we'll use GraphQL to include data from our API within the application.

## CHAPTER 23

GraphQL and React Native

At the Andy Warhol Museum in Pittsburgh, Pennsylvania, there is a permanent installation called "Silver Clouds." The installation is a sparse room with a dozen or so rectangular foil balloons, each filled with a mix of helium and regular air. The result is that the balloons will stay suspended longer than balloons filled with atmospheric air, but don't float to the ceiling like helium balloons. Patrons of the museum walk through the museum, playfully batting the balloons to keep them afloat.

Currently, our application is much like the room of "clouds." It's enjoyable to playfully click the icons and navigate around the app shell, but in the end it is a mostly empty room (no offense to Mr. Warhol). In this chapter, we'll begin to fill our application by first exploring how we can display content with React Native's list views. We'll then make use of Apollo Client (*https://www.apollographql.com/docs/react*) to connect to our data API. Once we've connected, we'll write GraphQL queries, which will display data on an app screen.

Running Our API Locally

The development of our mobile application will require access to a local instance of our API. If you've been following along with the book, you may already have the Notedly API and its database up and running on your machine. If not, I've added instructions in the book's Appendix A on how to get a copy of the API up and running along with some sample data. If you already have the API running, but would like some additional data to work with, run **npm run seed** from the root of the API project directory.

Creating List and Scrollable Content Views

Lists are everywhere. In life we keep to-do lists, grocery lists, and guest lists. In applications, lists are one of the most common UI patterns: lists of social media posts, lists of articles, lists of songs, lists of movies, and so on. The list (see what I did there?) goes on and on. It may come as no surprise, then, that React Native makes creating scrollable lists of content a straightforward process.

The two types of lists on React Native are `FlatList` and `SectionList`. A `FlatList` is useful for a large number of items in a single scrollable list. React Native does some helpful things behind the scenes, such as rendering only the items that are initially viewable to improve performance. A `SectionList` is much like a `FlatList`, except that it allows groups of list items to have a header. Think of contacts in a contact list, often grouped alphabetically beneath an alphanumeric header.

For our purposes, we'll be using a `FlatList` to display a list of notes, through which a user can scroll and tap a preview to read the full note. To achieve this, let's create a new component named `NoteFeed`, which we can use to display the list of notes. For now we'll use some stand-in data, but we'll connect it to our API soon.

To begin, let's create a new component at *src/components/NoteFeed.js*. We'll start by importing our dependencies and adding an array of temporary data.

```
import React from 'react';
import { FlatList, View, Text } from 'react-native';
import styled from 'styled-components/native';

// our dummy data
const notes = [
  { id: 0, content: 'Giant Steps' },
  { id: 1, content: 'Tomorrow Is The Question' },
  { id: 2, content: 'Tonight At Noon' },
  { id: 3, content: 'Out To Lunch' },
  { id: 4, content: 'Green Street' },
  { id: 5, content: 'In A Silent Way' },
  { id: 6, content: 'Lanquidity' },
  { id: 7, content: 'Nuff Said' },
  { id: 8, content: 'Nova' },
  { id: 9, content: 'The Awakening' }
];

const NoteFeed = () => {
  // our component code will go here
};

export default NoteFeed;
```

Now we can write our component code, which will contain a `FlatList`:

```
const NoteFeed = props => {
  return (
    <View>
      <FlatList
        data={notes}
        keyExtractor={({ id }) => id.toString()}
        renderItem={({ item }) => <Text>{item.content}</Text>}
      />
    </View>
  );
};
```

In the preceding code you can see that `FlatList` receives three properties that simplify the process of iterating over the data:

data

    This property points to the array of data that the list will contain.

keyExtractor

    Each item in the list must have a unique key value. We are using `keyExtractor` to use the unique `id` value as the key.

renderItem

    This property defines what should be rendered within the list. For now we are passing an individual `item` from our `notes` array and displaying it as `Text`.

We can view our list by updating our *src/screens/feed.js* component to display the feed:

```
import React from 'react';

// import NoteFeed
import NoteFeed from '../components/NoteFeed';

const Feed = props => {
  return <NoteFeed />;
};

Feed.navigationOptions = {
  title: 'Feed'
};

export default Feed;
```

Let's move back to our *src/components/NoteFeed.js* file and update `renderItem` to add some spacing between list items using a styled component:

```
// FeedView styled component definition
const FeedView = styled.View`
  height: 100;
  overflow: hidden;
```

```
  margin-bottom: 10px;
`;

const NoteFeed = props => {
  return (
    <View>
      <FlatList
        data={notes}
        keyExtractor={({ id }) => id.toString()}
        renderItem={({ item }) => (
          <FeedView>
            <Text>{item.content}</Text>
          </FeedView>
        )}
      />
    </View>
  );
};
```

If you preview our app, you'll see a scrollable list of data. Finally, we can add a separator between our list items. Rather than adding a bottom border via CSS, React Native enables us to pass an `ItemSeparatorComponent` property to our `FlatList`. This gives us fine-grained control to place any type of component as a separator between list elements. It also avoids placing a separator in unwanted places, such as after the last item in the list. For our purposes we'll add a simple border, created as a styled component `View`:

```
// FeedView styled component definition
const FeedView = styled.View`
  height: 100;
  overflow: hidden;
  margin-bottom: 10px;
`;

// add a Separator styled component
const Separator = styled.View`
  height: 1;
  width: 100%;
  background-color: #ced0ce;
`;

const NoteFeed = props => {
  return (
    <View>
      <FlatList
        data={notes}
        keyExtractor={({ id }) => id.toString()}
        ItemSeparatorComponent={() => <Separator />}
        renderItem={({ item }) => (
          <FeedView>
            <Text>{item.content}</Text>
```

```
        </FeedView>
      )}
    />
  </View>
);
};
```

Rather than rendering and styling our note's content directly in our `FlatList`, let's isolate it within its own component. To do so we'll introduce a new type of view called `ScrollView`. The functionality of a `ScrollView` is precisely what you'd expect: rather than conforming to the size of the screen, a `ScrollView` will overflow the content, allowing the user to scroll.

Let's create a new component at *src/components/Note.js*:

```
import React from 'react';
import { Text, ScrollView } from 'react-native';
import styled from 'styled-components/native';

const NoteView = styled.ScrollView`
  padding: 10px;
`;

const Note = props => {
  return (
    <NoteView>
      <Text>{props.note.content}</Text>
    </NoteView>
  );
};

export default Note;
```

Finally, we'll update our *src/components/NoteFeed.js* component to make use of our new `Note` component by importing it and using it within our `FeedView`. The final component code will be as follows (Figure 23-1):

```
import React from 'react';
import { FlatList, View, Text } from 'react-native';
import styled from 'styled-components/native';

import Note from './Note';

// our dummy data
const notes = [
  { id: 0, content: 'Giant Steps' },
  { id: 1, content: 'Tomorrow Is The Question' },
  { id: 2, content: 'Twilight At Noon' },
  { id: 3, content: 'Out To Lunch' },
  { id: 4, content: 'Green Street' },
  { id: 5, content: 'In A Silent Way' },
  { id: 6, content: 'Lanquidity' },
```

```
    { id: 7, content: 'Nuff Said' },
    { id: 8, content: 'Nova' },
    { id: 9, content: 'The Awakening' }
];

// FeedView styled-component definition
const FeedView = styled.View`
  height: 100;
  overflow: hidden;
  margin-bottom: 10px;
`;

const Separator = styled.View`
  height: 1;
  width: 100%;
  background-color: #ced0ce;
`;

const NoteFeed = props => {
  return (
    <View>
      <FlatList
        data={notes}
        keyExtractor={({ id }) => id.toString()}
        ItemSeparatorComponent={() => <Separator />}
        renderItem={({ item }) => (
          <FeedView>
            <Note note={item} />
          </FeedView>
        )}
      />
    </View>
  );
};

export default NoteFeed;
```

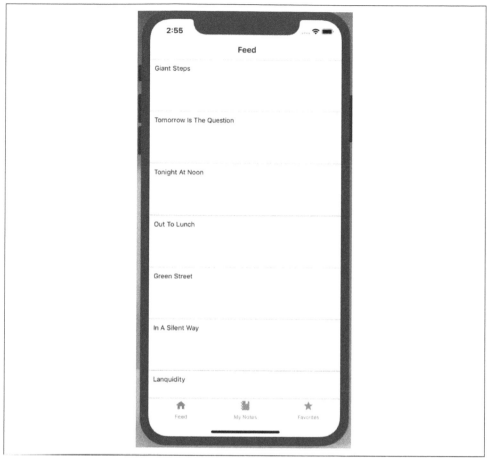

Figure 23-1. Using FlatList we can display a list of data

With this we've laid out a simple `FlatList`. Now let's make it possible to route from a list item to an individual route.

Making a List Routable

A very common pattern in mobile applications is to tap an item in a list to view more information or expanded functionality. If you recall from the previous chapter, our feed screen sits atop the note screen in our navigation stack. In React Native we can use the `TouchableOpacity` as a wrapper for making any view respond to user touches. This means that we can wrap the content of our `FeedView` in `TouchableOpacity` and route the user on press, the same way that we previously did with a button. Let's go ahead and update our *src/components/NoteFeed.js* component to do just that.

First, we must update our `react-native` import to include `TouchableOpacity` in *src/components/NoteFeed.js*:

```
import { FlatList, View, TouchableOpacity } from 'react-native';
```

Next, we update our component to use `TouchableOpacity`:

```
const NoteFeed = props => {
  return (
    <View>
      <FlatList
        data={notes}
        keyExtractor={({ id }) => id.toString()}
        ItemSeparatorComponent={() => <Separator />}
        renderItem={({ item }) => (
          <TouchableOpacity
            onPress={() =>
              props.navigation.navigate('Note', {
                id: item.id
              })
            }
          >
            <FeedView>
              <Note note={item} />
            </FeedView>
          </TouchableOpacity>
        )}
      />
    </View>
  );
};
```

We'll also need to update our *feed.js* screen component to pass the navigation properties to the feed. In *src/screens/feed.js*:

```
const Feed = props => {
  return <NoteFeed navigation={props.navigation} />;
};
```

With this, we can easily navigate to our generic note screen. Let's customize that screen so that it displays the ID of the note. You may have noticed that in our Note Feed component navigation, we're passing an `id` property. In *screens/note.js* we can read the value of that property:

```
import React from 'react';
import { Text, View } from 'react-native';

const NoteScreen = props => {
  const id = props.navigation.getParam('id');
  return (
    <View style={{ padding: 10 }}>
      <Text>This is note {id}</Text>
    </View>
```

```
    );
  };

  export default NoteScreen;
```

Now, we're able to navigate from our list view to a detail page. Next, let's take a look at how we can integrate data from our API into our application.

GraphQL with Apollo Client

At this point we are ready to read and display data within our application. We'll be accessing the GraphQL API that we created in the first portion of the book. Conveniently, we'll be making use of Apollo Client, the same GraphQL client library from the web portion of the book. Apollo Client offers a number of helpful features to simplify working with GraphQL within JavaScript UI applications. Apollo's client features include fetching data from a remote API, local caching, GraphQL syntax handling, local state management, and more.

To get started we'll first need to set up our configuration file. We'll store our environment variables in a file called *config.js*. There are several ways to manage environment and configuration variables in React Native, but I've found this style of configuration file to be the most straightforward and effective. To get started, I've included a *config-example.js* file, which you can copy and edit with our app values. In your terminal application, from the root of the project directory:

```
$ cp config.example.js config.js
```

From here we can update any dev or prod environment variables. In our case that will only be a production API_URI value:

```
// set environment variables
const ENV = {
  dev: {
    API_URI: `http://${localhost}:4000/api`
  },
  prod: {
    // update the API_URI value with your publicly deployed API address
    API_URI: 'https://your-api-uri/api'
  }
};
```

We will now be able to access these two values, based on Expo's environment, using the getEnvVars function. We won't dive into the rest of the configuration file, but it is well commented if you are interested in exploring this setup further.

From here we can connect our client to our API. In our *src/Main.js* file we will set up Apollo by using the Apollo Client library. If you worked through the web portion of the book, this will look very familiar:

```
import React from 'react';
import Screens from './screens';
// import the Apollo libraries
import { ApolloClient, ApolloProvider, InMemoryCache } from '@apollo/client';
// import environment configuration
import getEnvVars from '../config';
const { API_URI } = getEnvVars();

// configure our API URI & cache
const uri = API_URI;
const cache = new InMemoryCache();

// configure Apollo Client
const client = new ApolloClient({
  uri,
  cache
});

const Main = () => {
  // wrap our app in the ApolloProvider higher-order component
  return (
    <ApolloProvider client={client}>
      <Screens />
    </ApolloProvider>
  );
};

export default Main;
```

With this, there won't be a visible change in our application, but we are now connected to our API. Next, let's look at how we can query data from that API.

Writing GraphQL Queries

Now that we're connected to our API, let's query some of the data. We'll start by querying for all of the notes in our database, to be displayed in our `NoteFeed` list. We'll then query for individual notes to be displayed in our `Note` detail view.

The note Query

We'll be using the bulk `note` API query rather than the paginated `noteFeed` query for simplicity and to reduce repetition.

Writing a `Query` component works exactly the same way as in a React web application. In *src/screens/feed.js*, we import the `useQuery` and GraphQL Language (`gql`) libraries like so:

```
// import our React Native and Apollo dependencies
import { Text } from 'react-native';
import { useQuery, gql } from '@apollo/client';
```

Next, we compose our query:

```
const GET_NOTES = gql`
  query notes {
    notes {
      id
      createdAt
      content
      favoriteCount
      author {
        username
        id
        avatar
      }
    }
  }
`;
```

Finally, we update our component to call the query:

```
const Feed = props => {
  const { loading, error, data } = useQuery(GET_NOTES);

  // if the data is loading, our app will display a loading indicator
  if (loading) return <Text>Loading</Text>;
  // if there is an error fetching the data, display an error message
  if (error) return <Text>Error loading notes</Text>;
  // if the query is successful and there are notes, return the feed of notes
  return <NoteFeed notes={data.notes} navigation={props.navigation} />;
};
```

All together, our *src/screens/feed.js* file is written as follows:

```
import React from 'react';
import { Text } from 'react-native';
// import our Apollo libraries
import { useQuery, gql } from '@apollo/client';

import NoteFeed from '../components/NoteFeed';
import Loading from '../components/Loading';

// compose our query
const GET_NOTES = gql`
  query notes {
    notes {
      id
      createdAt
      content
      favoriteCount
      author {
```

```
        username
        id
        avatar
      }
    }
  }
`;

const Feed = props => {
  const { loading, error, data } = useQuery(GET_NOTES);

  // if the data is loading, our app will display a loading indicator
  if (loading) return <Text>Loading</Text>;
  // if there is an error fetching the data, display an error message
  if (error) return <Text>Error loading notes</Text>;
  // if the query is successful and there are notes, return the feed of notes
  return <NoteFeed notes={data.notes} navigation={props.navigation} />;
};

Feed.navigationOptions = {
  title: 'Feed'
};

export default Feed;
```

With our query written, we can update the *src/components/NoteFeed.js* component to
use the data passed to it via props:

```
const NoteFeed = props => {
  return (
    <View>
      <FlatList
        data={props.notes}
        keyExtractor={({ id }) => id.toString()}
        ItemSeparatorComponent={() => <Separator />}
        renderItem={({ item }) => (
          <TouchableOpacity
            onPress={() =>
              props.navigation.navigate('Note', {
                id: item.id
              })
            }
          >
            <FeedView>
              <Note note={item} />
            </FeedView>
          </TouchableOpacity>
        )}
      />
    </View>
  );
};
```

With this change, with Expo running, we will see the data from our local API displayed in a list, as shown in Figure 23-2.

Figure 23-2. Our API data displaying in our feed view

Right now, tapping a note preview in the list will still display a generic note page. Let's resolve that by making a **note** query in the *src/screens/note.js* file:

```
import React from 'react';
import { Text } from 'react-native';
import { useQuery, gql } from '@apollo/client';

import Note from '../components/Note';

// our note query, which accepts an ID variable
const GET_NOTE = gql`
  query note($id: ID!) {
    note(id: $id) {
```

```
        id
        createdAt
        content
        favoriteCount
        author {
          username
          id
          avatar
        }
      }
    }
  `;

  const NoteScreen = props => {
    const id = props.navigation.getParam('id');
    const { loading, error, data } = useQuery(GET_NOTE, { variables: { id } });

    if (loading) return <Text>Loading</Text>;
    // if there's an error, display this message to the user
    if (error) return <Text>Error! Note not found</Text>;
    // if successful, pass the data to the note component
    return <Note note={data.note} />;
  };

  export default NoteScreen;
```

Finally, let's update out *src/components/Note* component file to display the note contents. We'll add two new dependencies, `react-native-markdown-renderer` and `date-fns`, to parse the Markdown and dates from our API in a more user-friendly way.

```
  import React from 'react';
  import { Text, ScrollView } from 'react-native';
  import styled from 'styled-components/native';
  import Markdown from 'react-native-markdown-renderer';
  import { format } from 'date-fns';

  const NoteView = styled.ScrollView`
    padding: 10px;
  `;

  const Note = ({ note }) => {
    return (
      <NoteView>
        <Text>
          Note by {note.author.username} / Published{' '}
          {format(new Date(note.createdAt), 'MMM do yyyy')}
        </Text>
        <Markdown>{note.content}</Markdown>
      </NoteView>
    );
  };
```

```
export default Note;
```

With these changes, we'll see a list of notes in the application's feed view. Tapping a note preview will take us to the full, scrollable content of the note (see Figure 23-3).

Figure 23-3. With our GraphQL queries written, we can navigate between screens to view note previews and full notes

Adding a Loading Indicator

Currently when data is loading in our application, it flashes the word "Loading" on the screen. This may be effective at conveying the message, but is also a pretty jarring user experience. React Native supplies us with a built-in `ActivityIndicator`, which displays an operating system–appropriate loading spinner. Let's write a simple component that we can use as a loading indicator across our application.

Create a file at *src/components/Loading.js* and compose a simple component that displays the activity indicator in the center of the screen:

```
import React from 'react';
import { View, ActivityIndicator } from 'react-native';
import styled from 'styled-components/native';

const LoadingWrap = styled.View`
  flex: 1;
  justify-content: center;
  align-items: center;
`;

const Loading = () => {
  return (
    <LoadingWrap>
      <ActivityIndicator size="large" />
    </LoadingWrap>
  );
};

export default Loading;
```

Now we can replace the "Loading" text in our GraphQL query components. In both *src/screens/feed.js* and *src/screens/note.js*, first import the Loading component:

```
import Loading from '../components/Loading';
```

Then, in both files, update the Apollo loading state as follows:

```
if (loading) return <Loading />;
```

With this, our application will now display a spinning activity indicator when our API data is loading (see Figure 23-4).

Figure 23-4. Using ActivityIndicator, we can add an operating system–appropriate loading spinner

Conclusion

In this chapter we first looked at how we can integrate list views into a React Native application, making use of common application UI patterns. From there we configured Apollo Client and integrated the data from our API into the application. With this, we already have everything we need to build many common types of applications, such as a news app or integrating a blog feed from a website. In the next chapter, we'll add authentication to our app and display user-specific queries.

## CHAPTER 24

Mobile Application Authentication

If you've ever stayed with a relative, vacationed at a rental property, or rented a furnished apartment, you know what it's like to be surrounded by things that aren't yours. It can be hard to feel settled in these types of environments, not wanting to leave something out of place or make a mess. When I'm in these situations, no matter how kind or accommodating the host is, this lack of ownership leaves me on edge. What can I say? I'm just not comfortable unless I can put a glass down without a coaster.

Without the ability to customize or read user-specific data, our app might fill users with the same sense of discomfort. Their notes are simply mixed in with those of everyone else, not making the application truly their own. In this chapter we'll add authentication to our application. To accomplish this, we'll introduce an authentication routing flow, store token data using Expo's SecureStore, create text forms in React Native, and perform authentication GraphQL mutations.

Authentication Routing Flow

Let's begin by creating our authentication flow. When a user first accesses our application, we'll present them with a sign-in screen. When the user signs in, we'll store a token on the device, allowing them to bypass the sign-in screen on future application uses. We'll also add a settings screen, where a user can click a button to log out of the application and remove the token from their device.

To accomplish this, we'll be adding several new screens:

authloading.js
> This will be an interstitial screen, which users won't interact with. When the app is opened, we'll use the screen to check if a token is present and navigate the user to either the sign-in screen or the application content.

signin.js

This is the screen where a user can sign in to their account. After a successful login attempt, we will store a token on the device.

settings.js

In the settings screen, a user will be able to click a button and log out of the application. Once they are logged out, they will be routed back to the sign-in screen.

Using an Existing Account

We'll be adding the ability to create an account through the app later in the chapter. If you haven't already, it would be useful to create an account either directly through your API instance's GraphQL Playground or the web application interface.

For storing and working with tokens, we'll be using Expo's SecureStore library (*https://oreil.ly/nvqEO*). I've found SecureStore to be a straightforward way to encrypt and store data locally on a device. For iOS devices, SecureStore makes use of the built-in keychain services (*https://oreil.ly/iCu8R*), while on Android it uses the OS's Shared Preferences, encrypting the data with Keystore (*https://oreil.ly/gIXsp*). All of this happens under the hood, allowing us to simply store and retrieve data.

To begin with, we'll create our sign-in screen. For now, our sign-in screen will consist of a `Button` component that, when pressed, will store a token. Let's create a new screen component at *src/screens/signin.js*, importing our dependencies:

```
import React from 'react';
import { View, Button, Text } from 'react-native';
import * as SecureStore from 'expo-secure-store';

const SignIn = props => {
  return (
    <View>
      <Button title="Sign in!" />
    </View>
  );
}

SignIn.navigationOptions = {
  title: 'Sign In'
};

export default SignIn;
```

Next, let's create our authentication loading component at *src/screens/authloading.js*, which for now will simply display a loading indicator:

```
import React, { useEffect } from 'react';
import * as SecureStore from 'expo-secure-store';

import Loading from '../components/Loading';

const AuthLoading = props => {
  return <Loading />;
};

export default AuthLoading;
```

Finally, we can create our settings screen at *src/screens/settings.js*:

```
import React from 'react';
import { View, Button } from 'react-native';
import * as SecureStore from 'expo-secure-store';

const Settings = props => {
  return (
    <View>
      <Button title="Sign Out" />
    </View>
  );
};

Settings.navigationOptions = {
  title: 'Settings'
};

export default Settings;
```

With these components written, we will update our routing to handle the authenticated and unauthenticated states. In *src/screens/index.js*, add the new screens to our list of import statements as follows:

```
import AuthLoading from './authloading';
import SignIn from './signin';
import Settings from './settings';
```

We'll also need to update our react-navigation dependency to include createSwitchNavigator, which allows us to display a single screen at a time and switch between them. The SwitchNavigator (*https://oreil.ly/vSURH*) resets routes to the default state when a user navigates and does not offer back-navigation options.

```
import { createAppContainer, createSwitchNavigator } from 'react-navigation';
```

We can create a new `StackNavigator` for our authentication and settings screens. This will allow us to add subnavigation screens when or if needed in the future:

```
const AuthStack = createStackNavigator({
  SignIn: SignIn
});

const SettingsStack = createStackNavigator({
  Settings: Settings
});
```

We will then add our settings screen to the bottom `TabNavigator`. The rest of the tab navigation settings will stay the same:

```
const TabNavigator = createBottomTabNavigator({
  FeedScreen: {
    // ...
  },
  MyNoteScreen: {
    // ...
  },
  FavoriteScreen: {
    // ...
  },
  Settings: {
    screen: Settings,
    navigationOptions: {
      tabBarLabel: 'Settings',
      tabBarIcon: ({ tintColor }) => (
        <MaterialCommunityIcons name="settings" size={24} color={tintColor} />
      )
    }
  }
});
```

We can now create our `SwitchNavigator` by defining the screens to switch between and setting a default screen, the `AuthLoading`. We'll then replace our existing `export` statement with one that exports the `SwitchNavigator`:

```
const SwitchNavigator = createSwitchNavigator(
  {
    AuthLoading: AuthLoading,
    Auth: AuthStack,
    App: TabNavigator
  },
  {
    initialRouteName: 'AuthLoading'
  }
);

export default createAppContainer(SwitchNavigator);
```

All together, our *src/screens/index.js* file will appear as follows:

```
import React from 'react';
import { Text, View, ScrollView, Button } from 'react-native';
import { createAppContainer, createSwitchNavigator } from 'react-navigation';
import { createBottomTabNavigator } from 'react-navigation-tabs';
import { createStackNavigator } from 'react-navigation-stack';
import { MaterialCommunityIcons } from '@expo/vector-icons';

import Feed from './feed';
import Favorites from './favorites';
import MyNotes from './mynotes';
import Note from './note';
import SignIn from './signin';
import AuthLoading from './authloading';
import Settings from './settings';

const AuthStack = createStackNavigator({
  SignIn: SignIn,
});

const FeedStack = createStackNavigator({
  Feed: Feed,
  Note: Note
});

const MyStack = createStackNavigator({
  MyNotes: MyNotes,
  Note: Note
});

const FavStack = createStackNavigator({
  Favorites: Favorites,
  Note: Note
});

const SettingsStack = createStackNavigator({
  Settings: Settings
});

const TabNavigator = createBottomTabNavigator({
  FeedScreen: {
    screen: FeedStack,
    navigationOptions: {
      tabBarLabel: 'Feed',
      tabBarIcon: ({ tintColor }) => (
        <MaterialCommunityIcons name="home" size={24} color={tintColor} />
      )
    }
  },
  MyNoteScreen: {
    screen: MyStack,
    navigationOptions: {
```

```
        tabBarLabel: 'My Notes',
        tabBarIcon: ({ tintColor }) => (
          <MaterialCommunityIcons name="notebook" size={24} color={tintColor} />
        )
      }
    },
    FavoriteScreen: {
      screen: FavStack,
      navigationOptions: {
        tabBarLabel: 'Favorites',
        tabBarIcon: ({ tintColor }) => (
          <MaterialCommunityIcons name="star" size={24} color={tintColor} />
        )
      }
    },
    Settings: {
      screen: SettingsStack,
      navigationOptions: {
        tabBarLabel: 'Settings',
        tabBarIcon: ({ tintColor }) => (
          <MaterialCommunityIcons name="settings" size={24} color={tintColor} />
        )
      }
    }
  }
});

const SwitchNavigator = createSwitchNavigator(
  {
    AuthLoading: AuthLoading,
    Auth: AuthStack,
    App: TabNavigator
  },
  {
    initialRouteName: 'AuthLoading'
  }
);

export default createAppContainer(SwitchNavigator);
```

Right now, when we preview our app we'll only see loading spinner, since our Auth
Loading route is the initial screen. Let's update this so that the loading screen checks
for the existence of a token value in the application's SecureStore. If the token is
present, we'll navigate the user to the main application screen. However, if no token is
present, the user should be routed to the sign-in screen. Let's update *src/screens/*
authloading.js to perform this check:

```
import React, { useEffect } from 'react';
import * as SecureStore from 'expo-secure-store';

import Loading from '../components/Loading';

const AuthLoadingScreen = props => {
```

```
const checkLoginState = async () => {
  // retrieve the value of the token
  const userToken = await SecureStore.getItemAsync('token');
  // navigate to the app screen if a token is present
  // else navigate to the auth screen
  props.navigation.navigate(userToken ? 'App' : 'Auth');
};

// call checkLoginState as soon as the component mounts
useEffect(() => {
  checkLoginState();
});

return <Loading />;
};

export default AuthLoadingScreen;
```

With this change, when we load the app we should now be routed to the sign-in screen, since no token is present. For now, let's update our sign-in screen to store a generic token and navigate to the application when the user presses the button (Figure 24-1):

```
import React from 'react';
import { View, Button, Text } from 'react-native';
import * as SecureStore from 'expo-secure-store';

const SignIn = props => {
  // store the token with a key value of `token`
  // after the token is stored navigate to the app's main screen
  const storeToken = () => {
    SecureStore.setItemAsync('token', 'abc').then(
      props.navigation.navigate('App')
    );
  };

  return (
    <View>
      <Button title="Sign in!" onPress={storeToken} />
    </View>
  );
};

SignIn.navigationOptions = {
  title: 'Sign In'
};

export default SignIn;
```

Figure 24-1. Clicking the button will store a token and route the user to the application

Now, when a user presses the button, a token is stored via SecureStore. With the sign-in functionality in place, let's add the ability for users to sign out of the application. To do so, we'll add a button on our settings screen that, when pressed, will remove the *token* from SecureStore (Figure 24-2). In *src/screens/settings.js*:

```
import React from 'react';
import { View, Button } from 'react-native';
import * as SecureStore from 'expo-secure-store';

const Settings = props => {
  // delete the token then navigate to the auth screen
  const signOut = () => {
    SecureStore.deleteItemAsync('token').then(
      props.navigation.navigate('Auth')
    );
  };
```

```
  return (
    <View>
      <Button title="Sign Out" onPress={signOut} />
    </View>
  );
};

Settings.navigationOptions = {
  title: 'Settings'
};

export default Settings;
```

Figure 24-2. Clicking the button will remove the token from the device and return the user to the sign-in screen

With these pieces in place, we have everything we need to create an application authentication flow.

Be Sure to Sign Out

If you haven't already, tap the Sign Out button in your local app instance. We'll be adding proper sign-in functionality in the upcoming sections.

Creating a Sign-in Form

While we can now click a button and store a token on the user's device, we're not yet allowing a user to sign in to an account by entering their own information. Let's begin to remedy this by creating a form where a user can enter their email address and password. To do this, we'll create a new component at *src/components/UserForm.js* with a form using React Native's `TextInput` component:

```
import React, { useState } from 'react';
import { View, Text, TextInput, Button, TouchableOpacity } from 'react-native';
import styled from 'styled-components/native';

const UserForm = props => {
  return (
    <View>
      <Text>Email</Text>
      <TextInput />
      <Text>Password</Text>
      <TextInput />
      <Button title="Log In" />
    </View>
  );
}

export default UserForm;
```

Now we can display this form on our authentication screen. To do so, update *src/screens/signin.js* to import and use the component like so:

```
import React from 'react';
import { View, Button, Text } from 'react-native';
import * as SecureStore from 'expo-secure-store';

import UserForm from '../components/UserForm';

const SignIn = props => {
  const storeToken = () => {
    SecureStore.setItemAsync('token', 'abc').then(
      props.navigation.navigate('App')
    );
  };
```

```
      return (
        <View>
          <UserForm />
        </View>
      );
    }

    export default SignIn;
```

With this, we'll see a basic form display on the authentication screen, but it lacks any style or functionality. We can continue implementing the form in our *src/components/ UserForm.js* file. We'll be using React's `useState` hook to read and set the values of our form elements:

```
const UserForm = props => {
  // form element state
  const [email, setEmail] = useState();
  const [password, setPassword] = useState();

  return (
    <View>
      <Text>Email</Text>
      <TextInput onChangeText={text => setEmail(text)} value={email} />
      <Text>Password</Text>
      <TextInput onChangeText={text => setPassword(text)} value={password} />
      <Button title="Log In" />
    </View>
  );
}
```

Now we can add a few more additional properties to our form elements to provide users with the expected functionality when working with email addresses or passwords. Full documentation of the `TextInput` API can be found in the React Native docs (*https://oreil.ly/yvgyU*). We'll also call a function when the button is pressed, though the functionality will be limited.

```
const UserForm = props => {
  // form element state
  const [email, setEmail] = useState();
  const [password, setPassword] = useState();

  const handleSubmit = () => {
    // this function is called when the user presses the form button
  };

  return (
    <View>
      <Text>Email</Text>
      <TextInput
        onChangeText={text => setEmail(text)}
        value={email}
```

```
              textContentType="emailAddress"
              autoCompleteType="email"
              autoFocus={true}
              autoCapitalize="none"
            />
            <Text>Password</Text>
            <TextInput
              onChangeText={text => setPassword(text)}
              value={password}
              textContentType="password"
              secureTextEntry={true}
            />
            <Button title="Log In" onPress={handleSubmit} />
        </View>
    );
}
```

Our form has all of the necessary components, but the styling leaves a lot to be desired. Let's use the Styled Components library to give the form a more appropriate appearance:

```
import React, { useState } from 'react';
import { View, Text, TextInput, Button, TouchableOpacity } from 'react-native';
import styled from 'styled-components/native';

const FormView = styled.View`
  padding: 10px;
`;

const StyledInput = styled.TextInput`
  border: 1px solid gray;
  font-size: 18px;
  padding: 8px;
  margin-bottom: 24px;
`;

const FormLabel = styled.Text`
  font-size: 18px;
  font-weight: bold;
`;

const UserForm = props => {
  const [email, setEmail] = useState();
  const [password, setPassword] = useState();

  const handleSubmit = () => {
    // this function is called when the user presses the form button
  };

  return (
    <FormView>
      <FormLabel>Email</FormLabel>
```

```
        <StyledInput
          onChangeText={text => setEmail(text)}
          value={email}
          textContentType="emailAddress"
          autoCompleteType="email"
          autoFocus={true}
          autoCapitalize="none"
        />
        <FormLabel>Password</FormLabel>
        <StyledInput
          onChangeText={text => setPassword(text)}
          value={password}
          textContentType="password"
          secureTextEntry={true}
        />
        <Button title="Log In" onPress={handleSubmit} />
      </FormView>
    );
  };

  export default UserForm;
```

Finally, our `Button` component is limited to the default style options, with the exception of accepting a `color` property value. To create a custom-styled button component, we can use the React Native wrapper `TouchableOpacity` (see Figure 24-3):

```
const FormButton = styled.TouchableOpacity`
  background: #0077cc;
  width: 100%;
  padding: 8px;
`;

const ButtonText = styled.Text`
  text-align: center;
  color: #fff;
  font-weight: bold;
  font-size: 18px;
`;

const UserForm = props => {
  const [email, setEmail] = useState();
  const [password, setPassword] = useState();

  const handleSubmit = () => {
    // this function is called when the user presses the form button
  };

  return (
    <FormView>
      <FormLabel>Email</FormLabel>
      <StyledInput
        onChangeText={text => setEmail(text)}
```

```
      value={email}
      textContentType="emailAddress"
      autoCompleteType="email"
      autoFocus={true}
      autoCapitalize="none"
    />
    <FormLabel>Password</FormLabel>
    <StyledInput
      onChangeText={text => setPassword(text)}
      value={password}
      textContentType="password"
      secureTextEntry={true}
    />
    <FormButton onPress={handleSubmit}>
      <ButtonText>Submit</ButtonText>
    </FormButton>
  </FormView>
);
};
```

With this, we've implemented a sign-in form and applied custom styles. Let's now implement the form's functionality.

Figure 24-3. Our sign-in form with custom styles

Authentication with GraphQL Mutations

You may recall the authentication flow we've developed from the API and web application chapters, but before moving forward let's do a quick refresher. We will send a GraphQL mutation to our API that includes the user's email address and password. If the email address is present in our database and the password is correct, our API will respond with a JWT. We can then store the token on the user's device, as we've already been doing, and send it along with every GraphQL request. This will allow us to identify the user on every API request, without requiring them to constantly re-enter their password.

With our form in place, we can write our GraphQL mutation in *src/screens/signin.js*. First, we'll add the Apollo libraries as well as our Loading component to our list of imports:

```
import React from 'react';
import { View, Button, Text } from 'react-native';
import * as SecureStore from 'expo-secure-store';
import { useMutation, gql } from '@apollo/client';

import UserForm from '../components/UserForm';
import Loading from '../components/Loading';
```

Next, we can add our GraphQL query:

```
const SIGNIN_USER = gql`
  mutation signIn($email: String, $password: String!) {
    signIn(email: $email, password: $password)
  }
`;
```

And update our `storeToken` function to store a token string passed as a parameter:

```
const storeToken = token => {
  SecureStore.setItemAsync('token', token).then(
    props.navigation.navigate('App')
  );
};
```

Finally, we update the component as a GraphQL mutation. We'll also pass several property values to the `UserForm` component, allowing us to share the mutation data, identify the type of form we are calling, and make use of the router's navigation.

```
const SignIn = props => {
  const storeToken = token => {
    SecureStore.setItemAsync('token', token).then(
      props.navigation.navigate('App')
    );
  };

  const [signIn, { loading, error }] = useMutation(SIGNIN_USER, {
    onCompleted: data => {
      storeToken(data.signIn)
    }
  });

  // if loading, return a loading indicator
  if (loading) return <Loading />;
  return (
    <React.Fragment>
      {error && <Text>Error signing in!</Text>}
      <UserForm
        action={signIn}
        formType="signIn"
        navigation={props.navigation}
      />
    </React.Fragment>
  );
};
```

Now we can make a simple change in our *src/components/UserForm.js* component, which will enable it to pass the user-entered data to the mutation. Within the component, we will update our `handleSubmit` function to pass the form values to our mutation:

```
const handleSubmit = () => {
  props.action({
    variables: {
      email: email,
      password: password
    }
  });
};
```

With our mutation written and form complete, users can now sign in to the application, which will store the returned JSON Web Token for future use.

Authenticated GraphQL Queries

Now that our users can sign-in to their account, we'll need to use the stored token to authenticate each request. This will allow us to request user-specific data, such as a list of notes by the current user or a list of notes the user has marked as "favorites." To accomplish this, we'll update the Apollo configuration to check for the existence of a token and, when one is present, send that token's value with each API call.

In *src/Main.js*, first add `SecureStore` to the list of imports and update the Apollo Client dependencies to include `createHttpLink` and `setContext`:

```
// import the Apollo libraries
import {
  ApolloClient,
  ApolloProvider,
  createHttpLink,
  InMemoryCache
} from '@apollo/client';
import { setContext } from 'apollo-link-context';
// import SecureStore for retrieving the token value
import * as SecureStore from 'expo-secure-store';
```

We can then update our Apollo Client configuration to send the token value with each request:

```
// configure our API URI & cache
const uri = API_URI;
const cache = new InMemoryCache();
const httpLink = createHttpLink({ uri });

// return the headers to the context
const authLink = setContext(async (_, { headers }) => {
  return {
```

```
      headers: {
        ...headers,
        authorization: (await SecureStore.getItemAsync('token')) || ''
      }
    };
  });

  // configure Apollo Client
  const client = new ApolloClient({
    link: authLink.concat(httpLink),
    cache
  });
```

With the token sent in the header of each request, we can now update the mynotes
and favorites screens to request user-specific data. If you followed along through
the web chapters, these queries should look very familiar.

In *src/screens/mynotes.js*:

```
  import React from 'react';
  import { Text, View } from 'react-native';
  import { useQuery, gql } from '@apollo/client';

  import NoteFeed from '../components/NoteFeed';
  import Loading from '../components/Loading';

  // our GraphQL query
  const GET_MY_NOTES = gql`
    query me {
      me {
        id
        username
        notes {
          id
          createdAt
          content
          favoriteCount
          author {
            username
            id
            avatar
          }
        }
      }
    }
  `;

  const MyNotes = props => {
    const { loading, error, data } = useQuery(GET_MY_NOTES);

    // if the data is loading, our app will display a loading message
    if (loading) return <Loading />;
    // if there is an error fetching the data, display an error message
```

```javascript
  if (error) return <Text>Error loading notes</Text>;
  // if the query is successful and there are notes, return the feed of notes
  // else if the query is successful and there aren't notes, display a message
  if (data.me.notes.length !== 0) {
    return <NoteFeed notes={data.me.notes} navigation={props.navigation} />;
  } else {
    return <Text>No notes yet</Text>;
  }
};

MyNotes.navigationOptions = {
  title: 'My Notes'
};

export default MyNotes;
```

In *src/screens/favorites.js*:

```javascript
import React from 'react';
import { Text, View } from 'react-native';
import { useQuery, gql } from '@apollo/client';

import NoteFeed from '../components/NoteFeed';
import Loading from '../components/Loading';

// our GraphQL query
const GET_MY_FAVORITES = gql`
  query me {
    me {
      id
      username
      favorites {
        id
        createdAt
        content
        favoriteCount
        author {
          username
          id
          avatar
        }
      }
    }
  }
`;

const Favorites = props => {
  const { loading, error, data } = useQuery(GET_MY_FAVORITES);

  // if the data is loading, our app will display a loading message
  if (loading) return <Loading />;
  // if there is an error fetching the data, display an error message
  if (error) return <Text>Error loading notes</Text>;
```

```
  // if the query is successful and there are notes, return the feed of notes
  // else if the query is successful and there aren't notes, display a message
  if (data.me.favorites.length !== 0) {
    return <NoteFeed notes={data.me.favorites} navigation={props.navigation} />;
  } else {
    return <Text>No notes yet</Text>;
  }
};

Favorites.navigationOptions = {
  title: 'Favorites'
};

export default Favorites;
```

Figure 24-4. Passing the token in the header of each request allows us to make user-specific queries in our application

We are now retrieving user-specific data based on the token value stored on the user's device (Figure 24-4).

Adding a Sign-up Form

Right now a user can sign in to an existing account, but they have no way to create an account if one doesn't exist. A common UI pattern is to add a link to a registration form below the sign-in link (or vice versa). Let's add a sign-up screen to allow users to create a new account from within our application.

To begin, let's create a new screen component at *src/screens/signup.js*. This component will be nearly identical to our sign-in screen, but we'll call our signUp GraphQL mutation and pass a formType="signUp" property to our UserForm component:

```
import React from 'react';
import { Text } from 'react-native';
import * as SecureStore from 'expo-secure-store';
import { useMutation, gql } from '@apollo/client';

import UserForm from '../components/UserForm';
import Loading from '../components/Loading';

// signUp GraphQL mutation
const SIGNUP_USER = gql`
  mutation signUp($email: String!, $username: String!, $password: String!) {
    signUp(email: $email, username: $username, password: $password)
  }
`;

const SignUp = props => {
  // store the token with a key value of `token`
  // after the token is stored navigate to the app's main screen
  const storeToken = token => {
    SecureStore.setItemAsync('token', token).then(
      props.navigation.navigate('App')
    );
  };

  // the signUp mutation hook
  const [signUp, { loading, error }] = useMutation(SIGNUP_USER, {
    onCompleted: data => {
      storeToken(data.signUp);
    }
  });

  // if loading, return a loading indicator
  if (loading) return <Loading />;

  return (
    <React.Fragment>
```

```
      {error && <Text>Error signing in!</Text>}
      <UserForm
        action={signUp}
        formType="signUp"
        navigation={props.navigation}
      />
    </React.Fragment>
  );
};

SignUp.navigationOptions = {
  title: 'Register'
};

export default SignUp;
```

With the screen created, we can add it to our router. In the *src/screens/index.js* file, first add the new component to our list of file imports:

```
import SignUp from './signup';
```

Next, we will update our `AuthStack` to include the sign-up screen:

```
const AuthStack = createStackNavigator({
  SignIn: SignIn,
  SignUp: SignUp
});
```

With this, our component is created and routable; however, our `UserForm` component does not contain all of the necessary fields. Rather than creating a registration form component, we can make use of the `formType` property that we're passing to `User Form` to customize the form, depending on the type.

In our *src/components/UserForm.js* file, let's first update the form to include a username field when the `formType` equals `signUp`:

```
const UserForm = props => {
  const [email, setEmail] = useState();
  const [password, setPassword] = useState();
  const [username, setUsername] = useState();

  const handleSubmit = () => {
    props.action({
      variables: {
        email: email,
        password: password,
        username: username
      }
    });
  };

  return (
    <FormView>
```

```
            <FormLabel>Email</FormLabel>
            <StyledInput
              onChangeText={text => setEmail(text)}
              value={email}
              textContentType="emailAddress"
              autoCompleteType="email"
              autoFocus={true}
              autoCapitalize="none"
            />
            {props.formType === 'signUp' && (
              <View>
                <FormLabel>Username</FormLabel>
                <StyledInput
                  onChangeText={text => setUsername(text)}
                  value={username}
                  textContentType="username"
                  autoCapitalize="none"
                />
              </View>
            )}
            <FormLabel>Password</FormLabel>
            <StyledInput
              onChangeText={text => setPassword(text)}
              value={password}
              textContentType="password"
              secureTextEntry={true}
            />
            <FormButton onPress={handleSubmit}>
              <ButtonText>Submit</ButtonText>
            </FormButton>
        </FormView>
    );
};
```

Next, let's add a link at the bottom of the sign-in form that will allow a user to route
to the sign-up form when pressed:

```
return (
  <FormView>
      {/* existing form component code is here */}
      {props.formType !== 'signUp' && (
        <TouchableOpacity onPress={() => props.navigation.navigate('SignUp')}>
          <Text>Sign up</Text>
        </TouchableOpacity>
      )}
  </FormView>
)
```

We can then use styled components to update the look of the link:

```
const SignUp = styled.TouchableOpacity`
  margin-top: 20px;
`;
```

```
const Link = styled.Text`
  color: #0077cc;
  font-weight: bold;
`;
```

And in the component's JSX:

```
{props.formType !== 'signUp' && (
  <SignUp onPress={() => props.navigation.navigate('SignUp')}>
    <Text>
      Need an account? <Link>Sign up.</Link>
    </Text>
  </SignUp>
)}
```

All together, our *src/components/UserForm.js* file will now be as follows:

```
import React, { useState } from 'react';
import { View, Text, TextInput, Button, TouchableOpacity } from 'react-native';
import styled from 'styled-components/native';

const FormView = styled.View`
  padding: 10px;
`;

const StyledInput = styled.TextInput`
  border: 1px solid gray;
  font-size: 18px;
  padding: 8px;
  margin-bottom: 24px;
`;

const FormLabel = styled.Text`
  font-size: 18px;
  font-weight: bold;
`;

const FormButton = styled.TouchableOpacity`
  background: #0077cc;
  width: 100%;
  padding: 8px;
`;

const ButtonText = styled.Text`
  text-align: center;
  color: #fff;
  font-weight: bold;
  font-size: 18px;
`;

const SignUp = styled.TouchableOpacity`
  margin-top: 20px;
`;
```

```
const Link = styled.Text`
  color: #0077cc;
  font-weight: bold;
`;

const UserForm = props => {
  const [email, setEmail] = useState();
  const [password, setPassword] = useState();
  const [username, setUsername] = useState();

  const handleSubmit = () => {
    props.action({
      variables: {
        email: email,
        password: password,
        username: username
      }
    });
  };

  return (
    <FormView>
      <FormLabel>Email</FormLabel>
      <StyledInput
        onChangeText={text => setEmail(text)}
        value={email}
        textContentType="emailAddress"
        autoCompleteType="email"
        autoFocus={true}
        autoCapitalize="none"
      />
      {props.formType === 'signUp' && (
        <View>
          <FormLabel>Username</FormLabel>
          <StyledInput
            onChangeText={text => setUsername(text)}
            value={username}
            textContentType="username"
            autoCapitalize="none"
          />
        </View>
      )}
      <FormLabel>Password</FormLabel>
      <StyledInput
        onChangeText={text => setPassword(text)}
        value={password}
        textContentType="password"
        secureTextEntry={true}
      />
      <FormButton onPress={handleSubmit}>
        <ButtonText>Submit</ButtonText>
```

```
      </FormButton>
      {props.formType !== 'signUp' && (
        <SignUp onPress={() => props.navigation.navigate('SignUp')}>
          <Text>
            Need an account? <Link>Sign up.</Link>
          </Text>
        </SignUp>
      )}
    </FormView>
  );
};

export default UserForm;
```

With these changes, a user can both sign in and register for an account with our application (Figure 24-5).

Figure 24-5. A user can now register an account and navigate between the authentication screens

Conclusion

In this chapter we looked at how to bring authentication to an application. Through a combination of React Native's text form elements, React Navigation's routing capabilities, Expo's SecureStore library, and GraphQL mutations, we can create a user-friendly authentication flow. Having a solid understanding of this type of authentication also enables us to explore additional React Native authentication methods, such as Expo's `AppAuth` (*https://oreil.ly/RaxNo*) or `GoogleSignIn` (*https://oreil.ly/Ic6BW*). In this next chapter, we'll look at how we can publish and distribute a React Native application.

## CHAPTER 25

Mobile Application Distribution

In my high school in the mid-1990s, it was all the rage to download games for your TI-81 graphing calculator (*https://oreil.ly/SqOKQ*). Someone would get ahold of a copy of a game and then it would spread like wildfire, each of us taking turns connecting our calculator to another with a cord in order to load the game. Having a game on your calculator was a way to fill the hours in the back of a class or study hall while maintaining the appearance of doing schoolwork. As you can imagine, however, this distribution method was slow, requiring two students to remain connected for several minutes while others waited. Today, our digital pocket computers are capable of much more than my humble graphing calculator, in part because we can easily extend their capabilities through installable third-party applications.

With our initial application development complete, we can now distribute our application so that others may access it. In this chapter we'll look at how to configure our *app.json* file for distribution. We'll then publish our application publicly within Expo. Finally, we'll generate application packages that can be submitted to the Apple or Google Play stores.

app.json Configuration

Expo applications include an *app.json* file, which is used to configure application-specific settings.

When we generate a new Expo application, an *app.json* file is automatically created for us. Let's take a look at the generated file for our application:

```
{
  "expo": {
    "name": "Notedly",
    "slug": "notedly-mobile",
    "description": "An example React Native app",
```

```
      "privacy": "public",
      "sdkVersion": "33.0.0",
      "platforms": ["ios", "android"],
      "version": "1.0.0",
      "orientation": "portrait",
      "icon": "./assets/icon.png",
      "splash": {
        "image": "./assets/splash.png",
        "resizeMode": "contain",
        "backgroundColor": "#ffffff"
      },
      "updates": {
        "fallbackToCacheTimeout": 1500
      },
      "assetBundlePatterns": ["**/*"],
      "ios": {
        "supportsTablet": true
      },
      "android": {}
    }
  }
```

It is likely that most of these are self-explanatory, but let's review the purpose of each:

name
> The name of our application.

slug
> The URL name for publishing the Expo app at *expo.io/project-owner/slug*.

description
> A description of our project, which will be used when publishing the application with Expo.

privacy
> The Expo project's public availability. This can be set to either `public` or `unlisted`.

sdkVersion
> The Expo SDK version number.

platforms
> The platforms we are targeting, which can include `ios`, `android`, and `web`.

version
> Our application's version number, which should follow the Semantic Versioning standards (*https://semver.org*).

orientation

Our application's default orientation, which can be locked with `portrait` or `land scape` values, or match the user's device rotation with `default`.

icon

A path to the application icon, which will be used for both iOS and Android.

splash

The image location and settings for the app loading screen.

updates

A configuration for how our application should check for over the air (OTA) updates when the app is loaded. The `fallbackToCacheTimeout` parameter allows us to specify a length of time in milliseconds.

assetBundlePatterns

Allows us to specify the location of assets that should be bundled with our application.

ios and android

Enable platform-specific settings.

This default configuration provides us with a solid basis for our application. There are a number of additional settings, which can be found in the Expo documentation (*https://oreil.ly/XXT4k*).

Icons and App Loading Screens

The small squarish icons found on our devices have become one of the most recognizable designs in modern society. Close your eyes and I'm sure you can imagine dozens of them, down to a logo or a specific background color. Additionally, when a user taps an icon there is an initial static "splash screen," which is displayed while the application loads. Up until now we've used the default empty Expo icons and splash screen. We can replace those with custom designs in our application.

I've included a Notedly icon and splash screen in the *assets/custom* folder. We can make use of these by replacing the images in the *assets* directory with them or updating our *app.json* configuration to point to the files in the *custom* subdirectory.

App Icons

The *icon.png* file is a square 1024×1024px PNG file. If we point to this file with our *app.json* `icon` property, Expo will generate the appropriate icon sizes for various platforms and devices. The image should be exactly square and without any transparent pixels. This is the simplest and most straightforward way to include an application icon:

```
"icon": "./assets/icon.png",
```

In addition to the single cross-platform icon, we have the option to include platform-specific icons. The main draw of this approach would be to include separate icon styles for Android and iOS, particularly if you are interested in using Android's adaptive icons (*https://oreil.ly/vLC3f*).

For iOS, we would continue to use a single 1024×1024 png. In the *app.json* file:

```
"ios": {
  "icon": IMAGE_PATH
}
```

To make use of Android's adaptive icon, we would specify a `foregroundImage`, a `back groundColor` (or `backgroundImage`), and a fallback static `icon`:

```
"android": {
  "adaptiveIcon": {
    "foregroundImage": IMAGE_PATH,
    "backgroundColor": HEX_CODE,
    "icon": IMAGE_PATH
  }
}
```

For our use case, we can continue to use the single static icon.

Splash Screens

The splash screen is a full screen image that will briefly display while our application is booting on the device. We can replace the default Expo image with one found in *assets/custom*. Though device sizes vary within and across platforms, I've chosen to use a size of 1242×2436, as recommended by the Expo documentation (*https://oreil.ly/7a-5J*). Expo will then resize the image to work across device screens and aspect ratios.

We can configure our splash screen in the *app.json* file like so:

```
"splash": {
  "image": "./assets/splash.png",
  "backgroundColor": "#ffffff",
  "resizeMode": "contain"
},
```

By default, we are setting a white background color, which may be visible as the image loads or, depending on our selected `resizeMode`, as a border around the splash screen image. We can update this to match the color of our screen:

```
"backgroundColor": "#4A90E2",
```

The `resizeMode` dictates how the image should be resized for various screen sizes. By setting this to `contain`, we preserve the aspect ratio of the original image. When you use `contain`, some screen sizes or resolutions will see the `backgroundColor` as a border around the splash screen image. Alternately, we could set `resizeMode` to `cover`, which will expand the image to fill the entire screen. Since our application has a subtle gradient, let's set our `resizeMode` to `cover`:

```
"resizeMode": "cover"
```

Figure 25-1. Our application splash screen

With this, our icon and splash screen images are configured (see Figure 25-1). We are now ready to look at how to distribute our application to make it accessible to others.

Expo Publish

During development, our application is accessible to us in the Expo Client application on a physical device, over our local area network. This means that we can access the application as long as our development machine and phone are on the same network.

Expo enables us to publish our project, which uploads the application to an Expo CDN and gives us a publicly accessible URL. With this, anyone can run our application through the Expo Client app. This can be useful for testing or quick application distribution.

To publish our project, we can click the "Publish or republish project" link in the browser's Expo Dev Tools (see Figure 25-2), or type `expo publish` in our terminal.

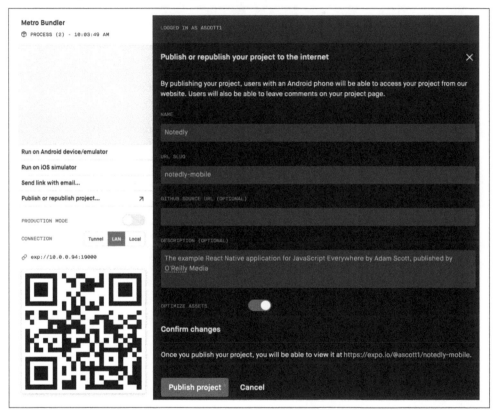

Figure 25-2. We can publish our application directly from Expo Dev Tools

Once the packaging has been completed, anyone can visit *https://exp.host/@<username>/<slug>* to access the application through the Expo Client App.

Creating Native Builds

While distributing directly through Expo is a great option for testing or quick use cases, we will most likely want to release our application through the Apple App Store or Google Play Store. To do so, we will build the files that can be uploaded to the respective store.

> **Windows Users**
>
> According to the Expo documentation, Windows users need to enable Windows Subsystem for Linux (WSL). To accomplish this, follow the Installation Guide for Windows 10 (*https://oreil.ly/B8_nd*) provided by Microsoft.

iOS

Generating an iOS build requires a membership to the Apple Developer Program (*https://oreil.ly/E0NuU*), which costs $99 a year. With an account, we can then add a `bundleIdentifier` for iOS in our *app.json* file. This identifier should follow reverse DNS notation:

```
"expo": {
"ios": {
    "bundleIdentifier": "com.yourdomain.notedly"
  }
}
```

With our *app.json* file updated, we can generate the build. In your terminal application, from the root of the project directory, enter:

```
$ expo build:ios
```

After running the build you'll be prompted to sign in with your Apple ID. Once you are signed in, you'll be asked several questions about how you would like to handle credentials. Expo is able to manage all credentials and certificates for us, which you can permit by selecting the first option at each of the following prompts:

```
? How would you like to upload your credentials? (Use arrow keys)
❏ Expo handles all credentials, you can still provide overrides
  I will provide all the credentials and files needed, Expo does limited validat
ion

? Will you provide your own Apple Distribution Certificate? (Use arrow keys)
❏ Let Expo handle the process
  I want to upload my own file

  ? Will you provide your own Apple Push Notifications service key? (Use arrow keys)
❏ Let Expo handle the process
  I want to upload my own file
```

If you have an active Apple Developer Program account, Expo will then generate the file, which can be submitted to the Apple App Store.

Android

For Android we can generate either an Android Package File (APK) or an Android App Bundle (AAB) file. Android App Bundles are the more modern format, so let's go that route. If you are interested, the Android developers documentation (*https://oreil.ly/mEAlR*) offers a detailed description of the benefits of App Bundles.

Before we generate the bundle, let's update our *app.json* file to include an Android package identifier. Similarly to iOS, this should be in reverse DNS notation:

```
"android": {
    "package": "com.yourdomain.notedly"
}
```

With this, we can generate the app bundle from our terminal application. Be sure to cd into the root of the project and run the following:

```
$ build:android -t app-bundle
```

App Bundles are required to be signed. Though we can generate a signature ourselves, Expo can manage the keystore for us. After running the command to generate the bundle, you'll see the following prompt:

```
? Would you like to upload a keystore or have us generate one for you?
If you don't know what this means, let us handle it! :)

   1) Let Expo handle the process!
   2) I want to upload my own keystore!
```

If you select 1, Expo will generate the App Bundle for you. At the end of the process, you can download the file, which can be uploaded to the Google Play Store.

Distributing to App Stores

Because of the shifting review guidelines and associated costs, I won't be walking through the specifics of submitting our application to the Apple App Store or Google Play Store. The Expo documentation (*https://oreil.ly/OmGB2*) does a nice job of collecting resources and guidelines and is a helpful, up-to-date guide on how to navigate the app store distribution process.

Conclusion

In this chapter we've looked at how to publish and distribute a React Native application. Expo's tooling allows us to quickly publish applications for testing and generate production builds that can be uploaded to app stores. Expo also provides us with options around levels of control for managing certificates and dependencies.

With this, we've successfully written and published a backend data API, a web application, a desktop application, and a cross-platform mobile application!

Afterword

Here in the United States it's common to give a new high school graduate a copy of Dr. Suess's *Oh the Places You'll Go!* as a graduation gift.

> Congratulations! Today is your day. You're off to Great Places! You're off and away!

If you've made it to the end of this book, a bit of a graduation celebration feels appropriate. We've covered a lot of material, from building a GraphQL API with Node through several types of UI clients, but we've only scratched the surface. Each of these topics fills books and countless online tutorials on its own. I hope that rather than feeling overwhelmed, you now feel equipped to more deeply explore the topics that interest you and build amazing things.

JavaScript is the little programming language that could. What was once a humble "toy language" is now the most popular programming language in the world. The result is that knowing how to write JavaScript is a superpower that enables us to build nearly any sort of application for any platform. Given that it's a superpower, I'll leave you with one last cliche (*https://oreil.ly/H02ca*):

> …with great power there must also come — great responsibility!

Technology can, and should, be a force for good. My hope is that you are able to apply the things you've learned in this book toward making the world a better place. That may include taking on a new job or side project that enables a better life for your family, teaching others new skills, or building a product designed to bring happiness or improve the lives of others. Whatever it may be, when you wield your powers for good, we are all better off.

Please do not be a stranger. I would love to see and hear about anything you create. Feel free to send me an email at *adam@jseverywhere.io* or join the Spectrum community (*https://spectrum.chat/jseverywhere*). Thank you for reading.

— Adam

Running the API Locally

If you've chosen to follow along with the UI portion of the book, but not the API development chapters, you will still need a copy of the API running locally.

The first step is to ensure that you have MongoDB installed and running on your system, as described in Chapter 1. With your database up and running, you can clone a copy of the API and copy the final code. To clone the code to your local machine, open the terminal, navigate to the directory where you keep your projects, and `git clone` the project repository. If you haven't done so already, it may also be helpful to create a *notedly* directory to keep the project code organized:

```
$ cd Projects
# only run the following mkdir command if you do not yet have a notedly directory
$ mkdir notedly
$ cd notedly
$ git clone git@github.com:javascripteverywhere/api.git
$ cd api
```

Lastly, you'll need to update your environment variables by making a copy of the *.sample.env* file and populating the information in the newly created *.env* file.

In your terminal, run:

```
$ cp .env.example .env
```

Now, in your text editor, update the values of the *.env* file:

```
## Database
DB_HOST=mongodb://localhost:27017/notedly
TEST_DB=mongodb://localhost:27017/notedly-test

## Authentication
JWT_SECRET=YOUR_PASSWORD
```

Finally, you can start the API. In your terminal, run:

```
$ npm start
```

After working through these instructions, you should have a copy of the Notedly API running locally on your system.

Running the Web App Locally

If you've chosen to follow along with the Electron portion of the book, but not the web development chapters, you will still need a copy of the web app running locally.

The first step is to ensure that you have a copy of the API running locally. If you haven't already, please reference Appendix A for running the API locally.

With your API up and running, you can clone a copy of the web app. To clone the code to our local machine, open the terminal, navigate to the directory where you keep your projects, and **git clone** the project repository:

```
$ cd Projects
# if keeping your projects in a notedly folder, cd into the notedly directory
$ cd notedly
$ git clone git@github.com:javascripteverywhere/web.git
$ cd web
```

Next, you'll need to update your environment variables by making a copy of the *.sample.env* file and populating the information in the newly created *.env* file.

In your terminal, run:

```
$ cp .env.example .env
```

Now, in your text editor, update the values of the *.env* file to make sure that it matches the URL of your locally running API. If everything is kept at the default values, you shouldn't need to make any changes.

```
API_URI=http://localhost:4000/api
```

Finally, you can run the final web code example. In your terminal application, run:

```
$ npm run final
```

After working through these instructions, you should have a copy of the Notedly web application running locally on your system.

Index

Symbols

.remove(), 69
<div> tag, 113
<Image>, 236
<Text>, 236
<view>, 236

A

AAB (Android App Bundle), 307
account creation flow, 55
Android App Bundle (AAB), 307
API (see application programming interface)
API deployment, 91-100
    application code deployment, 97-100
    hosting database, 91-97
    project setup, 97-99
    testing, 100
    to Heroku's servers, 99
Apollo Client, 135-152
    about, 135
    dynamic queries, 148-150
    GraphQL, 263-269
    pagination, 150-152
    querying an API, 138-147
    setting up, 136
Apollo GraphQL platform, 88
Apollo Server
    about, 17
    resolver functions, 26
ApolloProvider, 137
app icons, 225, 303
app stores, distributing to, 308
app.json configuration, 301-303
app.listen, 15

appId, 224
application authentication flow, 55
application code deployment
    project setup, 97-99
    testing, 100
    to Heroku's servers, 99
application programming interface (API), 9-12
    about, 9-10
    Electron, 213
    getting started with, 11
    GraphQL for, 10
    integrating authentication into, 59-64
    querying an, 138-147
    running locally, 136, 311-312
    turning server into an, 17-21
application styling, 121-133
    adding global styles, 127
    component styles, 129-132
    creating a button component, 125-127
    creating a layout component, 121-123
    CSS, 124-132
    CSS-in-JS, 124
args, defined, 26
arguments, 26
attaching headers to requests, 162
authenticated GraphQL queries, 289-293
authentication
    mobile application, 273-299
    resolvers, 61-64
    routing flow, 273-282
    user accounts and, 55-67
        (see also user accounts and authentication)
AuthenticationError, 70

authloading.js, 273

B

bcrypt, 57
browserWindow, 209
button component
    creating a, 125-127
    mobile application authentication, 285

C

Cascading Style Sheets (CSS), 124-132
    adding global styles, 127
    component styles, 129-132
    creating a button component, 125-127
    CSS-in-JS, 124
code signing, 226
collections, defined, 32
command-line prompts, terminal, 3
command-line tools (Mac only), 3
component styles, 129-132
conditional rendering, 151
content security policy (CSP), 219
context function
    CRUD operations and, 47
    defined, 27
CORS (cross-origin resource sharing), 84
create(), 40
create-react-app, 103
createBottomTabNavigator, 243
createSwitchNavigator, 275
cross-origin resource sharing (CORS), 84
CRUD operations, 45-53, 177-199
    creating new notes, 177-183
    date and time, 51-53
    deleting notes, 193
    reading user notes, 183-186
    resolvers, 49-51
    separating GraphQL schema and resolvers, 45-48
    toggling favorites, 195-196
    updating notes, 186-192
    writing GraphQL CRUD schema, 49
CSP (content security policy), 219
CSS (see Cascading Style Sheets)
CSS-in-JS, 124
cursor-based pagination, 85

D

data limitations, 87
database, 31-44
    about, 31
    MongoDB, 32-37
    reading/writing data from application, 37-44
DateTime function, 51-53
deleteNote mutation, 72, 193
deployment pipeline, 203-205
    hosting source code with Git, 203
    Netlify, 205
details, 83-89
    Apollo GraphQL platform, 88
    cross-origin resource sharing, 84
    data limitations, 87
    Express Helmet, 83
    pagination, 84-87
    subscriptions, 88
    testing, 88
    web application and express.js best practices, 83
developer tools, 211
development environment, 1-8
    about, 1
    command-line tools and homebrew (Mac only), 3
    ESLint, 8
    Expo, 7
    Git, 6
    installing and running MongoDB for macOS, 6
    installing and running MongoDB for Windows, 6
    installing Node.js and NPM for macOS, 4
    installing Node.js and NPM for Windows, 5
    MongoDB, 5
    navigating filesystem, 2
    Node.js and NPM, 4
    Prettier, 7
    terminal, 2
    text editor, 2
    using a dedicated application, 2
    VSCode, 2
distribution, mobile application, 301-308
dynamic queries, 148-150

E

Electron, 207-213

About the Author

Adam D. Scott is an engineering manager, web developer, and educator based in Connecticut. He currently works as the Web Development Lead at the Consumer Financial Protection Bureau, where he focuses on building open source web applications with his talented team. Additionally, he has worked in education for over a decade, teaching and writing curriculum on a range of technical topics. He is the author of *WordPress for Education* (Packt, 2012), the *Introduction to Modern Front-End Development* video course (O'Reilly, 2015), and the *Ethical Web Development* report series (O'Reilly, 2016–2017).

Colophon

The animal on the cover of *JavaScript Everywhere* is a common bronze-winged dove (*Phaps chalcoptera*), one of the most common members of the Columbidae family living in Australia. These birds are scattered throughout the continent in a wide range of habitats and will most likely be found foraging on the ground for the seeds of acacia shrubs.

Bronzewings are cautious birds—the slightest disturbance will trigger them to flap their wings in a loud flurry and retreat to the nearest mulga tree. On a bright day, sunlight will reveal iridescent patches of bronze and green on their wings. A yellow and white forehead with a pink breast indicates a male, while females have a light gray forehead and breast. Both, however, have a stark white line that curves from under their eyes toward the back of their nape.

A bronzewing nest measures about 10 inches across and 4 inches deep, just large enough to fit the two smooth, white eggs that are laid concurrently. After about 14–16 days, during which both parents incubate the eggs, they will hatch. Unlike most birds, both sexes of bronzewings share the responsibility of feeding their young, which involves secreting a milk-like substance from their "crop," a muscular pouch near the throat that is used for food storage.

While the bronze-winged dove's current conservation status is designated as of Least Concern, many of the animals on O'Reilly covers are endangered; all of them are important to the world.

The cover illustration is by Karen Montgomery, based on a black and white engraving from *Lydekker's Royal Natural History*. The cover fonts are Gilroy Semibold and Guardian Sans. The text font is Adobe Minion Pro; the heading font is Adobe Myriad Condensed; and the code font is Dalton Maag's Ubuntu Mono

O'REILLY®

There's much more where this came from.

Experience books, videos, live online training courses, and more from O'Reilly and our 200+ partners—all in one place.

Learn more at oreilly.com/online-learning

CPSIA information can be obtained
at www.ICGtesting.com
Printed in the USA
BVHW021006130121
597713BV00016B/368